Oxford Shakespeare Topics

Shakespeare and the Victorians

OXFORD SHAKESPEARE TOPICS

Published and Forthcoming Titles Include:

Oxford Shakespeare Topics

GENERAL EDITORS: PETER HOLLAND AND STANLEY WELLS

Shakespeare and the Victorians

STUART SILLARS

OXFORD
UNIVERSITY PRESS

OXFORD
UNIVERSITY PRESS

Great Clarendon Street, Oxford, OX2 6DP,
United Kingdom

Oxford University Press is a department of the University of Oxford.
It furthers the University's objective of excellence in research, scholarship,
and education by publishing worldwide. Oxford is a registered trade mark of
Oxford University Press in the UK and in certain other countries

© Stuart Sillars 2013

The moral rights of the author have been asserted

First Edition published in 2013
Impression: 1

Published in the United States of America by Oxford University Press
198 Madison Avenue, New York, NY 10016, United States of America

British Library Cataloguing in Publication Data
Data available

ISBN 978-0-19-966807-6 (hbk)
      978-0-19-966808-3 (pbk)

As printed and bound by
CPI Group (UK) Ltd, Croydon, CR0 4YY

Contents

List of Illustrations

Except where otherwise noted, all images are from the author's collection.

Author's Note

The Shakespearian edifice that the Victorians constructed for themselves was extensive, and had many mansions. Any attempt to do it justice in a small introductory volume will inevitably be selective, and for the areas that this one does not cover I would point readers to the Further Reading section with which it concludes, which gives advice on some of the more specialized areas of the subject that space has excluded here. After long and careful thought and discussion with the series editors, I have decided to return to the original policy of the series and not include footnotes, but instead to make sources clear in the text and then give full details with the other volumes suggested for further study. The illustrations have been selected to present a representative range of visual treatments of Shakespeare from the period, and also as far as possible for their relative absence from published sources. Most of the paintings referred to in Chapter 4 can be easily seen on the websites of the relevant galleries; consequently, images of contemporary engravings or of less familiar works have been included here.

A particular problem when writing about the Victorians lies in the choice of words that both reflect the usages of the time and remain clear to readers of the present day. For names of the plays and the characters I have retained earlier usages, with *2 Henry VI* rather than *The First Part of the Contention*, Falstaff not Oldcastle, and Imogen not Innogen. To reflect today's thinking I have used the word 'actor' for performers of both gender and, although the Victorians were quite happy about 'femininity', I have opted for the perhaps less contentious 'femaleness'. That said, I have retained stage names such as 'Mrs Patrick Campbell'. Since Henry Irving, Beerbohm Tree, and William Poel all devised their own stage names, it seemed ungracious to deny that right to their female partners—most particularly since a declaration of marriage was presumably an important statement of respectability of a kind as yet not always conferred on someone using the deeply ambivalent term 'actress' to describe her occupation.

Any work of this kind inevitably depends on the help of others, and it is a pleasure here to thank those who have contributed generously of their time and expertise. I am especially grateful to Stanley Wells and Peter Holland, initially for inviting me to write this book and subsequently for their guidance and kindness during its gestation. The poet and critic Clive Wilmer showed great kindness in helping the discussion of Ruskin and Shakespeare. As always, the librarians of the Rare Books Room, Cambridge University Library, were of very great assistance. In Oxford, Jacqueline Baker gave enthusiastic support from the outset, and Rosie Chambers oversaw the production process with great efficiency. Susan Frampton copyedited the text with precision, tact, and patience. To them all, I offer my sincere thanks, grateful for the pleasure and privilege of working with skilled professionals. For all errors, inaccuracies, and infelicities that remain, however, I take sole responsibility.

Shakespeare the Victorian

Many months before April 1864, local worthies and the great and good began planning how to celebrate with due decorum the tercentenary of Shakespeare's birth. Preparations were as extensive and methodical as every other Victorian venture, typifying the age's concern for propriety and order. When the eventful date arrived, the festivities themselves were equally revealing: to the later onlooker, they are a formidable, inclusive lens through which the period's construction of Shakespeare is refracted. That the plays themselves occupied only a small part of the celebrations, enfolded as they were within banquets, excursions, sermons, dances and concerts, the organisation and physical location of which reflected civic pride and due observance of social rank, makes them an immediate representative sample of the Victorian creation of what *Punch*, the comic magazine founded in the early years of the period, called 'Shakespeareanity'. That scholarly activities—lectures, publications, editions—were conspicuously absent from the celebrations evidences a division between critical endeavours and those of the stage and wider society, a separation remaining largely unbridged throughout the period.

On 23 April, the Stratford festivities began, not with a performance of a play but with a celebratory banquet and firework display; it was clear from this that, while Shakespeare was being celebrated, the celebrations themselves would be wholly Victorian in nature. The original scheme had been that the second evening would be the climax of the celebrations, but what transpired was not quite what had been planned. The Stratford committee, headed by the local brewing magnate and Shakespearian amateur Edward Flower, and composed of other civic dignitaries, had wanted a performance of *Hamlet*. But who should play the prince? Charles Kean, having completed his tenure at the Princess's Theatre, had departed for a tour of Australia, and had in any case been far from successful in the role. Samuel Phelps, famed for his Hamlet and innovative in his productions when managing Sadler's Wells in the 1840s and 50s, was now widely considered old-fashioned in his declamatory style. To many, his successor was Charles Albert Fechter, of whose début in the role the *Athenaeum* (23 March 1861) simply asserted 'Mr Fechter does not act; he is Hamlet'. In a tradition not uncommon among committees, both actors were invited. Phelps, already furious with Fechter, withdrew; Fechter, after promising faithfully to perform, pulled out much later.

What might seem an outbreak of offstage histrionics was a reflection of a larger uncertainty in the theatre at the time. Phelps's time had passed; Kean's tenure at the Princess's, where elaborate scenery was as important as personal performance, had ended in 1859. In the mid-1860s the theatre lacked a single dominant power. Fechter came close, but his popularity was limited for many by his nationality: of Anglo-German descent, he was brought up in France, where he established his reputation before coming to England. There were many other figures, but no outstanding leader: it was not until the 1880s that Henry Irving would emerge as the eminent tragedian, in the process making the profession respectable and becoming the first theatrical knight.

In an atmosphere of mingled relief and smug satisfaction that the Frenchman would be both unsuitable and untrustworthy, a double bill of *The Comedy of Errors* and *Romeo and Juliet* was given on the 27th. Such yoking together of tragedy and comedy, or even the inclusion of two or three quite different plays, was by no means unusual. The idea of a single play being the focus of an evening's theatre-going was as yet rare, developing a little later in the era of much larger theatres with associated bars and restaurants, and the longer intervals demanded by changes of ever more complex scenery. The evening also typified earlier production styles in using the same scenery for both plays—the sets and props for *Romeo* that had been used a few days before at the Princess's Theatre. In the comedy, the two Dromios were played by actors celebrated for the roles, the Brothers Webb, identical twins who gave the performance something of the quality of a Victorian circus. In the tragedy, as Juliet the French actress Stella Colas was generally thought beautiful in appearance but incomprehensible in diction; as Romeo, J. Nelson provided matching home-grown inadequacy, and it was left to George Vining as Mercutio and Mrs Henry Marston as the Nurse to carry the performance, to the general approval of the capacity audience of 3,000. Unusually for the period, it used the revision of the text by David Garrick in which Juliet recovers briefly to exchange final vows with Romeo. A century earlier this had been a great success, and Benjamin Wilson had painted the recovery scene being played by Garrick and George Anne Bellamy. Now, though, it was seen by many as unfashionable and by some as an inappropriate tampering with Shakespeare's text, the pursuit of the elusive authoritative original forms of the plays being a constant concern for scholars, editors, and some, though by no means all, performers.

Textual choices apart, both productions reflected the state of the theatre, its performers and its audiences, at the centre of Victoria's reign. The inclusion of foreign actors, either using their own language or speaking the parts with heavy accents, was frequent in London, balanced by visits of English actors to Europe, America or, in the case of the Keans, Australia. That a major female performer appeared under the name of 'Mrs Henry Marston' suggests the status of the actress at a time before individual identity was established by later women actors, notably Ellen Terry. A similar uncertainty of station was shown by Helen Faucit who, celebrated as Juliet and other major Shakespearian roles in the 1840s, and prized for her tenderness and womanly grace as Imogen, had in 1851 married the literary scholar Theodore Martin, and had increasingly moved away from the stage in consequence. She took no part in the tercentenary celebrations, only performing once at Stratford when, in 1879, she played Beatrice in *Much Ado About Nothing* in the recently completed Shakespeare Memorial Theatre.

The evening before the climactic double bill, *Twelfth Night* had been performed, followed by a more recent comic piece, *My Aunt's Advice*. Both were given by the company of the Theatre Royal, Haymarket, under the direction of its manager John Baldwin

Buckstone, one of a small but significant body of actor-managers whose companies balanced Shakespeare against more popular contemporary pieces in the somewhat precarious business of theatrical management. Buckstone took the role in which he was celebrated, Sir Andrew Aguecheek, with other members of his company in a reprise of their Haymarket roles. The Haymarket was one of many smaller theatres competing for audiences in the century's middle years. The theatre itself, built to a design by John Nash in 1821, had been remodelled in the succeeding decades, most notably in the shortening of the forestage, widening of the proscenium and the removal of proscenium doors to reflect changes in performance style. What was performed was also significant: the Haymarket had been one of the earliest theatres to challenge the restrictions on serious drama in theatres other than Drury Lane and Covent Garden, and was given a special licence for such productions before the 1843 Act allowed them in all theatres. Despite this, it was outside the narrow area of fashionable London, described in the 1850s as 'uncompromisingly in the foreign quarter' yet still 'generally acknowledged to be one of the best playhouses in London'. In design, repertoire, location and reputation, it was representative of the state of theatrical presentation in the middle years of Victoria's reign.

The setting of all these productions was a wooden Pavilion, specially constructed on the meadows beside the River Avon. In its design and the uses to which it was put it presented a forceful emblem of the place of Shakespeare in Victorian society (see Illustration 1.1). The building was a twelve-sided structure with two stages facing each other, one used for theatrical performances, the other as a space for aristocratic dining or, with part of its dais removed to form an orchestra pit, for choral-orchestral concerts. The auditorium, at floor level and in a gallery, offered seating of various kinds at different prices, from the silk-and-velvet chairs before the stage to the wooden benches of the higher galleries. This sharp demarcation of rank through differences in price reflected practice in London and in regional theatres housing touring companies, and the repertory companies of theatres built as part of the emerging civic identities of the industrial north. The building was essentially a physical embodiment of Victorian society, its structures of rank and its cultural forms, with Shakespeare's plays in a firm, but not dominant, position within them.

1.1 The interior of the Stratford Pavilion under construction for the tercentenary celebrations. The stage is in the distance, seen from the gallery where visitors could pay to see the opening banquet in progress; that the figures shown represent three clear layers of Victorian society is suggestive of the event's inclusiveness, but also its strict social divisions.

That it was a temporary rather than a permanent structure, like the rotunda built by Garrick for his celebrations nearly a century before, was further suggestive of the place of Shakespeare and the theatre in the national psyche: the Bard was a figure of national importance, but not one whose works were deserving of a permanent, still less a nationally supported, place of performance.

This reflects an ambivalence seen throughout the tercentenary celebrations, and the larger society they represent. Many were passionate in their support of the theatre and Shakespeare's place in performance. John Ruskin, the 'sage of Denmark Hill', who wrote and lectured profusely about art, society, and the need to return to a proper estimation of the working man, found it an essential means of combining entertainment with education, both aesthetic and moral. Others were less enthusiastic. The novelist and poet Thomas Hardy declined to contribute to the fund to build the Shakespeare Memorial

Theatre, saying that he valued Shakespeare as a man and a thinker, not a dramatist. Throughout the period, indeed, writers discussed Shakespeare as a moral guide rather than a practising poet and playwright. Thus the celebrations in Stratford and London were largely intended to mark the centenary of a great thinker, a great Englishman whose gifts were divinely inspired, so that performances of the plays, though important, were only one part of the celebrations.

To reflect this, the pavilion was the site of several other events during the celebrations. In the afternoon of 25 April Handel's *Messiah* was performed, with an amateur chorus of 500. Above all others, this was the work which enshrined the musical taste and practice of establishment England, its composer, forgiven for being of German origin by his long residence in London, the musician whose place in the public imagination was rivalled only by Mendelssohn. *Messiah*, held without question as his greatest work, had been performed annually by many of the music festivals that proliferated in the nineteenth century throughout the country. There is an important parallel with Shakespeare here. Just as Handel represented an ideal Englishness in music, so the plays were seen as something available for all, and the performance of the oratorio on the platform at the opposite end of the pavilion to its acting stage nicely presents this balance of cultural identities. In the evening of the same day there was a concert of music associated with Shakespeare's works, with items by the eighteenth-century composer Thomas Arne, and a specially composed overture, albeit not related to Shakespeare, by the conductor Alfred Mellon. Alongside them were important European compositions: Beethoven's *Coriolan* overture, pieces by Verdi, and Schubert's 'To Silvia', the song from *The Two Gentlemen*—a reminder of the international nature of much Victorian music-making, and the appreciation given to operatic and vocal settings by major European composers. This did not mean that native composers were unimportant; rather, they were regarded in a different light. Alfred Mellon was representative of a little-known and today almost totally forgotten group of musicians who composed, arranged, conducted, and played in the theatres of the period, their music aimed to reflect the mood of performances and, in consequence, as ephemeral as it was fitting.

Although standing at its centre, the pavilion was only one of the focal points of the Stratford celebrations. They began on the 23rd with a procession to the site proposed for a national monument to Shakespeare, headed by the Tercentenary Committee, an embodiment of the Victorian love of committees, rituals, and monuments that both made the tercentenary celebration possible and dominated its events. There followed a formal banquet, with speeches, at which the committee and honoured guests sat on the stage, while others who had paid 21 shillings were served in the auditorium. The less well off could pay five shillings for a seat in the gallery to watch the proceedings. A firework display ended the day's entertainments. On the following day, Sunday, there were two services in Holy Trinity Church, with sermons appropriate to the occasion. At Matins, the Reverend Chenevix Trench spoke on the text 'every perfect gift is from above', reflecting the common idea that, while Shakespeare was the embodiment of all things English, he was also a gift sent from God to 'mould a nation's life' to ensure that it would be 'animated and quickened to heroic enterprise and worthiest endeavour', as well as offering 'ideals of perfect womanhood'. He did not, however, find it necessary actually to quote anything from the works of Shakespeare in support of these noble thoughts. In the evening Charles Wordsworth spoke on Shakespeare's knowledge and use of the Bible, bringing together the two volumes that, with the possible addition of *The Pilgrim's Progress*, stood on every Victorian bookshelf, with bindings appropriate to the station of their owners.

Stratford town offered further enticements, most prominently Shakespeare's Birthplace in Henley Street, still retaining much of its external form within a row of houses, part of which was an alehouse. A further attraction within it was a portrait recently discovered by a W. H. Hunt, the town clerk of Stratford, encased in a fire-proof iron case with a frame of wood, a painted announcement claimed, from 'the old structure of Shakespeare's house'. Adherents claimed it was the original life portrait on which the bust in Holy Trinity was modelled; the *Athenaeum* dismissed it as 'a modern daub, possibly a tavern sign, a "Shakspear's head," probably made up for some purpose connected with the jubilee'. Controversy about the authenticity of portraits of Shakespeare was to remain prominent throughout the period, and far beyond. Adjoining the ruins of New

1.2 'Exhibition of Shakspeare Pictures and Relics in the Townhall', *Illustrated London News*, 1864. That the case of 'relics' is attracting more attention than the paintings perhaps suggests that the cult of 'Shakespeare the Man' was already well developed.

Place, Shakespeare's last home in Stratford, was the Shakespeare Museum, housing a collection of local documents and other elements purporting to come from Shakespeare's time or, much more rarely, from his own home or possessions. The Town Hall was the setting for an exhibition of paintings and other materials associated with the dramatist (see Illustration 1.2). Queen Victoria lent Thomas Lawrence's portrait of Kemble as Hamlet, and other exhibits included trinkets made from the mulberry tree in the garden of New Place, and the chair in which Shakespeare had reputedly sat. The range of these elements testified to the central importance of physical memorabilia to the mythic identity of the young Shakespeare—an importance that continued throughout the celebrations, and throughout the reign, by the sale of objects avowedly made from the mulberry tree, commemorative ribbons, Staffordshire ceramic figurines of actors in Shakespearian character and Shakespeare himself, and other impedimenta without which no serious Victorian parlour was complete (see Illustration 1.3).

1.3 Lead-glazed earthenware figure of Shakespeare, made in Staffordshire at about the start of the Victorian period. About 12 inches high, and based loosely on Scheemakers' life-size sculpture in Westminster Abbey, it offered Victorians an object of veneration for their own home.
© Victoria and Albert Museum, London

Other attractions were a short distance away. A procession of carriages took the affluent to see Charlecote, in celebration of Shakespeare's allegedly having poached deer from the estate, a story so longstanding as to have become an essential element of the Shakespeare myth. The building traditionally known as 'Anne Hathaway's Cottage' was a popular destination, with Mrs Mary Baker, purportedly the last survivor of the Hathaway family, in loving attendance. In fact a fairly substantial farmhouse, the building was traditionally known as a 'cottage', a shift that suggests a liking for the picturesque rural ideal, far removed from the damp, rat-infested actuality, that was celebrated by painters like William Allington and Randolph Caldecott. Together, these attractions remained powerful elements of Victorian Shakespeare, holding sway over the public imagination and making Stratford increasingly a place of attraction, and in many cases pilgrimage, for anyone in search of cultural fulfilment, almost a cut-price version of the European grand tour followed by young aristocrats.

After a performance of *As You Like It*, with James Bennett, a local actor, as the exiled Duke Senior, the pavilion was the setting for a fancy dress ball, the final event of the celebrations. Again, spectators were allowed in the gallery for five shillings; they would have seen dancing to music composed by Alfred Mellon by the Flower family and other guests, including the Lord Lieutenant of Warwickshire and the Mayor of Stratford who went, with remarkable imagination, in costumes as the Lord Lieutenant and the Mayor. But the celebrations did not quite end there. The following week was given over to popular entertainment, with events including a pageant with horses, knights in armour, and a procession of characters from the plays, at last enacting the one planned by Garrick a century earlier that was abandoned in heavy rain. Special trains were run from all over the country, in a nice example of the latest technology facilitating a mythic invention of the past, something far from uncommon in the Victorian frame of mind. *Othello* and *Much Ado* were performed, and the trial scene from *The Merchant of Venice*, testimony to the frequent use of Portia's 'Quality of Mercy' speech as an elocution-piece and moral homily in schools and academies throughout the age.

Those who could not attend the Stratford celebrations were offered rather more limited events in London. There were concerts and dramatic readings, performances of the plays, and separate scenes from them. A 'Colossal Tercentenary Bust' made by Charles Bacon was unveiled; the Chandos portrait of Shakespeare, a much worthier contender as life portrait than Mr Hunt's offering, was exhibited in the temporary home of the new National Portrait Gallery; Samuel Phelps, recovered a little from his rebuff at Stratford, recited the first act of *The Tempest*. At the Crystal Palace, William Paxton's masterpiece of glass and iron, a ceremony was held around the great statue of Shakespeare that had been made, like the Palace itself, for the Great Exhibition of 1851.

All these were similar in manner and kind to the events at Stratford, revealing again the ways in which the idea of Shakespeare the man and the works of Shakespeare the dramatist were embedded in Victorian culture and society. But one event presented a rather different set of relationships, albeit largely by chance. On 23 April the Working Men's Shakespeare Committee organized a 'Grand Miscellaneous Entertainment and Monster Demonstration of the Working Classes'. This merged with a large-scale political demonstration, with a crowd estimated at 4,000 protesting against the departure of the Italian statesman Garibaldi who, it was felt, had been urged to leave England for political reasons that ran counter to democracy. Later, some would see it as a preparation for the great Hyde Park demonstration of the following year, when thousands of working men assembled to demand reform of the electoral system. That the protests occurred simultaneously with Samuel Phelps planting a commemorative oak tree on Primrose Hill was a chance coincidence, but a revealing one. Shakespeare was part of the national consciousness, it seemed, in ways that went far beyond ideals of identity and moral guidance. There was, in the coming together, just a hint that his plays might contain ideas counter to those of established rank and order, and that those who had read speeches from the plays in the National Schools, or bought cheap editions of them as a means of self-improvement, would reject the social structures of which the plays had, in the minds of the Stratford and London tercentenary committees, been an inseparable, God-given part.

* * * * *

While the events, structures, and sites of the tercentenary celebrations should not be regarded as encyclopaedic in revealing Victorian approaches to Shakespeare, they offer enough that is representative to make them a secure starting point for larger discussions. The events make clear that in Victorian society 'Shakespeare' meant both far more and far less than a collection of literary and dramatic texts. One of the earliest poems by Matthew Arnold, a foremost intellectual and social critic of the age, is a sonnet entitled 'Shakespeare' (1844):

> Others abide our question. Thou art free.
> We ask and ask—thou smilest and art still,
> Out-topping knowledge

The opening lines suggest the status of the dramatist at the time, as something beyond human measure. The poem's conclusion, a tercet which places 'all pains', 'all weakness' and 'all griefs' within Shakespeare's understanding, is a summation of the period's veneration of the dramatist as a latter-day philosopher king. That the poem is itself a sonnet is a form of homage, a reflection of the influence of Shakespeare on literary production of the time. Sonnets of all kinds were written and published, some popular and about love, many less so, and engaging with political issues. The novel, especially in its more serious forms, examined the problems of the day through modifications of Shakespearian plot trajectories. Even the most popular, and least avowedly intellectual, made use of quotations and allusions as a way of establishing a bond between text and reader. In *The Manchester Man*, by Mrs G. Linnaeus Banks (1876), a whole chapter is devoted to 'How the Rev. Joshua Brookes and Simon Clegg interpreted a Shakespearian text' with no mention of the text itself. The episode relates to the confusion over naming a child at baptism, the title assuming that readers will immediately associate this with the 'What's in a name?' speech from *Romeo and Juliet*. A more specifically theatrical novel, Howard Merrick's *The Actor Manager* (1898), repeatedly puts quotations from the plays into the speech and thought of the central male character, and contains a scene in which the main female figure goes through proof prints of photographs of herself in Shakespearian roles to select the most appealing—both elements depending on the reader's knowledge of the plays and their production.

Such writings were one way in which a Victorian man or woman would probably have encountered the aesthetic construction known as 'Shakespeare'. Performance was another major part of their experience, and in the major metropolitan centres and county towns it was something available for people of all ranks, usually, albeit in carefully separated in seating locations, in the same theatres. Certainly, not all the plays were equally popular. Of the tragedies, *Hamlet* and *Macbeth* were the staples, with *King Lear*—perhaps because of the tradition, from Charles Lamb, of its being too great for the theatre—and *Othello* less so. Among the histories the second tetralogy was popular, especially *Henry V*, its history seen wholly in providential, patriotic terms; *Richard III* retained its popularity from Garrick through the sheer force of the central character. *King John* was also a favoured play, not only because of the sentimental scenes with Arthur and Hubert, and Constance's mourning, but because of the Magna Carta scenes inserted by Charles Kean and others as a way of celebrating English democracy. *As You Like It* and *A Midsummer Night's Dream*, the latter especially in the later years, where special effects were dominant, remained popular. Through the popularity of the trial scene and Portia's role, as well as some spectacular stagings including real canals and real gondolas, *The Merchant of Venice* was of major importance— although the final act, with the complexities of the ring conceit, met with bafflement and was often severely curtailed or even omitted. *The Taming of the Shrew* had the same popularity as today with theatregoers, Victorians finding the concluding speeches of Katherine untouched by irony. The works later described as 'problem plays', not surprisingly, were less often staged, *Measure for Measure* being produced only twice (in 1846 and 1850, both times at Sadler's Wells)— although Isabella's speech on chastity was highly regarded and often used as a recital piece, of the kind discussed in Chapter 7. *Troilus and Cressida* did not reach the English stage until 1907, and then in a form closer to a rehearsed reading directed by Charles Fry's Thersites. *Titus Andronicus* and *Timon of Athens* were barely mentioned and almost totally absent from the stage, the first because of its Senecan horror, the second because of its complex plot manoeuvres, and both because they were thought not wholly by Shakespeare. In combining romance and tragedy, *Romeo and Juliet* was a constant, sure-fire success. For most of the period Shakespeare's poetry was largely overlooked, with the exception of a score or so of the sonnets that, carefully selected, appeared in anthologies, often linked with some of the songs from the comedies. While the complete texts of the poems appeared in the popular editions of the works, they were often printed without annotation or scholarly discussion of the kind that followed the plays. In the editions of Charles Knight and Barry Cornwall, both issued serially between 1838 and 1843 and with the plays heavily illustrated, there are only one or two small wood-engravings showing rather embarrassed putti in woodland settings for the poems. The *Sonnets* as a whole were discussed largely within a biographical frame, *Venus and Adonis* and *Lucrece* hardly at all. Only later in the period did the poems come to be taken more seriously as literary texts.

During the eighteenth century, a tentative relationship developed between textual scholarship and editing and the stage performances through which actors gradually moved away from the adapted forms of the plays to those that more closely approached current thinking about their authentic texts. During Victoria's reign the process continued with, as mentioned above, a reaction against the use of earlier forms such as Garrick's ending for *Romeo and Juliet*. Yet the plays on stage and page do not necessarily grow closer together. The emphasis on antiquarianism that in part drove researches into Shakespeare's texts was also an impetus behind stage productions emphasizing historical authenticity to the periods in which plays were set. This was not only apparent in costumes: it also manifested itself in what Charles Kean called 'Historical Episodes', tableaux such as processions that were inserted within the action. Inevitably this extended the plays' duration, necessitating cuts from the texts—so that, at the same time as the play texts were being recovered from eighteenth-century adaptations, they were being altered in line with Victorian tastes. Omissions and rearrangements in performance were also frequent according to the preferences of individual actors and, increasingly, actor-managers. The power of the latter increased considerably from the beginning of the period so that, by the century's end, they were much closer in power and function to present-day directors, with the further complication that the choice of plays was driven by their own performing styles and preferences, and the suitability of key roles for their own performance.

The scholarly study of the plays was, in the early years, a confused and confusing coming together of linguistic analysis, source-hunting, biographical antiquarianism, and textual editing, the same figures being active in areas today largely discrete. Editing was a major concern of many, with its own disputes and controversies. Old versus contemporary spelling, Folio versus Quarto readings, the acceptance of conjectural readings, and the proper degree of annotation and introductory material, to say nothing of the expurgation of texts for younger readers, were all live and contentious issues for most of the period, until in the final decades some kind of consensus was reached. As passages of the plays were increasingly excised and used as educational tools, learning by rote became a common practice, though for reasons as much concerned with training the memory and developing proper enunciation as for valuing their poetic forms. Less intimidating, perhaps, were reading circles: the *Girl's Own Paper* in 1885 published a two-page letter headed 'Our Shakespeare Society' detailing the proceedings of one such group. A sentence from its first paragraph reveals another motive:

But I should say to everyone above the age of childhood—study Shakespeare; not because it is a proper thing to do, but because his works yield never-failing strength, delight, and inspiration. The characters he draws are living creations, whose springs of thought and action repair unending study. For the more they are scrutinised, the more wealth they will yield to the earnest, inquiring seeker.

Strength, delight, inspiration, wealth; the earnest, inquiring seeker: the vocabulary is typically Victorian in its aims and endeavours, and could reasonably be said to embody the whole approach to the plays. It exemplified the project of self-advancement made explicit by Samuel Smiles' *Self-Help*, first published in 1859 and popular throughout the period, and given narrative form in most of the novels of Charles Dickens as well as in the mythology erected around his own move from bottle-factory minion to gentleman novelist. Shared by both genders, at times it was given a sharper inflection: Mary Cowden Clarke, compiler of an important concordance (1845) and twice editor of the plays, first by herself in 1859–60 and later, in 1864–9, with her husband Charles, wrote on 'Shakespeare as the Girl's Friend' in another number of the *Girl's Own Paper* (1887). Often the moral thrust of the plays is presented through collections of quotations, as if their initial occurrence in plays is regrettable; the

Puritan rejection of the theatre was, though, moderated by many, Charles Kean regarding Shakespeare on the stage as a means of teaching history, John Ruskin seeing the plays in performance as intellectual and emotional nourishment essential for the good of working people.

This, then, is the immediate force of Shakespeare as dramatist and poet; but the presence of Shakespeare in Victorian life moves way beyond the stage and the study, so that it is hard to name an area of intellectual or social life in which the works did not feature. Two quite unrelated instances suggest this. The comic journal *Punch*, founded in 1841, repeatedly used references to Shakespeare's plays as captions to cartoons showing current political or social events. Clearly, unless readers could recognize the quotations and their incongruity in the new settings, the jokes or satirical thrust would be completely lost. The second example demonstrates the spread of interest in a more individual manner. In 1848 the engineer Isambard Kingdom Brunel moved into a new house in Duke Street, overlooking St James's Park in London. To decorate the main drawing room he commissioned paintings on Shakespearian themes from some of the most popular Victorian artists including Augustus Leopold Egg, C. R. Leslie, and Sir Edwin Landseer. The paintings remained in the room until sold at auction after his death.

Underlying such endeavours is the concept that a knowledge of Shakespeare's plays was essential for the possession of any kind of cultural maturity. In physical terms this was evidenced in the deluge of editions of the plays that poured from the new steam-operated printing presses, using paper made from wood-pulp, cased in embossed card bindings, from the very beginning of the period. Over the years the editions became progressively cheaper until in 1890 Ward and Lock issued a single-volume Complete Works for the price of sixpence. At the other end of the scale were privately printed limited editions of individual plays in original spelling, or large format volumes with specially commissioned illustrations. These were not only, or at least not principally, intended for private reading. Recitation of passages from the plays was a common educational pursuit, and this was linked with the use of Shakespeare's plays as a repository of moral and ethical truths. Anthologies appeared giving suitable lines under various subject headings; as the educational system developed towards compulsory elementary education, passages from the plays were prescribed as ways of testing reading and speech at various levels.

At the same time, the cult of 'Shakespeare the man' developed on many levels. Serious biographies, either extending the earlier myths surrounding the youth in Stratford or building on newly-discovered—and in some cases freshly-invented—documents appeared regularly throughout Victoria's reign. A visit to the town of Stratford-upon-Avon, with the house where Shakespeare was born and the school where he studied, became an essential rite of passage to cultural maturity.

Interest in the author was balanced by interest in his characters. Often, critical writing mingled character description with exploration of plot and language; some performers, most notably Helen Faucit, wrote of their sensations and reactions when presenting—or, in the term of the day, 'personating'—the characters on stage. Another approach was the invention of their childhood, matched with the retelling of the plays for children and young adults. One aspect of the growing interest in painting scenes from the plays was the production of portraits, mainly of women characters. Some took a more specialized interest. John Charles Bucknill, MD, London, and Superintendent of Devon County Lunatic Asylum, published *The Medical Knowledge of Shakespeare* in 1860, concluding that Shakespeare had been 'a diligent student' of medical practices of his day. In the previous year he had published *The Psychology of Shakespeare*, analysing a series of characters according to the methods of the time. In 1867, the same book was reissued as *The Mad Folk of Shakespeare*, perhaps suggesting a desire to increase sales rather than reflecting its sympathetic approach. But one comment stands out from its pages: 'All critical study of Hamlet must be psychological'. The view was shared by John Conolly who, in *A Study of Hamlet* (1863), concluded that the character had 'completely relapsed into distraction'. All these approaches would climax in the lectures of A. C. Bradley, published as *Shakespearian Tragedy* in 1904: it was perhaps the most influential fruit of the newly professionalized academic study of Shakespeare within University Departments of English Literature.

Such elevated approaches were matched by others more pragmatic. The burghers of Stratford were quick to exploit the town's connection with 'the Bard', so that it rapidly became a place of fashionable resort, combining the pleasures of sightseeing offered by increasing leisure time and railway travel with a veneer of cultural advancement. Flower himself capitalized on the connection, with beer mats proudly depicting the dramatist's head. Musical settings of songs in the plays and arrangements of pieces used in performance were published for amateur pianists to play in their own homes. Cheap prints, and increasingly, as the technology developed, photographs, depicted characters and performers. All demonstrated the fervour with which Victorians, at every social level, valued the advancement of culture through the accumulation of material objects.

Towards the end of the period, reaction set in. William Poel began to stage the plays in something approaching the manner of Shakespeare's time, without elaborate scenic devices and with music of Shakespeare's time. The *Sonnets* assumed greater importance and were read as important texts in their own right, without the earlier obsessive concern for rearranging their order to align with an imagined biography. In the last decades, writers began explicitly to reject the obsession with Shakespeare the man and instead focused on the plays themselves as literary and dramatic texts. When the Queen died in January 1901, English Literature had established itself as a major independent subject of study at university level, and editions of the plays and poems, with texts generally accepted as standard and authentic, were cheaply and reliably available. Yet this should not be seen as an inevitable process. At every moment, the Victorian period had Shakespearian activity of some kind at its core, and studying Victorian Shakespeare cannot be separated from studying Victorian society, and its views on history, culture, morality, and ethics. If it is possible to study Shakespeare without the Victorians, it is impossible to study the Victorians without being aware of their reading, appropriation, and exploitation of Shakespeare. What follows is an introduction to these processes.

2

Scholarship, Editing, and Criticism

From the appearance of the First Folio edition of Shakespeare's plays in 1623, perhaps even from the publication of the early Quartos, the relationship between the plays in print and on the stage has been one of uncertainty and controversy. Beginning with Nicholas Rowe in 1709, editors endeavoured to find and explain the ideal single text that was the dramatist's final intention, while performers strove to present the plays as they thought fitting for their audiences. In consequence, at times it seemed that the history of the plays was proceeding along two distinct paths, each constructed by different specialists for quite different consumers. The later seventeenth and early eighteenth centuries saw the two paths at their most divergent, with rewritings of the plays by William Davenant, Nahum Tate, Colley Cibber and others presenting them as 'made fit' for contemporary playgoers while Rowe, Samuel Johnson, George Steevens and Isaac Reed strove towards establishing, and in some cases inventing, a single authoritative text. Although introducing some new directions of divergence, overall the Victorian period saw the two paths coming closer together. The more extreme acts of adaptation gradually vanished from the stage, while the results of scholarly research began, with the aid of new publishing techniques and the Victorian thirst for knowledge and advancement, to be more freely available to a wider public. The debates of a later period over the plays' essence existing in performance or in print were not insistent for the Victorians; rather, the theatre and the library were tacitly accepted as two distinct places, at times complementary but rarely the cause of either union or dissent. Each was essential to Victorian Shakespeare activity, pursued with equal vigour by specialists in each field: that they are discussed separately in these pages reflects this difference. That scholarship is discussed before performance is the result of the demands of linear narrative rather than conceptual hierarchy—although the presence of this volume, and the discipline of study to which it contributes, is in some measure a continuation of the work of Victorian scholars rather than that of their contemporaries in the theatre.

At the start of the period, scholarship of all kinds retained its earlier identity as the preserve of wealthy amateurs; almost immediately, however, important figures made its results available to increasingly wide readerships through editions resting on principles developed from the editing of Greek and Roman texts. As the years passed, while controversies and debates continued, scholarship increasingly became a professional activity, so that at the century's close the study of Shakespeare at universities and in schools rested on the secure footing of scholarly research, editing, and critical analysis. Many of the major Shakespeare figures worked across the boundaries of what are now quite separate fields, collecting and publishing documents related to Shakespeare's life, editing individual plays, entering debates about spelling and chronology, and offering critical interpretations—the lives and work of such figures make intriguing subjects for intellectual biography. The logic of the activities, however, suggests that they are best explored separately. Scholarship provides the raw materials of plays, poems, and their historical frames; from this mass of material, editing selects and constructs texts and annotations; and from these materials critics produce wider interpretations, drawing them into larger conceptual frames that surround both Shakespeare's age and that of the critics themselves, and which are directed to readerships that steadily expand with the growth of the Victorian educational system.

Victorian Shakespeare scholarship revolved around a number of topics. That which drew most directly on earlier interests in antiquarianism concerned itself with searching for documents related to Shakespeare's life, partly to aid in biography but also to assist in establishing the dates of the plays' composition and, in many cases, their legitimacy as works of Shakespeare, either alone or with collaborators. The dating of the plays rested on close analysis of the metrical forms employed, as well as references to contemporary events—political, social, and even meteorological—in the effort to establish the pattern of the plays' growth through time. One branch of such enquiry was the identification and publication of the sources of many of the plays—historical chronicles, prose romances, earlier dramatic treatments—which spread further out into literary history. All such endeavours intersected with aspects of Shakespeare's life, raising important questions. How did Shakespeare know about rhetorical structures and verse forms? Did he read the story that became the source of *Othello* in the original Italian of Giraldo Cinthio's collection *Gli Hecatommithi*, or in a French translation? How involved was he with the earliest printings of the plays? Even from this brief listing it should be clear that scholarship often slanted heavily towards questions of identity and authorship, occupying a middle ground between biography and textual study. While many scholars were wholly absorbed with seemingly abstract minutiae of expression, it is nonetheless clear that few aspects of Shakespeare scholarship were quite distinct from the larger human concerns that circled around the playwright for almost the whole of the period. Issues of biography will be dealt with later; here, though, it is important to note that aspects today often kept separate were far more deeply connected in the Victorian period, a link that in itself reveals the preoccupation of the age with self-improvement and justification, Shakespeare's career path offering a model trajectory for the Victorian pattern of identity-making.

One of the ways in which matters of textual origins and forms were addressed was through meetings of learned individuals, and their publication either privately or by subscription. This was the formula followed by the Shakespeare Society, established in 1840 with, as its leading members, John Payne Collier and James Orchard Halliwell. Their *Shakespeare Society Papers* and *Shakespeare Society Publications* reveal much about the concerns of early Victorian scholarship. Halliwell produced an edition of the 1602 version of *The Merry Wives of Windsor* (1842) and *Illustrations of Fairy Mythology* (1845), designed as a historical supplement to the understanding of *A Midsummer Night's Dream*. Other publications included editions of the Chester cycle of mystery plays, *Edward IV*, *The Taming of A Shrew*, and the diaries of Philip Henslowe, builder of the Rose Playhouse and perhaps the most important theatre owner of Shakespeare's time. These fed into editing and criticism: in the 1840s Halliwell also produced *Some Notes on Passages in Shakespeare*, and in 1843 Collier published an edition of the plays. But the work of both scholars also had a darker side, as a later part of this chapter will reveal.

While the Shakespeare Society produced valuable work, some still important for researchers today, the work of individuals was increasingly significant, a change partly reflected in the disbanding of the Society in 1853. The retrieval of documents, the publication of sources, and the editing of plays by Shakespeare's contemporaries became important separate directions for a large number of scholars. In 1875, for example, Macmillan published an edition of Sir Thomas North's translation of Plutarch's *Lives*, carefully separating the new annotations from North's original marginal summaries, which were retained but presented in modernized spelling. That the editor was 'The Rev. Walter W. Skeat, M.A., Formerly Fellow of Christ's College, Cambridge' suggests that activity of this kind was not yet the preserve of full-time academic scholars: that Skeat is now principally known for his six-volume edition of the works of Geoffrey Chaucer (1894) reveals that in the Victorian period literary scholarship was not always focused as precisely on individual periods and authors as it has since become.

In the century's middle years, a major concern was the investigation and codification of Shakespeare's language. Edwin Abbott Abbott's *A Shakespearian Grammar* first appeared in 1869 and was reissued in enlarged form in 1870. The revised edition contained 451 separate paragraphs covering linguistic forms, arranged alphabetically from 'Adjectives used as adverbs' to 'Verbs, moods of', and including 'Double negatives', 'Adverbial compounds', and such exotica as 'Nominative implied from participial phrases'. A separate section on 'Prosody' explored contractions, pause accents, and other variations of accent and syllable, all elements increasingly of value in attempts to establish the dates of the plays. That the book included at its close a section of 'Notes and Questions' suggests a very specific, very rigorous linguistic discipline, but the verse analysis clearly also has value for performers and amateur readers. The volume thus locates itself within both the study of language and a larger, more general current of criticism. Alexander Schmidt's *Shakespeare-Lexicon* of 1874–5 was more concerned with linguistic history, harnessing the Victorian concern for system and explication to reveal the differences between Shakespeare's language and that of the mid-nineteenth century. It was perhaps also influential on some aspects of editorial practice, notably editions aimed at schools and colleges, many of which included a glossary as an appendix. Its approach was extended in C. T. Onions's *Shakespeare Glossary* (1911) which, through later reprints, continued the method well into the next century and remains in print.

Scholarship of this kind is related to, and for many scholars facilitated by, concordances to the works of Shakespeare, in which every word used in the plays, with the exception of articles and prepositions, is listed and its appearance cited in each of the plays. The value of this goes beyond linguistic tabulation: it is invaluable for anyone exploring the discussion of particular themes and concepts in the plays—and again, in this multiple value shows the ways in which scholarship moved outwards to affect wider approaches to Shakespeare. Although concordances had been compiled at the very end of the eighteenth century, Victorian scholars produced more thorough versions. Most important of these was that compiled by Mary Cowden Clarke in 1845, displaced only in 1895 by that of John Bartlett, which used the line numbering of the Globe edition, discussed later in this chapter.

In the final quarter of the century the question of Shakespeare's spelling, particularly its use in preference to an increasingly standardized, national orthography, became a matter of some controversy. In 1873 the New Shakspere Society was founded, the spelling of the name reflecting its eagerness to use earlier forms. Prominent members were the textual scholars Frederick James Furnivall and Frederick Gard Fleay, the Shakespeare biographer Sidney Lee, the critic R. G. Moulton, the actor-manager William Poel, and the Ben Jonson scholar C. H. Herford. Its plans included several series of publications, covering the relative authenticity of the Quartos and Folio as textual originals, plays by Shakespeare's contemporaries, the sources of the plays, and documents offering evidence of Shakespeare's life and times. Some of these achieved publication, although many of the Society's endeavours, especially in publishing the Quartos, were eclipsed and finally displaced by the work of individuals such as Israel Gollancz, who produced editions of the Quartos and edited historical documents and source texts, adding considerably to the material available for editors and readers. Although announced at a meeting of the society in 1880, its 'Old Spelling' edition did not materialize for many years, its first volume appearing in 1904.

The production of Shakespeare editions using the original spelling, aside from Gollancz's editions of the Quartos, was a cause that soon lost impetus, encountering opposition from scholars and readers who saw it as mere antiquarianism or, with more logical justification, pointed out that since spelling in Shakespeare's time lacked consistency it would offer more confusion than clarification to later readers. Related to this in the Society's deliberations were issues of verse-metrics, Fleay in particular analysing the play's metrical structures in an effort to establish both chronology and authorship, a process that became known as 'disintegration' since it claimed as much to identify passages in the plays not written by Shakespeare as to engage with larger concerns of authorship of whole plays. This led in the most extreme cases to the suggestion that *Julius Caesar* had been written by Ben Jonson from an earlier version by Shakespeare, now lost, and was allied with the proposals of those who sought to find another author for the canon in general—although these, as a later chapter will make clear, relied as much on external as textual evidence. While the process of verse analysis is now often rejected as positivist and reductive, it was a movement of importance in establishing a chronology for the plays, and in this was a major step forward in Shakespeare studies. The Society's work is still resonant in some of the more contentious issues of chronology; and, as will become clear later in this chapter, scholarship of this kind overlapped with critical reading of the plays, most notably in the work of Edward Dowden.

Probably the single most influential figure in the search for an accurate chronology was the German scholar Georg Gottfried Gervinus, a reminder that the British Isles were not nearly as insular as popular belief might have it, something reinforced by the interchange of performers and theatre companies that will be discussed in Chapter 3. The four-volume *Shakespeare* (1849–50), translated into English as *Shakespeare Commentaries* in 1863, was a thorough and detailed application of metrical tests to the plays, resulting in their categorization into four periods. This was taken up by Furnivall and other major English scholars, and arguments over chronology, and its construction through internal evidence of metrical forms, references to contemporary events in the plays or external evidence such as performance records, remained a major concern throughout the period and for many scholars is still significant today. What is also striking about Gervinus' approach is that it combines analysis of this acute statistical variety with writing about the aesthetic qualities of the plays, and the moral and ethical considerations that may be inferred from them. It is tempting, but reductive, to see in this both the inclusiveness of much Victorian Shakespearian activity, mingling close textual study with larger human reflections, and the threefold division—scholarship, editing, criticism—towards which it moves. Particularly resonant is the link between the aesthetic and the moral: the conceptual, even theological, linking of these elements was characteristic of much Victorian thought, and at a more local level the exploration of the plays' characters through explication of the ethical foundations of their important speeches—beauty of mind in beauty of utterance—was central to the use of Shakespeare in educational settings. But in some of these comments may be discerned the roots of a later kind of critical analysis. Discussing Hamlet's exchange with the actors, for example, Gervinus glances towards a critical discussion of the play within a larger historical setting, before moving to larger statements of moral approbation:

His praise of Pyrrhus sustained in the old Seneca-like style is perfectly serious, it distinguishes him from Polonius, whom a jig pleases better; this, as well as his instructions to the players, exhibits him as a man of cultivated mind and taste, as that judge whose single appreciation is worth more than that of all the rest of the theatre.

What is also implicit here is the approach to character. Taking in the highly Victorian notion of 'a man of cultivated mind and taste'—the translation by F. E. Bunnett is rich with its own cultural assumptions—the discussion of Hamlet continues a stream of enquiry begun by, among others, William Richardson in the eighteenth century. Gervinus was influential in taking this approach: as the final part of this chapter will make clear, it was something that, developed in various ways by different writers, became a dominant feature of Shakespeare study in the century's later years.

* * * * *

Seen in the longer processes of Shakespeare study, probably the most important elements of Victorian scholarship concerned the detailed exploration of the texts of the plays, particularly the relationship between the Quartos and the First Folio of 1623 in the hunt for a single authoritative version, a model as seductive as it was elusive. This work makes explicit what has become increasingly apparent in the preceding paragraphs; a great deal of Victorian scholarship was concerned with procedures preparatory to, or as major parts of, the process of editing. While it is tempting, and in part valid, to see the Victorian period as one in which Shakespeare editing moved to take on the shapes familiar in present-day processes, this would be to overlook many other aspects characteristic of its age, perhaps most notably in the identities of its editors, their intended readers, and the ways of reading they presented. Certainly, the business of editing moved from the preserve of wealthy amateurs to professional scholars, whose endeavours were aided by developments in the mechanics of publishing, and increasingly the editions themselves were directed towards readers at schools and universities. Yet there were also a large number of editions aimed at more extensive readership among those who, benefitting from improved education and a concern for self-improvement, sought to share in the cultural maturity offered by a knowledge of the plays. This balance between scholarly prowess, educative zeal and genuine hunger for advancement, an equation of increasing importance as the period moved on, was an essentially Victorian one, increasingly rejected in more recent years. Thus, while editing moved towards the practices now prevalent in universities throughout the world, it also embraced larger cultural, moral, and to some degree commercial imperatives peculiar to the age. By the end of the period, the foundations of twentieth- and twenty-first-century editing had been firmly laid; but it would be a mistake to see this as the only, or even the most important, result of the age's editorial practices. Nor was the division absolute between the popular and the scholarly. Many editions often dismissed as 'popular' made significant contribution to scholarship of sources and interpretation of theme and idea, and deserve serious consideration alongside those aimed at specialist readers.

All the practices so far discussed were component threads in the larger fabric of textual editing. The most immediate in practical terms were the acceptance of Folio or Quarto texts, or a compromise like that established by eighteenth-century precedent, the use of original or later spelling, and the clarification of meaning or metaphor by linguistic analysis aided by grammatical studies and concordances. Accompanying these at a greater distance were considerations of the dating of the plays based on metrical or circumstantial evidence, speculation around authorial intent—the establishment of a final authoritative text—the clarification of allusions within the plays by reference to scholarly work on historical events and related documents, and the identification of sources. All of these, with varying degrees of relative depth according to the individual play, the intended reader, and the practical limits and demands of the publication format, came together in the final text, annotations, and introductory material.

Some of the patterns of relative emphasis within editing procedures emerged fairly early in the period. Notions of shared authorship, prominent in the twenty-first century, were of less immediate concern to editors, and only rarely resulted in the omission of passages of doubtful provenance: the authorship debate was more one of biography, focusing on the identity of the man Shakespeare. Scholarship regarding sources flourished on the ground prepared by earlier antiquarianism and grew with the increased professionalization of history as a discipline and the concern for a larger sense of national identity. The debate about spelling was in general of little concern to many of those editing the complete works, and although from the 1830s there was a fashion for older versions of the dramatist's name, even in popular editions, the use of older orthography rarely went beyond the title page of any but the most specialized editions.

Whatever the concerns of editors, and whatever their intended readers, all Victorian editions were greatly assisted by new processes of book-production. Paper made by machine from wood-pulp and esparto grass; stereotype printing plates that copied whole pages of print made up from individual metal letters; pictorial engraving on wood blocks; various processes of facsimile reproduction, leading to the use of photography in the final quarter of the century; and mechanical steam presses all facilitated rapid and cheap production of the plays. The result was that, by the period's end, it seemed that every conceivable market sector had been offered its own volume that bore the culturally prestigious words 'Shakespeare: Complete Works' on its spine. This, of course, refers to efforts to establish the canon of the works as a fixed entity, for study, performance, or as national monument. Other editorial imperatives led elsewhere. Facsimile editions of the Quartos and Folio were one of these, combining antiquarian precision with a desire for textual authenticity, aided by increasing techniques of reproduction. As the century passed, larger individual volumes of the single plays became more frequent, some including greater critical and textual annotation, others offering the text for performance. Still more were tailored for individual readers, generally those studying a play for educational reasons and the examinations of the Board Schools, universities or the Home or Foreign Civil Service.

All Victorian editions had not only to engage with the varieties of Quarto and Folio texts, but with the versions constructed from them and annotations erected around them by earlier editors. The most significant of these was the first variorum edition, often called Boswell's Malone, published in 1821. The was a revision of Malone's text of 1795–6, itself a revised version of the work of Johnson and Steevens, completed by James Boswell, the son of Johnson's friend and biographer. Extending to 21 volumes, it presented the plays in their conjectured order of composition, except for the histories which unfolded in chronological order of subject, using texts constructed from both Quartos and Folio, with meticulous engagement with the editorial decisions of its predecessors. In doing this and including a life of Shakespeare and the prefaces of all the major earlier editions, it followed precedent; in emphasizing the importance of Shakespeare's language, examining in detail the plays' chronology, and in including the *Sonnets* as part of the main body of annotated work, it broke new ground. It thus offered the Victorian editor both a series of possible beginnings and a clear ending: the inclusion of all earlier prefatory material soon became far too cumbersome, and the practice had ceased by mid-century, finally eradicated by the so-called 'Cambridge Shakespeare', of which more later.

One of the earliest editors of the period is also one who perhaps displays most directly the ethos of the age. Charles Knight was an immensely prolific writer, editor, and publisher, embodying the Victorian drive to educate and enlighten through many ventures including a *Penny Magazine* (1832–46), a history of London (1841–44), and a history of England (1855–62), all aimed at those seeking self-advancement in all intellectual and cultural areas. That all of these were serial publications also reveals them as the most up-to-date productions of their age in idea and form: they used the most modern techniques and materials, harnessed new methods of distribution, and ensured an immediate income for the publisher. Knight's *Pictorial Shakspere* (1838–43) also demonstrates concerns recurrent through the period. The plays followed Boswell's Malone in the order in which the plays were presented; the edition broke new ground by taking the Folio as its base text, with frequent emendations from the Quartos. Rejecting the earlier practice of beginning with lengthy prefaces and a biography, it instead had brief introductory passages for each play, while a later volume presented a new life of Shakespeare by Knight himself. A small number of footnotes, on a range of textual and interpretive issues, were supplemented by three- to four-page sections of 'Illustrations' after each act, combining visual material clarifying allusions with longer explanatory discussions. Visual material was strictly controlled, restricted to a headpiece and tailpiece for each act, intended to show 'the realities on which Shakespeare's imagination rested', although the illustrated title pages and 'persons represented' were more imaginative in interpreting the texts. Its serial parts used the most up-to-date production methods, and from the outset stereo plates were exported to America and editions printed from them to avoid import duty. Serial publication suggests its classification as a popular venture, but this is misleading: many scholarly works were published in this way. The genuine engagement with textual issues, especially the major reliance on the Folio, suggests its larger importance, and Knight's edition is only now coming to be taken more seriously as a contribution to the tradition of scholarly editing.

Quite different was the approach of 'Barry Cornwall', the pseudonym of Brian Proctor, whose edition was issued serially at exactly the same time as Knight's and is now remembered, if at all, for the images

2.1 Title-page to *Julius Caesar* from Charles Knight's *Pictorial Shakspere*, 1838–43, combining two scenes of the play with fasces, bundles of sticks emblematic of the emperor's power—techniques of presentation used in the opening images of all the plays in the edition.

of Kenny Meadows, avoiding Knight's strict historicism and verging on the bizarre in their presentation of scene and character (see Illustration 2.1). That both editions were extensively illustrated reveals the concern for the visual that in many ways dominated the age. For Knight, this was filtered through a concern for antiquarianism that would later flourish on the stage, and aided by the costume historian James Robinson Planché, who contributed notes on dress to each play. Cornwall's approach was far closer to imaginative constructions developed elsewhere in painting that placed the texts within the visual imagination of their own time—although Meadows' style was something rarely approached by other artists of his time, except possibly Richard Dadd. In their own, very different, ways, each edition offered a unified experience of the plays in word and image that, for many, was the initial encounter with Shakespeare. To dismiss something that cost 2/6 per monthly part, totalling £7, as aimed at a popular readership is seriously to misrepresent its aims: the editions of Knight and Cornwall predominantly offered Shakespeare to the emerging middle classes, a financial stratum above those who clubbed together to find the sixpence for each part of the novels of Dickens, issued at exactly the same time as these Shakespeare editions.

In this intended readership, these two editions are quite different from other aspects of editing activity with which they were contemporary, largely the concern of wealthy amateurs engaged in debates that, to many outside their charmed circle, seemed remote and obsessive in their detail. Ironically, an early force in this was the most notorious Shakespeare forger of the age, John Payne Collier, whose *Reasons for a New Edition of Shakespeare's Works* (1842) essentially stated the terms of a debate that would last through the century. Here, as often in books from before the twentieth century, the full title is suggestive. It goes on to include *Notices of the defects of former impressions, and pointing out the lately acquired means of illustrating the plays, poems, and biography of the poet*. The conjunction of academic rivalry, claims of new discoveries, and the folding back of all these to reveal the life of the dramatist, suggests many of the forces driving academic editing in the mid-century. The volume itself addressed what had always been the central issue of editing, that of establishing the author's final intention and presenting it in print. Collier argued that greater weight should be given to Quarto texts, going beyond their value in contest with the Folio to explore running changes made within printing so that individual copies differed—a complex issue only explored with anything like completeness in the online *Hamlet*

Quartos project of the first decade of the twenty-first century. Collier also had other concerns: chronology, punctuation, and metre, and specific 'errors' in editions of individual plays and—unusually for this period—the poems.

The three editions he produced (1842–4, 1853, and 1858) rested on these principles; but his editorial work was largely overshadowed by a much darker aspect of his activities. Part of Collier's editorial processes rested on the 'Perkins Folio', a copy of the Second Folio of 1632 with annotations by a figure, purportedly a relative of an actor in the King's Men, who became known as 'The Old Corrector'. In 1852 Collier claimed to have discovered this in a London bookshop, and presented it as an authentic source for textual emendation. A vigorous exchange followed, its contributors including Charles Knight, culminating with N. E. S. A. Hamilton's *Inquiry into the Manuscript Corrections* (1860), and the annotations were finally exposed as being in his own hand. After Collier's death, several other documents he claimed to have found were revealed as forgeries; meanwhile, he continued to work as a scholar, claiming that he was the victim, not the perpetrator, of the forgery. But the whole episode is intriguing because of its bringing together the most advanced forensic examination techniques with the plot intricacies of the burgeoning detective novels.

In consequence of this activity, Collier is often bracketed with J. O. Halliwell, who in 1872 changed his name to Halliwell-Phillipps to ensure his wife's inheritance from a father who despised her chosen spouse. This was not without cause. Early in his career Halliwell had stolen some manuscripts from Trinity College, Cambridge, and then sold them to the British Museum; later, he borrowed and mutilated a first Quarto of *Hamlet* from his prospective father-in-law. Despite this, he produced between 1853 and 1865 a 15-volume edition of the plays, lavishly illustrated by F. W. Fairholt, and limited to 150 sets, and was important in the production of facsimiles of the Quartos (see below). He is also notable for his work on Shakespeare's life, discussed in Chapter 6. Despite the nefarious activities of their creators, the works of Halliwell and Collier contributed further to the controversies that drove Victorian Shakespeare editing: the Folio and Quarto dilemma, the degree of annotation needed, and the underlying question of purpose—was editing the plays a preserve of amateurs, or an activity of professional publishers intent on spreading the word of the Bard as a cornerstone of national identity?

Probably the closest approach to answering these questions came in the 1860s with the appearance of what was known as the Cambridge edition, although its nine volumes, appearing between 1863 and 1866, were published by the London firm of Macmillan. The name derives from its being the work of Cambridge scholars printed by Cambridge University Press, marking a major shift in Shakespeare activity into the hands of professional academics, in this case all from Trinity College: William George Clark, John Glover, and William Aldis Wright. The textual position was clearly stated: it would be collated from Quartos and the First Folio, but in all cases textual variants would be made clear in annotations and—crucially—there were no changes resting on rhythmic or grammatical consistency, or on conjectural authorial intention. Where the Quarto differed significantly from what was termed 'the received text', its text was given in smaller type immediately afterwards. Spelling and punctuation were, however, modernized; and it was the first edition to contain line numbers, introducing the system of citation by act, scene, and line that remained the primary form of reference until the growing use of through line numbers (TLNs) at the very end of the twentieth century. After each play came a short section of notes, to explain variant readings, justify any deviations from the edition's stated principles, or offer clarification of complex passages. Those for *The Tempest*, for example, ran to six pages, and concerned matters of grammar, punctuation, or meter. In all these ways, the edition set the standard approach that would be followed throughout the century and long into the next. The absence of the lengthy introductory material, common in all earlier editions, and the abbreviated annotation immediately threw the interest onto the text itself, making it immediately less intimidatory—something much aided by the nicely proportioned page design and clear font of its nine volumes.

The impact of the Cambridge edition was extended by the use of its text in the 'Globe' edition (1864), a single volume with no critical apparatus except a closing glossary extending to 83 double-column pages. It was, however, of great importance in presenting the text of a major scholarly edition for a mere 3/6—a price calculated on an estimated print run of 50,000 in three years, again demonstrating the essential presence of financial calculus alongside academic scholarship. The eventual print run, including the last edition of 1911, was a touch short of a quarter of a million, by which time it had established itself as the reference standard for general readers as well as for the increasing numbers of those studying Shakespeare for academic purposes as English literature began to establish itself as a separate, if not universally respected, discipline of study at the older, as well as the more recently established, universities.

This did not mean that its primacy was immediately established. During the 1850s and 60s two extensively illustrated editions appeared in serial form, curiously paralleling the earlier pairing of Cornwall and Knight. These were produced by Howard Staunton, with illustrations by Sir John Gilbert (1856–60), and Mary and Charles Cowden Clarke, with images designed by Henry Courtney Selous (1864–9). These differed from their earlier equivalents by including far more images, all cut into the text (see Illustration 2.2). Gilbert's were powerfully effective in placing the onlooker within the action, Selous's by translating events into the visual vocabulary of the popular illustrated magazine. That both rejected the aesthetic sophistication of the so-called 'sixties style' woodcuts produced to illustrate expensive editions of Tennyson and others was not the point: they allowed more immediate progress into the words of the play as a product of the reader's imagination and, in Gilbert's case, were reproduced in a large number of other editions, of all formats and prices, for the next two decades.

The simultaneous availability of these two illustrated editions and the Globe and Cambridge is perhaps the most direct evidence of a parting of the ways between editions directed for study and those intended for general reading—for individual pleasure or for reading aloud in the family or by groups of friends. This fissure would widen in the remaining years of the century, to be matched by others in which editions of particular types would emerge to satisfy specialized groups of readers and ways of reading. By the end of the century it seemed that every possible aspect of the Shakespeare market had been covered. In 1864 John Dicks produced a serial edition at one penny per part, offering for a further seven pence a separate case binding into which the completed set could be sewn on completion. The text itself is near-microscopic, and presumably read by many

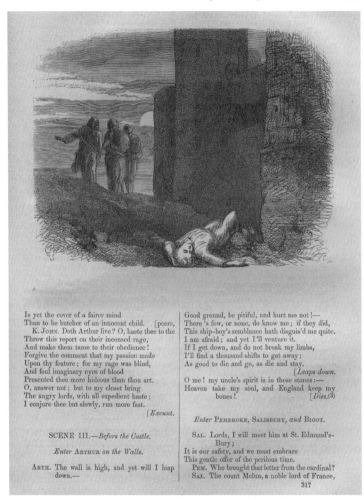

Is yet the cover of a fairer mind
Than to be butcher of an innocent child.   [peers,
  K. JOHN. Doth Arthur live? O, haste thee to the
Throw this report on their incensed rage,
And make them tame to their obedience!
Forgive the comment that my passion made
Upon thy feature; for my rage was blind,
And foul imaginary eyes of blood
Presented thee more hideous than thou art.
O, answer not; but to my closet bring
The angry lords, with all expedient haste;
I conjure thee but slowly, run more fast.
                                         [*Exeunt.*

                SCENE III.—*Before the Castle.*

              Enter ARTHUR *on the Walls.*

  ARTH. The wall is high, and yet will I leap
down.—

Good ground, be pitiful, and hurt me not!—
There's few, or none, do know me; if they did,
This ship-boy's semblance hath disguis'd me quite.
I am afraid; and yet I'll venture it.
If I get down, and do not break my limbs,
I'll find a thousand shifts to get away;
As good to die and go, as die and stay.
                                    [*Leaps down.*
O me! my uncle's spirit is in these stones:—
Heaven take my soul, and England keep my
      bones!   [*Dies.*(3)

        Enter PEMBROKE, SALISBURY, *and* BIGOT.

  SAL. Lords, I will meet him at St. Edmund's-
      Bury;
It is our safety, and we must embrace
This gentle offer of the perilous time.
  PEM. Who brought that letter from the cardinal?
  SAL. The count Melun, a noble lord of France,
                                              317

2.2 A page from *King John*, edited by Howard Staunton and illustrated by John Gilbert. Image and text work together here, the former suggesting the action that will shortly follow, thus both delaying the reading process and anticipating an emotional response to events in one of the most popular plays for the Victorians.

with aid of a magnifying glass; but the illustrations, generally of two characters, that preface each play are astute in the presentation of key encounters (see Illustration 2.3). Even here, marketing was of the essence, the serial parts matched by a casebound copy at two shillings and an early paperback version for half that. Dicks claimed a total sale of 700,000 of all these variants in a two-year period. In 1890 Ward and Lock offered a casebound volume for sixpence, after which the battle for the cheapest edition that could actually be read reached its conclusion. Yet we should not ignore the miniature editions, about a third the size of a present-day paperback, that became fashionable near the century's close and were designed to be carried in ladies' reticules, or came encased in miniature bookcases. And these mark another climax: surely nobody actually read the plays in these minute volumes, so that they are the most complete, as well as the most diminutive, statement of the play's ownership as cultural marker.

Many other collected editions appeared in the second half of the century, some using quite new textual procedures but most building on earlier work. Remarkable among them were the four editions of Nikolaus Delius, appearing first in 1854 with text and commentary in English but, in subsequent editions of 1854–61, 1864, and 1872, supplementing the same text with a commentary in German, evidencing the continuing importance of Shakespeare's work in that country. The latest English edition presented the text without annotation, a brief comment explaining that these might 'distract the reader's attention'. The text prepared by Delius was also employed in the Leopold Shakespeare of 1877, so called because of its dedication to Prince Leopold, the youngest son of Queen Victoria. The edition was notable for two other reasons: its introduction in which Frederick J. Furnivall expounded his theories concerning Shakespeare's versification and the dating of the plays, discussed later in this chapter, and the inclusion of both *The Two Noble Kinsmen* and *Edward III* as canonical plays—although it should be noted that Charles Knight had included both these and a number of others in a supplementary volume, titled 'Apocryphal Plays', to his edition of the 1840s.

The Delius and the Leopold were both avowedly scholarly editions, but the identity of that by Henry Irving and Frank A. Marshall, known as 'The Henry Irving Shakespeare' (1888–90), is less clear. Dowden provided a general introduction and each play had a brief

2.3 Title page to *All's Well that Ends Well* from John Dicks' *Complete Works of Shakspere*, 1864. This functioned as cover, dramatis personae and frontispiece for each serial part.

introduction by a different critic, with some unexpected choices such as Arthur Symons on *Measure for Measure*. The prefatory 'Advertisement' to the subscription edition promised a text 'given entire, without garbling or mutilation', and assured readers that 'the best readings have been adopted' for doubtful passages. The text itself is full of lines enclosed between square brackets to signify cuts that might be made in production, relying heavily on those made by Irving himself. This would not make it unique as an edition based on performance. John Bell's editions of 1774–5 used the prompt books from Drury Lane and Covent Garden, and Charles Kean's editions scrupulously recorded the text and, more important, the additional scenic episodes, from his Princess's Theatre productions of the 1850s. Yet the function of Irving and Marshall's volumes as performing editions is undermined both by the presence of approaching 600 illustrations by Gordon Browne— son of Hablôt Knight Browne, Dickens's 'Phiz'—quite unrelated to stage production, and through the suggestion that the bracketed passages are those that might be omitted in performance, not those actually excised at the Lyceum. In short, the volumes seemingly aim to combine theatrical kudos with scholarly respectability, a not unlikely reflection of the late-Victorian move to make the theatre more credible as a serious occupation. This was not the only later edition to use illustrations. In the 1870s, Charles Knight issued his 'Imperial Shakespeare,' using his earlier text with reproductions, as steel engravings, of many of the best-known Shakespeare paintings of the age, and Howard Staunton's edition with John Gilbert's illustrations was reissued in large-paper format, significantly changing the rhythmic placement of images within the play text to offer some intriguing juxtapositions of character and event.

Despite the profusion of popular texts and the seeming dominance of the Cambridge edition, battles over relative primacy of competing early texts and issues of spelling and punctuation struggled on, and the antiquarian impulse in editing was undiminished. Facsimile editions, editions of the Quartos, and editions of individual plays with profuse annotation all multiplied, taking advantage of new methods of production to make available both texts and the issues they raised to a wider community of readers and scholars. Between 1862 and 1864 Lionel Booth issued the first facsimile of the First Folio, a typeset reproduction that meticulously reproduced not only lineation but also broken type and apparent errors in the original. Howard Staunton was the first to produce, between 1864 and 1866, a true facsimile using photolithography, following this with a version in reduced size in 1876. These were of considerable value, but did not take notice of the many variations between individual copies of the Folio—the small changes and corrections made by the typesetter during the course of production, in effect making each printed copy unique.

At the same time, work was being done to make available the texts of the Quartos, the first series of facsimiles being issued by E. W. Ashbee and James Halliwell between 1861 and 1871. The production of the 48 volumes, all in photolithographic facsimile, was a major publishing undertaking, including *Hamlet* Quartos of 1603, 1604, and 1605 and multiple versions of other plays, including the so-called 'Pavier Quartos' issued by Thomas Pavier in 1619. The undertaking did something to restore Halliwell's scholarly reputation, and he continued to publish critical papers and editions of source documents, some in single-figure limited editions, maintaining to the end the position of aristocratic antiquarianism. A further series of the Quartos, with some differences and the inclusion of some variant copies, was produced by W. Griggs and C. Praetorius between 1880 and 1891. These rejected photographic reproduction in favour of producing lithographic plates by making tracings, by hand, of each letter of each page, an extraordinarily laborious and time-consuming undertaking, the advantages of which are not immediately obvious. While the earlier series was privately published, each volume costing five guineas (£5/5/-), the later cost only five shillings for each volume, which came with a critical introduction. This was a considerable advance, but the texts were still restricted to a wealthy few. It would not be until the Malone Society series of the twentieth century, and later scholarly editions such as those of Cambridge University Press, that the full texts of the Quartos were available more freely.

The continuing availability and use of these editions, and that of the Cambridge and Globe volumes, well into the twentieth century suggests that, by the close of the reign, the form in which Shakespeare's texts were presented to readers, if not the actual identity of the texts themselves in the words on the printed page, was now defined with relative consistency. Instead of the eighteenth-century practice of beginning each successive edition with the prefatory matter of each earlier one from the First Folio onwards, a life of Shakespeare and a series of documents in which Shakespeare's will was prominent, the pattern was now concentrated more directly on the plays themselves. The reader of a collected edition at the end of the century might expect an introductory exposition of the dating of the plays; a discussion of sources; some notes about the theatre in which they were originally performed, and perhaps something approaching a critical introduction stressing their unique literary, moral and national value. Single-play volumes often extended these elements in depth. The battle between Quarto and Folio had in general resulted in a compromise solution, with editors selecting the most convincing of the available alternatives, often presented as the most seemingly authorial. Annotation, where used, would offer explanations of unfamiliar words or difficult passages, and in some cases give variant readings of Quarto and Folio or suggestions of earlier editors. While the general move was away from conjectural emendation, some of the earlier constructions—called the 'received text' in the Cambridge edition—remained. Malvolio's 'Some are born great' speech, slightly adapted by Nicholas Rowe's edition, remained, as did Mistress Quickly's 'a babbled of green fields,' Lewis Theobald's lovely but entirely imagined replacement for 'a table of green fields', the latter only coming under question in the late twentieth century. Annotations appeared either at the foot of the page or collected at the end, along with a glossary, with the aim of making the initial reading more immediate in a manner, we should remember, recommended by Samuel Johnson himself.

Single-play editions aimed at student readers began to appear in large quantities nearer the end of the period. The earliest was the 15-volume *Collins School and College Classics* series, edited by several scholars led by Samuel Neil, which appeared between 1873 and 1879. Also important were the single-play editions of *The Oxford and Cambridge Shakespeare*, 'prepared specially for the Oxford and Cambridge Local Examinations'. Typical is the *As You Like It* (1884). The volume opens with a scene-by-scene summary, which compares its events to the major source in Thomas Lodge's *Rosalynd*, and the text itself has footnote comments clarifying issues of grammar and allusion as well as clarifying complex passages. There is a short

Glossary, a list of proper names, and, most revealing to later readers, a series of questions taken from the Oxford and Cambridge examination papers (see Illustration 2.4). These reveal a great deal about the ways in which the plays were taught and examined at the end of the century; few present-day students would find them straightforward. While these volumes aimed at those in the growing numbers of local authority schools, a different group was addressed by the small volumes of 'The Rugby Shakespeare', initially produced for use at Rugby School. Far less extensive in their introductions and annotations, they are interesting for what they reveal about reading and teaching practices in the public schools of the period. In some cases the texts are expurgated. In *Hamlet* (1885), for example, the passage playing on 'country matters' between Hamlet and Ophelia before the Players perform 'The Mousetrap' is excised, although it was at the time freely available in the Cambridge and Globe texts. By contrast, *The Tempest* (1876) includes the account of Caliban's attempt to rape Miranda. Does this, perhaps, suggest that to young gentlemen sexual violence is quite appropriate to a 'salvage and deformed slave', but bawdy wordplay unthinkable for the young Prince of Denmark? Some attitudes to character seem similarly concerned to extend ideas of rank and duty: 'the folly of Lear never seems for a moment to rob him of his royalty of nature', we are confidently told. Occasionally contemporary issues intervene. Referring to Gervinus' comment that 'Hamlet is Germany', the volume editor, the Rev. Charles E. Moberly (Late Assistant Master in Rugby School) expresses the hope that 'the political life of revived Germany will be as strong, as fruitful and as enlightening as her literary research has hitherto been'. In these and similar passages the editions are suggestive about the place of Shakespeare in the education of the upper middle classes.

　The textual modifications of these editions rest on quite a different premise from those of the edition of Henrietta and Thomas Bowdler, begun in 1818 but completed in a version of 1853 which achieved widespread popularity. Whereas the Rugby volumes are aimed at boys in public schools, the Bowdlers' texts deleted phrases, and in some cases whole scenes, deemed unfit for family reading. Although largely the work of Henrietta, forces of decorum demanded that her name be withheld: if passages were deleted as unseemly for sensitive feminine eyes, the work of their identification could surely not be

26. Restore the following passage to its original form as it stands in the text, and paraphrase it :

'I must have liberty withal, as large a charter as the wind, to blow on whom I please ; for so fools have ; and they that are most galled with my folly, they most must laugh. And why, sir, must they so ? The "why" is plain as way to parish church : he that a fool doth wisely hit doth very foolishly, although he smart, (not to) seem senseless of the bob : if not, the wise man's folly is anatomized even by the squandering glances of the fool. Invest me in my motley.'

27. Give the etymology of *roynish, fond, churlish, charlot, naught, not, graff, leer, atone, troth, eyne, se'nnight.*

28. Scan the following lines, and comment on the prosody of them :

(1.) 'But justly, as you have exceeded all promise.'
(2.) 'Her very silence and her patience.'
(3.) 'And churlish chiding of the winter's wind,
        Which, when it bites and blows upon my body.'
(4.) 'Stood on the extremest verge of the swift brook.'
(5.) 'Alack, in me what strange effect
        Would they work in mild aspect !
        Whiles you chid me I did love ;
        How then might your prayers move ?'
(6.) 'In second childishness and mere oblivion,
        Sans teeth, sans eyes, sans taste, sans everything.'

29. From what earlier work is the plot of this play taken, and what are the chief alterations made by Shakespeare ?

30. Recount the events and motives which bring Oliver to Arden and reconcile him to Orlando.

31. State what incidents of the play seem to you most strikingly improbable, and criticize their effect from a dramatic point of view.

32. Comment on the following, with particular reference to the state of society in Shakespeare's age :

(1.) 'Love . . . . deserves as well a dark house and a whip as madmen do.'
(2.) 'By my life, I do ; which I tender dearly, though I say I am a magician.'
(3.) 'Sir Oliver Mar-text.'
(4.) 'Like as halfpence.'
(5.) 'We quarrel in print, by the book, as men have books for good manners.'
(6.) '*Ros.* (as epilogue). If I were a woman.'

33. Write a short description of the characters of Jaques and Touchstone. What rank does the latter hold amongst Shakespeare's clowns ? Mention the best of them, and the plays in which they take part.

2.4 Questions from the Oxford and Cambridge edition of *As You Like It*, 1884. The range of themes is formidable, among others including etymology, narrative sources, scansion, social history, and dramatic effect, demonstrating the nature of Victorian secondary education at its highest level.

presented as that of a woman. Often reviled as the epitome of Victorian prudery, the work deserves more charitable treatment: it was never intended to displace fuller texts in serious study, and did much to encourage the habit of reading aloud in the family, an introduction to the plays for many Victorians.

Towards the end of the century two projects began that, in developed and extended form, remain essential to the process of reading and studying the plays. That one took place in America and the other in Britain itself reveals the degree to which Shakespeare studies and performance had become international. This was the Variorum Shakespeare, begun by Horace Howard Furness in 1871, with *Romeo and Juliet*. In 1928 the founder's son edited *Coriolanus*, bringing to an end the first Variorum series, although not completing the canon, work on which is still proceeding. The aim, then as now, was simply to record every item of textual and scholarly study written about the play since its first appearance, along with all instances of textual variation between Quartos and Folio. The second venture was more diverse: the introduction of individual volumes aimed at students studying Shakespeare at a higher level in teacher-training college and university departments of English Literature.

The earliest of these was the Clarendon series, published by Oxford University Press between 1868 and 1897, eventually comprising 17 of the most often studied plays, edited by Aldis Wright, working with Clark for the first four volumes and using a sometimes modified version of their Cambridge Shakespeare text. Cambridge University Press, presumably relying instead on their authoritative collected edition, came late to individual plays, beginning with the Pitt Press Shakespeare in 1890 and continuing it until 1936, when it was replaced by the New Shakespeare edited by John Dover Wilson. Then came the Warwick Shakespeare (1893–1938) under the editorship of C. H. Herford, also involved in the magisterial collected edition of the works of Ben Jonson, which remained in use, highly valued for its annotations and introductions, well into the next century. All were serious endeavours, making available the most scholarly texts and often containing original introductory material. Aldis Wright's Clarendon *Tempest* (1874), for example, contains in its eighteen-page preface discussion of the date, sources in Montaigne and the Summers Bermuda venture, an engagement with some recent critical comments, discussion and rejection of some possible narrative sources, the Dryden-Davenant adaptation of 1770, and various other explicatory matter. Along with the endnotes, occupying 86 pages in contrast to the text's 67, this presents the volume as an impressive tool for the critical understanding of the text by senior high school, certificate, and undergraduate students. It might also, one hopes, have given food for thought to those preparing for the Colonial Civil Service examinations.

In 1899 appeared Edward Dowden's edition of *Hamlet*, the first volume of the Arden Shakespeare, a new series under the general editorship of W. J. Craig. With the single play editions of Oxford and Cambridge University Presses it would form the holy trinity of twentieth-century Shakespeare editions in the United Kingdom. As Victoria's reign drew to its end, the essential raw materials for engagement with Shakespeare's plays, at initial and advanced levels of study, had thus been established. So, too, was the practice of single volumes presenting the whole canon for general readers and, between these extremes, a barely measurable diversity of published versions of the texts, each aimed at a clearly identified readership defined by gender and rank. Together, they constituted a remarkable achievement that brought together fundamental aspects of Victorian society—its mechanical inventiveness, rigorous scholarly endeavour, antiquarianism, and not least the ceaseless drive for self-advancement and national cultural identity.

* * * * *

With the rapid increase of editions, writing about Shakespeare began to proliferate in both kind and volume. The single major form this took rested on earlier work on verse forms and linguistic structures to form a chronology of the plays, separated into periods, to explore the plays' growing complexity. The work of Gervinus has already been noted; this was supplemented by writers in England. W. S. Walker published *Shakespeare's Versification* in 1854, Charles Bathurst followed this in 1857 with *Difference in Shakespeare's Versification at Different Periods of his Life* in 1857, and these were given more rigorous, tabulated form by Frederick Gard Fleay in the New Shakespeare Society's *Transactions* of 1874. This used metrical analysis as the basis of critical study, showing how the greater freedom of the later plays evidenced Shakespeare's increasing insight into human nature, taken from personal experience rather than rhetorical exercise, while also revealing the qualities of his own mind. In the work of certain writers this merged with discussions of the plays' dramatic structures; yet it bore little resemblance to the techniques of later critical analysis that addressed language, metaphor, and idea.

This combination of critical aims, apparent in the work of many Victorian critics, owes much to the *Commentaries* of Gervinus, discussed earlier in relation to their dating of the plays. In their final chapter, the author extends the discussion into areas of character and morality, beginning by placing Shakespeare on the same level as Homer, in achieving in drama what his predecessor did in the epic, and continuing with these words:

As the rarest judge of men and human affairs, he is a teacher of indisputable authority, and the most worthy to be chosen as a guide through the world, and through life.

Shakespeare is not without fault, however: Gervinus makes clear his shortcomings, especially in the earlier plays, which include:

his marks of a perverted and uncultivated taste in his indelicacies, his laboured plays upon words, and his odd conceits, or in the cutting off of heads, and putting out of eyes on the stage.

These 'disfigurements' are however forgiven because, in the contest between 'taste and truth', Homer, like Shakespeare, 'would not have hesitated': it is the greater human understanding that wins through.

How, though, is this achieved? In discussing individual plays Gervinus is very assertive about character but imprecise in detail. Of Olivia's place as 'the central point of the whole action' of *Twelfth Night*, for example, he claims simply that 'her relation to the self-loving trait in the Duke's character, is unusually and skilfully woven'. In discussing *The Merchant of Venice*, he refers to Jessica as 'delicately feminine', seeing her theft of her father's jewels as 'a new relation in possession ... that of the inexperienced child'. Elsewhere he talks of the 'high moral spirit' of the plays, and the balance between characters within them as reflecting 'the original indivisibility of nature', in which 'the single character can properly only be a means to the aim of the whole'. This results from Shakespeare's essential realism which, avoiding any overtly stated creed or system, instead rests on his belief that 'the laws of morality' are 'written plainly enough on the tablet of the human heart'. Implicit within all this is the assumption of a moral view shared by Shakespeare, Gervinus, and their readers: there is no need to explain further, least of all through any analysis of linguistic or dramatic form, because the essential nature of humanity is already understood. Just as the editors of the Cambridge edition did not see the need to explain their methods of achieving their final text, so Gervinus sees no need to say how the words and movements of the plays convey their truth: universality of understanding does not, by direct implication, need any explanation. It is this truth universally acknowledged that permeates Shakespeare criticism, something demonstrably Victorian in its assurance.

Occasionally, though, Gervinus moves close towards the critical readings of a later period. Here, for instance, is part of his discussion of *The Tempest*:

It is not impossible, that Shakespeare in this piece, and especially in regard to Caliban (whose name is a near anagram of Cannibal) meant to answer the great question of the day, concerning the justifiableness of European usurpation over the wild aborigines of the new world.

Continuing by saying that the Earl of Southampton, Shakespeare's patron, was a major figure in the Virginia Company, Gervinus comes close here to a kind of political historicism that would be significant in the following century, and which moves away from what can sometimes feel a rather cosy, unquestioning acceptance of a consensual view of morality in the pages of the *Commentaries* as translated by Bunnett.

A similar approach is taken by Furnivall in his introduction to the Leopold Shakespeare. There, discussion of character is related more to the differences in the periods of the plays and what they reveal of Shakespeare's life and thought, with a touch of Victorian sentiment about character. Here, for example, is Furnivall on *The Tempest*:

No play brings out more clearly than *The Tempest* the fourth-period spirit; and Miranda evidently belongs to that time; she and her fellow, Perdita, belong to that time, being idealisations of the sweet country maidens whom Shakespeare would see about him in his renewed family life at Stratford.

It is not just 'the spirit' that marks off the periods of the plays: Furnivall makes specific distinctions between the metrical structures of the earliest and the latest writings. The mature works contain a far greater proportion of run-on lines, central pauses, lines with eleven syllables and those with weak endings; Shakespeare 'soon gave up the doggrel [sic], the excessive word-play, quip and crank... puns, conceits, and occasional bombast' as he moved to control his fantasy and subdue his rhetoric. Seen from a distance, the movement reflects something of the Victorians' own concern for progress, even perhaps a hint of Darwinist evolution, as the plays are shown within a carefully structured and meticulously tabulated development. Furnivall's introduction is important for more than comments of this kind, though: he offers advice on the best books to read on Shakespeare, compares the division of the texts into periods by Gervinus and Dowden, and in general offers a rounded critical introduction to the plays themselves, anticipating the range, if not the content, covered by editors in much more recent editions.

In 1880 the poet Algernon Charles Swinburne published *A Study of Shakespeare*. Notorious for poetry that, for the Victorians, was explicit in its exploration of erotic themes—'Dolores, our lady of pain' was his most celebrated lyric—Swinburne here follows very much the same direction as Gervinus in concentrating on character and morality. He divides the plays into three periods, Lyric and Fantastic, Comic and Historic, and Tragic and Romantic, discussing in turn each of the plays within these categories. Rather than relying on metrical tests, he instead stresses the importance of 'the mere text itself', and the qualities that reveal it as early, middle, or late to any sensitive reader, advocating 'study by ear alone'. Again there is adulatory assertion, with little analytic support. The second period is 'the national side' of Shakespeare, the *Henry IV–V* sequence 'the great national trilogy' presented through 'the heroic vein of patriotism'. Perhaps developing Gervinus' idea of the balance between character and whole, Swinburne describes *Othello* and *Hamlet* as complete entities, whereas 'Constance is the jewel of *King John*, and Katherine is the crowning blossom of *Henry VIII*'. Of Arthur in *King John* and Cordelia in *Lear* he writes 'The place they have in our lives and thoughts is not one for words'. Sometimes plays are rejected without explicit reason: the ending of *Measure for Measure* 'completely unsatisfactory'. Where any kind of critical evaluation is made, it is through comparison with classical drama: the third period plays differ from those of Aeschylus because their 'fatalism is of a darker and harder nature', and consideration of the sociopolitical frame of *Coriolanus* is dismissed as a waste of time. Character is all. Cleopatra is 'the perfect and the everlasting woman', and Cordelia and Imogen are figures of wonder: 'Godlike though they be, their very Godhead is human and feminine; and only therefore credible, and only therefor adorable'. The discussion of the plays ends with Imogen, 'the woman above all Shakespeare's women'.

What is apparent throughout the book is Swinburne's mistrust of academic critics, whom he dismisses as 'Cantabrigian Magi, led by the star of their goddess Mathesis'. The volume's appendix develops this more fully. Titled 'Report on the Proceedings on the first anniversary session of the Newest Shakespeare Society', it pokes fun at the activities of Furnivall and others, including a debate on 'the lameness of Shakespeare—was it moral or physical?' and another establishing George Peele as the author of *Romeo and Juliet*. It is witty and inventive, but underlying it is a serious rejection of an approach to the plays that Swinburne thought extreme in its concern for minutiae of structure or source.

A related concern for character, chronology, and morality of texts and authors is evident in the work of the other major writer of the period, Edward Dowden. His first work, *Shakspere: A Critical Study of his Mind and Art* (1875) was followed by a much shorter but more widely read *Shakespeare Primer* (1877). Both divide the work into four periods, each explored to suggest what it revealed of Shakespeare's critical and moral intelligence. In many instances Dowden engages directly with earlier scholars' concerns about dating the plays, but moves beyond them to explain their significance in terms of character-drawing or larger ethical force—for example, he agrees with Gervinus that *Timon of Athens* is a very late play, completed by another hand, but uses this to explore the character of Timon as evidence of Shakespeare's insight. Dowden's later *Shakspere* gives titles to each of the periods which suggest his approach, a mixture of literary analysis, intellectual biography of the dramatist, and awareness of larger moral function. The sequence moves from 'In the workshop' to 'In the world', through 'Out of the depths' to 'On the heights'. Each of these stages depends on a reading of the plays with the aim as much of revealing the growing maturity and changing experience of their author as clarifying their literary and dramatic identities. Often the plays are employed primarily to evidence Shakespeare's changing nature, and show how it reveals the plays' developing human understanding and moral purpose. While the stance might seem outmoded, and was sharply attacked by C. J. Sisson's *The Mythical Sorrows of Shakespeare* (1934), similar approaches were followed by later writers. Wilson Knight's sequence of books rest on similar assumptions, as does the much more recent *Shakespeare the Thinker* (2007) by A. D. Nuttall. Dowden also showed a broader understanding of the work of the critic. His essay 'Some Old Shakespearians' showed an awareness of the history of Shakespeare criticism from the eighteenth century onwards, and in 'Shakespeare as a man of Science' he disposed with clinical efficiency of the claims of such identity, most immediately as advanced by Judge Webb, as spurious and ill-founded.

Concerns with the plays as theatric or literary structures do not figure prominently in the Victorian reading of Shakespeare. One early example, little known but in its way quite innovative, was a small volume published in 1849 by the Reverend N. J. Halpin, titled *The Dramatic Unities of Shakespeare*. The title itself engages with the largely invented 'classical unities', for the rejection of which Shakespeare was first castigated and then lionized as the embodiment of English pragmatism in the eighteenth century: but Halpin's idea of unity is quite different. He suggests that the plays work like dramatic landscape paintings, their action in detail in the foreground with supporting events and figures sketched more lightly at the rear, the result achieving a harmony of event and idea that is the real dramatic unity of the plays. Now almost wholly forgotten, the work is interesting because it continues an earlier controversy about the plays and suggests the importance of visual structures to a contemporary critic, something that will become increasingly dominant in the plays' performance from the 1850s onwards.

In 1885 Richard G. Moulton, a member of the New Shakspere Society, published a volume whose subtitle makes its aims abundantly clear: *Shakespeare as a Dramatic Artist: A Popular Illustration of the Principles of Scientific Criticism*. This claimed to rest on inductive reasoning rather than earlier notions of taste or judgment and, after a rigorous and methodical rejection of these in the history of

Shakespeare criticism, presented a series of 'Principles of inductive criticism'. The volume then goes on to analyse the construction of five plays, eventually extended to nine in subsequent editions, in a variety of ways, including plot and underplot, action, irony, and character construction, both singly and in dramatic interaction. This is not a complete change of approach, as the titles of some chapters suggest: 'How nemesis and destiny are interwoven in "Macbeth"'; 'How the Play of Julius Caesar works up to a climax at the centre'; 'How "As You Like It" presents varied forms of Humour in conflict with a single conventionality'. Certainly there is concern with larger elements of human behaviour; but that the majority of the chapter titles begin with 'How' suggests a much larger concern with method than was present in earlier criticism. That Moulton began his career as a lecturer to the Board of Extension Studies at Cambridge is suggestive: it reflects the greater emphasis placed on literary study as a distinct method in the newer universities and their departments existing for part-time students, than in the older universities where the concern was more with complexities of editing and, until the century's closing decades, with the study of classical literature.

When Victoria's reign drew to its close, Shakespeare editing had adopted many of the forms of the century that followed, resting on scholarly examination of sources, grammatical and rhetorical structures, and the dating of the plays, while criticism developed some of these areas in addressing the plays. But in them all, the stamp of the Victorian mind is deeply imprinted. Its near-obsession with identification and naming, of placing within a tabular structure, is one feature of this. Alongside it are constructions of identity, personal in the life of the author, generic in the discussion of characters, and the larger issues of national distinctiveness, with its implications of duty and rank. Paradoxically, too, there is a strong force of sentiment, especially in the discussion of women characters. These are topics that will recur throughout this book, and are apparent, albeit modified by generic impulses, in the performance of the plays, the subject of the next chapter.

3

Performance

In 1843, the Theatre Regulation Act was passed, repealing the Licensing Act of 1737 that restricted the performance of spoken drama to the two patent theatres, Drury Lane and Covent Garden. That this was the result of a government enquiry, at a time when there was as yet no compulsory education system, let alone a school-leaving age, and the cessation of child labour in mines was less than a decade old, says much about the priorities of the establishment. It also reveals something uniquely Victorian; the importance of cultural forms as a way of offering moral guidance to the people. That Shakespeare was the single most important dramatist whose works were thus released for more widespread performance is by no means incidental: already established in the preceding century as the greatest statement of English values, the works were increasingly becoming a means of moral guidance and instruction, as their adaptation for reading by children and the growing number of editions aimed at popular readership make clear. Just as the desire to read the plays was not restricted to the wealthier, more educated classes, the hunger for Shakespeare on stage was pervasive across boundaries of rank. Although many of the new, or newly-enfranchised, theatres were in less fashionable areas of London, this did not mean that they were all disreputable music halls, nor that the patent theatres were not also visited by poorer people eager for entertainment that would stimulate and offer cultural advancement. This was, though, progressively reflected in theatre design, with the various areas of seating differently priced and rigidly separated, with separate entrances and, as the theatres grew in size, separate refreshment areas.

As this paragraph suggests, the course of Shakespeare performance was in part decided by forces other than those concerned only with the business of acting; but it would be a mistake to see the two as wholly separate. At the beginning of Victoria's reign, theatres and the performance styles they encouraged had changed little since the middle of the preceding century. The restriction of drama without music to two London theatres throughout the eighteenth century meant that, to accommodate the audiences, the auditoria had become extremely large, both housing around 3,000 at the start of Victoria's reign. Even in 1846, when Covent Garden was refurbished, it was capable of seating this number, and such structures inevitably impacted on styles of performance. Speeches were delivered in a declamatory sing-song, and gestures were flamboyant, semaphoring emotion to the distant galleries. These elements combined with the cult of individual actors to produce performances in which others clustered around the main performer, with little sense of dramatic interaction or what would later become known as ensemble performance. This effect, of isolated recitals rather than an integrated progress of language, response, and event, was heightened by the paucity of rehearsals.

Although stages were now lit with lime, not candles, the action was largely, as in the eighteenth century, conducted on an apron stage, flanked by boxes that brought the most affluent audience members within touching distance of the cast. The stage itself would be covered in green baize, and scenery was of the 'wings and drop' sort—flats at the side of the stage jutting further across it as they receded towards the back wall, itself adorned with a painted cloth. All designs would be more generic than specific, with sets related to interior or exterior scenes. If there were any changes of scene, they would be done quickly, in full view of the audience. Costumes were still in many instances the standard court dress of earlier times—an equivalent of modern dress—which resulted in curious but not unsuggestive parallels, Othello being dressed, for example, exactly the same as Macbeth. This, then, was the state of Shakespeare production at the beginning of the period.

The six decades between the 1843 Act and the end of Victoria's reign saw radical changes in every aspect of Shakespearian performance. The first and probably most far-reaching was the great increase in the number of productions with the end of the monopoly. This must surely also have contributed to changes in styles of acting, since the non-patent theatres were much smaller and made the remote rhetoric of the two patent theatres unnecessary. Rapid advances in the technology of the stage were another force for change. Limelight had been largely displaced by gas in the 1850s, and in 1881 the Savoy Theatre became the first to be lit wholly by electricity. These changes worked with increasingly sophisticated scenic devices, some of which were already being developed at the start of the period. The apron stage was almost completely outmoded by 1860, replaced by a fixed proscenium or 'picture frame' behind which flats had been progressively replaced by shutters, screens hung from rails above the stage and running in grooves within it, which extended across the whole width of the stage. These allowed rapid but effective changes of setting, simply by being drawn apart to reveal a scene within, often a drop curtain painted with increasing concern to its aesthetic richness and relation to the individual play in which it appeared, instead of following the earlier practice of general views. The movement farther upstage was further accelerated by greater sophistication in lighting, which accentuated perspective to add realism of setting, and allowed subtler effects of changing time of day or season.

The use of drops made of translucent gauze allowed other effects. Combined with lighting and the use of mirrors they made possible elaborate projections: Charles Kean conjured the vision of Queen Katherine in *Henry VIII* by such means in his 1855 production. Cycloramas, scenes painted on vast rolls of fabric which were unfurled horizontally across the back of the stage, made possible both changes of setting and the illusion of movement. One of the earliest was designed by Clarkson Stanfield for Macready's 1839 *Henry V*, showing the passage of the English fleet across the channel as background to the words of the Chorus. In 1855, the group of artists known as the Grieve Family designed a shifting diorama of forest scenes for Charles Kean's *Midsummer Night's Dream*. Theatrical make-up became more sophisticated, changing in response to the new forms of lighting. Powder was at first still the main medium, but Ludwig Leichner founded his company producing sticks of grease paint in 1873, and by the 1890s this was the usual choice for actors in London. All these elements were enhanced by the practice, begun in

Wagner's Bayreuth, of dimming the house lights during performance. This made impossible the practice of following the text, popular with some earlier audiences; but the larger knowledge of the plays, through the increasing number of cheap editions, made this progressively less necessary.

These technical changes were closely related to the upsurge of interest, growing from earlier antiquarianism, in productions resting on concepts of historical authenticity—meaning authentic visual presentation of the periods in which the plays were set, not that in which they were written. In the 1820s the costume historian James Robinson Planché had begun to produce meticulously researched volumes of drawings and descriptive texts each relating to one of Shakespeare's plays. Later he added notes on costumes to Knight's *Pictorial Shakspere*; and his work formed the basis of many costumes worn on stage. From the 1850s onwards, authenticity had become the established aim of scenography and costuming. In the 1870s, E. W. Godwin wrote a series of articles titled 'The Architecture and Costumes of Shakespeare's Plays' in the periodical *The Architect*, a setting revealing the close intersection between Shakespearian activity and other fields of endeavour so prevalent in the period. All of the plays, including comedies apparently beyond any specific period, were meticulously dated and detailed advice given on appropriate designs. Scene-painting became an art in itself through the work of William Capon, Frederick Lloyds, the Grieve Family, and Hawes Craven. Again, this was related to other areas of intellectual and artistic life: an early work of Augustus Welby Northmore Pugin, the dynamic force behind the Gothic revival and later designer of the interior of the new Houses of Parliament, comprised some designs for Charles Kemble's 1831 *Henry VIII* showing the choir and the medieval exterior of the Abbey.

Authenticity reached its geometric climax from the 1850s in the use of built-up, practicable stages—houses, bridges, gardens, and even the canals of Venice—to enhance the sense of realism. Since many of these visual devices originated with pantomime, melodrama, or dramatized forms of sensational novels, many observers felt them inappropriate, even demeaning, to the staging of the national dramatist. Others saw them as essential to the educative function of the plays in developing a sense of history in the audiences. The new structures demanded the use of an act-drop curtain just behind the proscenium to conceal scene changes. Since these could easily take twenty or thirty minutes to perform, intervals became longer, and texts were cut, in ironic contrast to the avowed fidelity of the staging. At the end of the century, the total time spent at the theatre could amount to five hours, with performances ending after midnight, with as much of the evening spent in scene-changing as in acting. At first this was accomplished by curtailing the evening's entertainment to a single play since, even in the later years, short plays would often be performed before or after a work by Shakespeare. In 1880, for example, Henry Irving simply cut the final act of *The Merchant of Venice* to allow a performance of the Gilbert and Sullivan operetta *Iolanthe*. And the longer intervals were welcomed by some theatre-goers: they provided more time for social engagements, and more recent theatres reflected this by providing seating areas and crush bars in every area of the building. As late as 1900, Herbert Beerbohm Tree's *Midsummer Night's Dream* developed this to the full with detailed forests, real grass and live rabbits. Paradoxically, Sir Lawrence Alma-Tadema's designs for Irving's *Coriolanus* that opened in the following year but which were first drawn in the 1880s, followed a much simpler form that employed wings and flats as well as some built-up sets for the home of the central character.

These movements were not exclusive to the theatre in London. Even before the 1843 Act, local magistrates could license performances of spoken drama for up to sixty days. This was exploited by 'stock companies' that offered a different play each night from a repertoire in which Shakespeare was well represented. As the railway network developed rapidly in the 1840s and 50s, these were increasingly threatened by touring companies, although at roughly the same time the larger cities began to expand their own buildings and companies as a mark of cultural identity and civic pride. Longer distances could also be travelled: the first transatlantic steamer service began in 1838, allowing exchanges of actors between England and America, and a few performers including Charles and Ellen Kean ventured as far as Australia. The European interest in Shakespeare, building on translations made during the Romantic period, facilitated similar exchanges, notably with France and Germany.

Legislation, education, publishing, antiquarianism, stage design, transport: all are significant elements in propelling, as well as responding to, the changing nature of Shakespeare performances. Since their nature and form often proceeded through a pattern of innovation, reflection, imitation, and revolt, they are best discussed chronologically. Here, though, there is another curious reflection of Victorian ideologies: it is fitting in both literal and symbolic terms that in an age obsessed with self-advancement the dominant forces of theatre are the actor-managers. These were men—and some independently-minded women—who, true to the Victorian spirit, established their own identities both by taking on Shakespearian roles and in building careers in the complex activity of managing a theatre, with its combination of business enterprise, aesthetic invention, and the supervisory and nurturing skills involved in working with groups of men and women of strong individual temperament.

In London, the major figures form an impressive list, the names of the theatres they managed illustrative of the range and growth of the theatre world, and the sometimes short periods of occupancy indexing the commercial perils of their work. William Charles Macready managed Covent Garden from 1837 to 1839, and Drury Lane from 1841 to 43; Samuel Phelps, with whom he is often compared, built his company at Sadler's Wells between 1844 and 1862; less well remembered, but just as important, was Madame Vestris, who followed Macready's tenancy at Covent Garden for three years and much later (1847–55) took over the running of Drury Lane. The century's middle years, and many of the production features of succeeding decades, were dominated by Charles Kean at the diminutive Princess's Theatre in Oxford Street (1850–59). Earlier accounts talk of the subsequent years as a period of inactivity in the London theatre, and Chapter 1 has discussed the absence of a single clear leading figure. But there were instead several important individuals. The work of Squire and Marie Bancroft at the Prince of Wales's and the Haymarket is important in continuing the methods of Kean and the traditions he established, as well as moving them into the less fashionable parts of London and so satisfying the growing audience for Shakespeare's plays. The same is true of Charles Calvert at the Theatre Royal, Manchester (1859–75), Edward Saker at the Alexandra in Liverpool, (1863–88) and several others away from the capital;

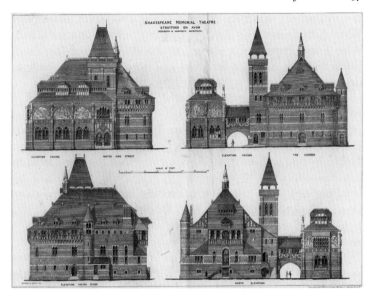

3.1 Architects' drawings of the Shakespeare Memorial Theatre, Stratford-upon-Avon, from *The Building News*, 22 September 1876. That its high Gothic-revival architecture makes it look rather like a church is wholly fitting to Stratford's identity as a shrine.

and there were also important figures who led itinerant companies to smaller theatres outside the larger cities, among whom Ben Greet, Frank Benson, and Barry Sullivan were probably the best known.

Rather different in identity and function was the Shakespeare Memorial Theatre (see Illustration 3.1), opened in Stratford-upon-Avon in 1879 and largely funded by the Flower brewing family. Built in a meadow adjoining the river, and thus at the geographic centre of Victorian creation of the Shakespeare myth, it yet remained in many ways peripheral to the tradition of production that was being developed in London and elsewhere. Inside its pseudo-Renaissance, towered and crocketed exterior, the auditorium seated only 800 and had excellent acoustics. Yet it had no permanent company and was dark for the majority of the year—an echo, perhaps, of the curious Victorian phenomenon of raising the dramatist to the status of a national hero while not being too concerned with his plays. The theatre's major productions occurred during a two-week Shakespeare Festival, first under the direction of Barry Sullivan and then, from 1886, Frank Benson. Its place, literal and conceptual, embodied the ambiguous nature of Stratford as a town, a series of paradoxes demonstrated in many ways that will be discussed in Chapter 6.

Around the time that the Memorial Theatre opened, the work of two actor-managers in London effectively brought Victorian styles of production to their climax. Beerbohm Tree took over the Haymarket in 1887, and remained there until opening Her Majesty's in 1897. Henry Irving had been at the Lyceum since 1878, but was forced by financial difficulties to relinquish his tenancy in 1898, selling his wardrobe and scenic collection, but remaining there as a performer: even at the end of the period, and for one of the most celebrated figures, the theatre was riven with financial difficulties. While both were essentially Victorian in performance and management style, Tree also had a small but highly significant function in more modern performance when in 1899 he acted four scenes from *King John* before a silent film camera. Only that showing the death of the king survives. The scene lasts only a few seconds, yet is a fascinating document in preserving what to later views is an extremely exaggerated performance, Tree thrusting and shuddering grotesquely in his death throes, within a medium that will in a few decades threaten the existence of many theatres and radically change performance practices in those that continued. But by then, styles were already changing: William Poel's New Shakespeare Society offered productions resting on aesthetic principles quite different from those of Tree and Irving, aiming to return to something approaching the staging practices of Shakespeare's time. These will be discussed in Chapter 8.

So much for the locations: what of the productions? The first major performer of the Victorian period, William Charles Macready, known in his lifetime as 'the eminent tragedian', forms a bridge with earlier acting styles (see Illustration 3.2). Famous during the 1820s, acting with John Philip Kemble and Sarah Siddons, his productions at Covent Garden were important in moving away from many earlier acting editions of the plays. In 1838 he restored the role of the Fool in his production of *King Lear*—a move that gained the approval of the Prime Minister, Lord Melbourne—as well as rejecting most of Nahum Tate's revisions of the play, and also deleting many of Colley

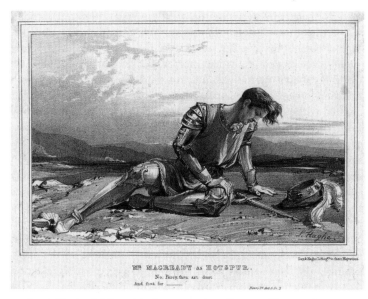

MR MACREADY as HOTSPUR.
No. Percy, thou art dust
And food for

3.2 Louis Haghe: William Charles Macready as Hotspur. This wood-engraving shows Macready in the attitude of a dying hero in a classical statue, suggesting the actor's approach to the part.
© Trustees of the British Museum

Cibber's changes to *Richard III*. A crucial difference between his approach and those of his successors, however, was his adherence to the repertory system in which plays were regularly rotated during a season, rather than retained for as long as the audience demanded. Partly this was for commercial reasons; alternating Shakespeare with popular plays and pantomimes ensured financial security. One result of this was that scenery and effects were kept to a minimum to allow changes of repertoire; but this did not mean they were not important, although much less extensive than later settings. In many ways his work can be seen as the foundation of Victorian and later practice, as the actor-manager became increasingly important in taking control of each production. Macready also compiled voluminous diaries and memoirs, early examples of the two genres in combining the intensely personal with the historically revealing.

While Macready moved some way towards reform, Samuel Phelps was perhaps the first to present himself as the figure who took charge of performances by a group rather than the central performer around whom the others clustered. In the year of Queen Victoria's accession he had already made a key innovation: the abandonment of acting 'points'. These were individual moments of declamation or business made their own by individual actors, and often later passing into tradition in later performances, expected by audiences who often felt cheated without them. Macready was one of the first to move away from these moments, favouring instead a more continuous, integrated approach to character and text. At the start of 1837 his performance as the title role in *Richard III* was praised for his 'strong and nervous acting' that revealed 'a mind capable of entering into the very spirit of the author'. That this prefers 'author' over character reveals the greater integration of the performance; that it was written in review of a performance at the Exeter Theatre, in the west of England county of Devonshire, is an important reminder that not all the most important developments happened in London, nor did all the major actors begin their careers there. On the passage of the Regulation Act, with the financial aid of Mary Hudart Warner, Phelps set up his own company at Sadler's Wells Theatre in Islington, then a suburb beyond the fashionable area of the London theatre. Although a centre for pantomime and low comedy, it was already offering Shakespeare to its primarily working-class audiences. Phelps developed this side of its activity, playing to full houses in the 1600-seat auditorium. In this his voice was a major asset. Trained in elocution and singing, he spoke the verse according to its rhythmic forms, with 'no pouting, no pointed ranting, no misdirected energy' as a reviewer claimed of his Macbeth. Other accounts speak of his sensitivity and tenderness, alternating with 'bouts of passionate anger' as Lear, in a 'mixture of elocutionary power and deep feeling'. What seems clear from these is that Phelps drew what he needed from the declamatory tradition, placing the language of the plays at the centre of his performance, but moulding it into a more thorough approach to the role by the avoidance of points and a greater integration of character, situation, and overall design. This unity had another consequence. Instead of the rounds of applause that greeted the 'points' of earlier actors, encouraged by carefully judged pauses that gave us the word 'claptrap', audiences began to demand the presence of the company at the end of the performance, in the curtain calls that were already fashionable in France. But, as Chapter 1 has suggested, his style was deemed outdated by some and too placid by others, and perhaps unfairly he suffered from comparisons with the more visually extravagant production style of Charles Kean. In a pattern recurrent in theatre history, the acting styles hailed as natural by one generation seemed stilted to the next.

Phelps' reforming work was also apparent in his approach to management. Although he still allotted roles, in the manner of the old stock companies, according to known skills of individual actors— First Old Man, Low Comedian and others—he was concerned, through meticulous rehearsal, to ensure that the text prevailed over the individual, coining the expression 'truth of illustration' to describe the way his plays presented the texts. His staging was conservative, retaining the apron, flats, and drop of his predecessors, and his *King John* rested heavily on the designs of Macready. But Phelps could also be innovative, for example in using gauzes to allow a slow reveal for the ghosts before the battle of Bosworth in *Richard III*, and then dividing the stage so that the figures of Richard and Bolingbroke were presented with equal weight. Building on Macready's return to greater textual authenticity he presented *Macbeth* without the singing and dancing witches added by Davenant, and went further in returning overlooked plays to the stage, with *Antony and Cleopatra* in 1849 and, more remarkably, *Timon of Athens* in 1851, claimed to be the first-ever performance of the play in something approaching its original form.

Many historians trace a direct line from Phelps to Kean, minimizing the importance of the first major woman actor-manager, Lucia Elizabeth Vestris, always known simply as Madame Vestris. Seen from the present, her work is contradictory. Her opening production at Drury Lane brought *Love's Labour's Lost* to the stage for the first time since the early seventeenth century, she herself playing Rosaline. This would suggest a reforming zeal; yet her next production, *The Merry Wives of Windsor*, included some interpolated songs that she performed herself, using her fine singing voice as a further draw for audiences. The mixture continued with her *Midsummer Night's Dream*, restored, albeit with cuts, in place of Garrick's *The Fairies* and the other adaptations popular in earlier decades. The reformist designer James Robinson Planché produced some authentic Athenian costumes, but alongside them were 52 fairies in gauze and spangles, while Oberon and Titania rode a flower-covered chariot. Her decision to play Oberon herself, setting a precedent for female casting that would last until the end of the century, was either an imaginative piece of cross-dressing or an intelligent manipulation of gender, designed to attract audiences by allowing a display of her figure through close-fitting tights and her voice through the addition of songs. Many of these contradictions suggest the ambivalent place of women in the theatre, in the need to exploit what would then be termed their femininity when performing while retaining their identity as professional individuals—an issue that recurs in the careers of later figures, most notably Ellen Terry. They also betray the precariousness of Shakespearian production on the grand scale: with just under 200 employees working on scenery and another 119 in the wardrobe, Vestris filed for bankruptcy, left Covent Garden, and turned to popular theatre.

Charles Kean is often presented as both Phelps's rival and his successor, but this is to oversimplify. Certainly Kean was more concerned with the visual aspects of the plays, but this was not from a desire for spectacle for its own ends. One of his proudest achievements was his election as a Fellow of the Society of Antiquaries, and a major aim was to bring history alive on the stage. In this he followed the example of Charles Knight in meticulously identifying the date in which each of the plays was set and presenting them with appropriate sets and costumes. Paradoxically this worked against his fidelity to Shakespeare's text: his addition of 'Historical Episodes', most famously the entry of Richard II into London, demanded the excision of the scene as described by York and the presentation of the procession exactly as contemporary sources recorded it. The procession also exemplified one of Kean's major innovations: the use of practicable, built-up sets aligned diagonally across the stage. This allowed buildings to be inhabited to give greater verisimilitude; more importantly, it moved away from the rigid, four-square geometry of the older theatre that privileged those seated directly in front of its vanishing point. Now, all audience members were equally involved, as each had a uniquely valid viewpoint, akin to the situation in the street watching the procession. That this may have been the result of the narrow stage at the Princess's does not lessen its effect: for a generation, the geometry was followed by almost all actor-managers who sought to produce Shakespeare in an avowedly realist manner.

Kean's desire for authenticity, expressed through extremely elaborate scenography, did not stop with the histories. *A Midsummer Night's Dream* opened with a drop showing ancient Athens, and moved to a carpenter's shop with authentic tools of the period, through the Grieve Family's elaborate cyclorama for the scenes in the wood. *The Winter's Tale* included an additional masque scene; *The Merchant of Venice*, a practicable canal, on which Bassanio and Jessica escaped by gondola before the stage was taken over by supernumeraries enacting the Venetian carnival. The climax came with *Henry V*, where battle scenes building on designs used by Macready were followed by another 'Episode' in which Henry V returned in triumph to London in a procession including dignitaries from the city of London, military and ecclesiastical figures, young women dressed as angels, and crowds of wives and children greeting the heroes as they returned over London Bridge. Kean's educative zeal also led him to provide extensive printed descriptions of his productions. Although known as playbills, these went far beyond the earlier advertising sheets of the same name, moving towards the extensive programme notes of much later productions. Among the many who were enthusiastic about Kean's productions, and his own acting, was Queen Victoria, who visited the Princess's frequently and also, in the 1850s, invited Kean and his company to give performances in a specially adapted room at Windsor Castle. This, and the introduction of Royal Command Performances, begun in 1848, did much to raise the prestige of the acting profession, as well as increasing already strident professional rivalries within it.

Kean's innovations were followed by the Bancrofts in London, Calvert in Manchester, and Saker in Liverpool. Bancroft's *Merchant of Venice* used a carefully reduced version of Kean's practicable set, including its navigable canal; Calvert's *Henry V* replicated the triumphal return scene added for the Princess's Theatre. But it was in the two final decades of the century that the theatre of extreme naturalism reached its climax (see Illustration 3.3), in the work of Henry Irving and Beerbohm Tree. This was only one aspect of their extension of the role of actor-manager, taking control of every facet of production so that they effectively founded what would later

3.3 'In Fairyland', by R. Caton Woodville, a lithograph dating from 1885. Perhaps showing a performance of *A Midsummer Night's Dream*, it reveals something of the complexity of Victorian staging and, in the group on the left, a little of the social life surrounding the wings.

become known as director's theatre—although the term 'producer' was first used, as more appropriate to the greater involvement in the physical putting together of the play. As both continued to play leading roles in their productions, there were inevitable conflicts of interest: both already known as 'star' performers, their relationships with other actors, especially those good enough to pose threats, often led to tensions in performance.

Early reviews of Henry Irving stress his physical awkwardness and poor delivery, and his idiosyncratic acting style continued to be controversial throughout his career. Henry James described his 1875 Macbeth as 'incomplete and amateurish', and throughout regarded his linguistic performance as inadequate, calling him instead a 'picturesque' actor. Throughout his career, audiences and critics were divided between those who found his language a major fault and those who found his visual appearance compelling. Many accounts record his strangely elongated vowels—'faaace', 'nao'—and sounded r consonants that resembled a West Country accent. He developed a remarkable skill in facial and bodily effects that presented extreme psychological states, first noted in his melodramatic performance in the popular play *The Bells*, developed in the roles of Shylock and Cardinal Wolsey, and manipulated with greatest power, and to most controversial effect, as Hamlet. Contemporary reviews all share a difficulty in explaining how these effects worked, whether as outward expressions of complex character and situations or in some way presenting them as physical metaphors. Perhaps it was their sheer inexplicability that made them so powerful, coupled with Irving's ability to reproduce them with near-identical precision for every performance—a magnetic combination of the mystical and the professional. Such intensity, and the precision with which it was learned and presented, was often contrasted with the performing and even the personal style of his contemporary, Beerbohm Tree; but the two were alike in other ways. One was the extremity of their performances in both success and failure, the latter notable in Irving's Othello and Tree's Macbeth; the other was the extreme degree to which they took control of their productions, managing every aspect including scenography while maintaining their own place as the central performer, making often drastic cuts to other parts to ensure their own supremacy.

Tree is often ridiculed in the popular memory for the most extreme manifestations of stage realism—remember the rabbits—but his work at the century's end probably comes closest to the present-day idea of a single directing intelligence at work in the planning and execution of a production. Yet here again there is the contradiction found with Irving between the magnetism of the individual performer and the incongruity and at times inadequacy of the performance. His 1898 *Julius Caesar* exemplified this most completely. While the production as a whole was praised, Tree's performance as Marc Antony drew contradictory responses from audience and critics. Much praised for the vigour and spontaneity in the comic roles in which he seemed more at home, his Antony was felt by many to be inappropriate to the role's rhetorical complexities, especially in the speech to the plebeians that featured largely in his heavily cut and rearranged version of the play, with a very elaborate, built-up set. Like Irving, his total control over the conception and execution of each production included his own location at its very centre: in 1899 the performance of Lewis Waller as the Bastard in *King John* was so successful that it outshone Tree's King, and shortly afterwards Waller left by mutual agreement to start his own company at the Lyceum, where he achieved great success as Henry V in 1901. Tree's 1900 *Midsummer Night's Dream* might easily appear as the apogee of the actor-manager and the exaggerated naturalistic set: that Tree himself played Bottom, exhibiting what one critic called 'a blank wall of vanity', itself offered an ironic undermining of the star performer-manager. That the scenes are recalled as much for the rabbits and grass as for the confusions of the lovers taking place before them suggests that this was in literal terms a stage too far.

Tree's conflict with Waller draws attention to the growing numbers of actors who achieved considerable personal success as individual performers rather than by dominating productions as actor-managers. Although he later took on such a role, Waller's earlier performances as Othello, Romeo, Henry V, and Brutus were those for which he was celebrated, the degree of his adulation approaching twenty-first century proportions, with a group of women describing themselves as 'K.O.W.' (Keen on Waller). A similar figure was Johnston Forbes-Robertson who, following success in New York as Orlando, played

Romeo and Hamlet with great success in London. He was also a successful painter whose portraits, including a fine one of Phelps as Cardinal Wolsey (1878: Garrick Club, London) offer a further view of the late-Victorian Shakespearian stage. Others came to prominence through managing touring companies alongside their own acting roles. Barry Sullivan made tours in England between 1841 and 1852, managed a theatre in Aberdeen for three years, acted Hamlet at the Haymarket, performed in New York and toured Australia, played Richard III in Liverpool and was Benedick to Helen Faucit's Beatrice at the newly-opened Shakespeare Memorial Theatre in 1879. Ben Greet ran a highly successful touring company throughout England, as well as mounting open-air productions of Shakespeare. There were also figures who, rejecting star status, did much to establish professionalism of a kind less conspicuous than that of Irving and Tree by adapting themselves to a wide range of parts and playing them with conviction and precision. One such was Lyn Harding, whose roles ranged from Aguecheek to Prospero, Cassius to Bolingbroke.

These, then, are the details of the main actor-managers and their approaches to Shakespeare's texts and scenography; but it should be remembered that live theatre is always dependent upon the responses of those who witnessed the performances and brought to them their own personal responses. In this regard, the growth of theatre reviewing, illustration, and theatrical diaries, biographies and memoirs during the Victorian period (see Illustration 3.4) is both intensely valuable and ultimately unsatisfying. The age saw a rapid proliferation in theatrical reviews, many written by figures who became celebrated in their own right, not least Henry James and George Bernard Shaw. Reviewing is always personal; illustration is done rapidly and with specific audiences in mind; life writing of all kinds is essentially—if often quite fascinatingly—distorted by personal bias. While biographies and reminiscences are written from personal experience, they have the weaknesses as well as the strengths of such intimacy, and the theatre reviews and recollections of such notable figures as George Henry Lewes, Hesketh Pearson, and W. Graham Robertson are all striking for these complexities, despite their marked differences in style and stance. Finding anything like a valid account of performers in action will always remain out of reach,

THEATRICAL TIMES

MONDAY, JANUARY 8, 1849.

No. 139.

ONE PENNY.

CONTENTS.

MRS. W DALY, AS THE NURSE, IN "ROMEO AND JULIET."

PORTRAIT OF MRS. W. DALY.

No. 1, Vol. 4.

3.4 *The Theatrical Times*, 8 January 1849, with an anonymous wood-engraving of Mrs W. Daly as the Nurse from *Romeo and Juliet*. That the periodical appeared every week suggests the popularity of theatre, and the degree to which individual performers were known and followed by its readers.

perhaps most markedly so when it seems most convincing because revealing a deeply-felt, immediate personal response. Writing and artistry of this kind is better considered as an aesthetic object in its own right than respected as an impartial historical source, a stance that should be kept firmly in mind in reading the paragraphs that follow.

That said, for many of the chief performers and performances there is a degree of consistency in response that allows a reasonable awareness of styles, stances, and strengths, together with individual elements of interpretation or stage business that deepened or modified the reading of the plays, or reacted sharply against earlier forms and processes. There is, for example, general agreement that Charles Kean's acting did not come near that of his father Edmund in quality, and that he was regarded more highly as a manager than an actor; that Irving's performances offered a quality of the uncanny never far from disturbing; or that Tree's were as much brilliant improvisation as meticulous preparation. And in many cases, reviews combine imaginative and witty use of language with genuine insights into the performances they discuss. 'Our captious critic', the anonymous writer for *The Illustrated Sporting and Dramatic News*, addressed Wilson Barrett's 1884 Hamlet (see Illustration 3.5) by combining comment on the conception of the role and its relation to what he terms 'the ordinary text' with some rather less analytical language: 'Mr Barrett delivers the text of Hamlet trippingly from the tongue like macadam slowly dribbling over the tailboard of a cart on to a hard road'. The outstanding example here is George Bernard Shaw, whose reviews often say more about himself than the play they ostensibly discuss, but whose sharp insights gave many performers cause to breathe more easily when he moved to the other side of the footlights in writing his own plays. Equal partners in the reviewing process were the artists and wood-engravers who produced images of the plays. As these generally showed either an individual performer or an important scene, they are influential in directing their readers towards a particular element of the play. They also exist within forceful constraints of design and production, images modified by personal view and production medium rather than impartial evidence of performance, the tension between these two offering teasing possibilities of interpretation for the later observer and historian. The evidence

3.5 Review of Wilson Barrett as Hamlet, *The Illustrated Sporting and Dramatic News*, 25 October 1884. On the reverse of this page is an engraving of Cardiff Horse Exchange and an item on 'Hunting in Leicestershire', suggesting the breadth of interest of the magazine's readers.

offered by photographs is perhaps even more uncertain, as Chapter 4 will suggest.

As well as involving a considerable degree of movement within England, Victorian Shakespeare performance took place through a series of international exchanges. In 1848 Charles and Ellen Kean crossed the Atlantic and performed in New York, and when they relinquished the lease of the Princess's Theatre they made a tour of Australia. There was also movement in the other direction. In 1861 Charles Fechter, brought up in France, appeared as Hamlet at the Princess's Theatre in a performance that was immediately recognized as groundbreaking. *The Times* (22 March) praised the complete rejection of earlier 'points' and conventions, marking out the care with which the soliloquies had been prepared, building on 'a vast expense of thought' to produce a performance 'marked by the subtlest variations'. Yet it still found something lacking, especially in the play and closet scenes, a quality only possible in an English actor; in this it summed up the duality with which the actor, and especially his performance in this role, would be most commonly regarded. In 1899 Sarah Bernhardt appeared in the role at the Adelphi in London, gaining praise for the unique quality and sensitivity of her voice and movement. Tommaso Salvini acted as Othello, Macbeth, Lear and—for two performances only—Hamlet in 1884, gaining responses that praised his direct emotion and sensual involvement with the parts, of which Othello was seen as the most effective. The Polish actress Helena Modjeska spent six months studying English while performing in California; her two-year stay in England (1880–82) was marked by a partnership with Forbes-Robertson in *Romeo and Juliet*.

Visits of individuals were matched by those of whole companies, notably the Saxe-Meiningen Theatre Company in the 1880s, which demonstrates a genuine exchange of influence and idea between England and Europe. Their *Julius Caesar*, performed at Drury Lane in 1880, is often regarded as building on Kean's use of supernumeraries in the histories, later influencing Tree's production and, at a larger level, throwing a bridge between English theatre and continental European ensemble practice. That the play was performed in German did not seem to dampen the enthusiasm of London audiences and critics. A different kind of internationalism was demonstrated by the American impresario Augustin Daly, who in 1893 opened a theatre in London, with Ada Rehan, a stalwart member of his New York company, as Katherina in *The Taming of the Shrew*. The company produced several other Shakespeare plays under his direction, using approaches more familiar to an earlier generation in style of declamation and gesture.

Although Squire Bancroft and Beerbohm Tree would both subsequently receive knighthoods, it was the gift of this honour to Henry Irving in 1895 that made acting finally become respectable. On Irving's death *The Times* credited him with making the stage equal to professions such as medicine and the law. That much of his career involved Shakespearian roles was a major part of this change, as if adding the approval of the greatest Englishman to their work. That Irving, like Tree, had risen from humble beginnings, both changing their names as their careers progressed, was perhaps the most complex statement of the Victorian idea of self-improvement and identity creation, though here with the added irony that the individuals created their own identities by repeatedly, and professionally, creating the identities of others on the stage.

Such transformations were if anything more complex in the case of women actors. Ellen Terry's career demonstrates even greater changes of identity and inventions of personhood. Married at the age of 16 to the artist G. F. Watts, then 40 years her senior, she epitomized the Victorian child-bride. The marriage soon failed, and for a short while Terry returned to the stage. She then lived with the architectural historian and stage designer E. W. Godwin, with whom she had a daughter and a son who in adult life, with a changed name, was the actor, designer, and dramatic theorist Edward Gordon Craig. In 1875 she played Portia at the Prince of Wales's Theatre, thus beginning the most successful period of her acting career. The review in the *Daily News* (19 April 1875) began 'This is the Portia that Shakespeare drew' and continued to praise 'the bold innocence, the lively wit, and quick intelligence, the grace and elegance of manner, and all the youth and freshness of this exquisite creation'. In 1878 she played Ophelia to Irving's Hamlet, and formed with him an important and long-lasting theatrical and personal partnership. In reviewing the production for the 1879 *Dramatic Notes*, Charles Eyre Pascoe described her performance as one of 'purity, charm and grace', qualities repeatedly praised in her performances of Shakespeare's heroines.

The painter W. Graham Robertson, for example, wrote in his memoirs of her as 'lovely and gracious, she was Cordelia as she had been Portia'.

Terry's autobiography, *The Story of My Life* (1907), reveals in its title as well as its contents and tone the careful construction of a personality through equally careful rejection of any such effort, an art concealing art that is apparent in the repeated references to innocence and effortlessness in her performance. The bare facts of her life, studiously omitted from her autobiography, are not unlike the plot of a Victorian sensation novel: that, through the strength of her own performances and refusal to conform to many contemporary models, she established herself as the major woman actor of her generation, and the second to be created a Dame (albeit not until 1925), is a major transformation. Unlike Irving and Tree, she had to overcome the still considerable prejudice against actresses, and independent women in general, endemic in English society at that time. Or perhaps English Society: within the lower orders, especially the working classes where women had long been expected to work, and where changes of marital relationship were more frequent, the path would have been unexceptional save for the nature of employment. Her acting ability was the essence of her success; but her extensive performances in leading Shakespearian roles was surely a major factor in her recognition and, by extension, the acceptance of acting as a suitable job for a woman.

While the most celebrated, Terry's career was not unique. Helen Faucit began her professional life with Macready in 1837, acting Constance, Imogen, Cordelia, Desdemona, Rosalind, and Hermione under his Covent Garden management. In the 1840s she performed with him in Paris, where Edouard Thierry wrote of her in the *Messager* (5 January 1845) '*on n'avait imaginé Ophélia ni plus touchant, ni plus gracieux*'. The words are significant—'touching, gracious' are terms applied to her acting almost as frequently as to that of Ellen Terry, suggesting that a particular kind of acting was popular, perhaps reflecting a particular ideal of womanhood, in France and England during the high Victorian period. Of her Rosalind at the Haymarket, the *Athenaeum* (8 November 1845) wrote that it 'charmed us by the simplicity, the delicacy, the purity of the delineation'. Later, when she had relinquished the stage, Faucit wrote a book about Shakespeare's women characters from the experience gained on the stage, discussed in Chapter 7. It is instructive to compare the tone of her writing and that of Terry's autobiography. Both avoid any hint of formality or scholarship and instead adopt an intimate, anecdotal style with frequent use of exclamation marks, words italicized for emphasis and direct address to the reader. The popularity of both books suggests that this was what was expected as a womanly, or to use the term of the day a feminine, approach. Twenty or thirty years later, a new generation of women would seek independence in quite opposite ways, rejecting the implicit naturalness and charm affected by Terry and Faucit as cover for the professionalism and sheer hard work that was the core of their success: ironically, it was the assumption of artlessness that was so successful for both.

Although Terry and Faucit were most prominent in defining their profession, in earlier years there were many other women performers who approached the task more directly, concentrating on their acting roles with professionalism and dedication without seeking publicity or defining their specific roles off the stage. Significant in this regard is Ellen Tree, better known as Mrs Charles Kean. As well as working with her husband in managing the Princess's Theatre in the 1850s, and surviving serious illness, she took many important Shakespearian roles. Writing of these, Theodor Fontane, the German author and critic today best known for the novel *Effi Briest*, described her as 'in any case a better actor than her husband'. That he found her acting at times 'too much of a good thing' in its 'extremity of emotion' may say as much about Fontane as about Tree; but that he described as 'outstanding' the scene in which, as Constance in *King John*, she denounced the Archduke, and the power of her performance as Queen Katharine in *Henry VIII*, largely delivered in a whisper, as 'a subdued dying fall of humility' suggests a clear and consistent reading of a part. That the trial scene 'took on too much the character of a state occasion' so that her performance was largely obscured suggests both Charles Kean's concern for overwhelming historical scenography and the great power he wielded as actor-manager.

Kate Terry, sister of Ellen, shared the stage of the Princess's with Ellen Tree when, at the age of eight, she played Arthur in *King John*. She went on to play Ophelia with Fechter's Hamlet, and a range of other Shakespearian roles, of which her Juliet was most widely admired. The *Athenaeum* (7 September 1867) praised 'the independence of her conceptions', sensing in her a 'fine poetic appreciation and a subtle judgment which satisfied the taste of the more refined among the audiences'. Reviews also commented on her slight physique and 'want of power', but as Juliet, towards the close, she became 'a strong, self-reliant woman'. Today far less celebrated than Ellen Terry, both performers typify, in their own sharply distinguished styles of acting, the range, imagination, and professionalism of women performers in the middle decades of the period.

Many began their careers in the provinces before moving to London. Ellen and Kate Terry both first appeared at the King Street Theatre, Bristol before making the change, as did Marie Wilton, better known as Marie Bancroft after her marriage to Squire Bancroft. Sharing with him in managing the Prince of Wales Theatre, she also continued an important Shakespearian acting career with roles including Juliet, Rosalind, and most of the comedic heroines. In the 1890s Mrs Patrick Campbell acted the same roles, and was a powerful Ophelia to Forbes-Robertson's Hamlet. Less well known was Sarah Thorne, who appeared at the Theatre Royal, Dublin with Charles Kean, playing Desdemona, Portia, and Juliet, both there and in touring productions in Ireland and Scotland, before repeating them at the Royal Standard Theatre in London. Later she took over the lease of the Margate Theatre for seven years, engaging many performers who would later move to London. The American-born Geneviève Ward made her debut as Lady Macbeth at the Theatre Royal, Manchester in 1873: the *Manchester Guardian* praised her 'perfect ease and a most scrupulously exact knowledge of her part'. She would later act with Frank Benson's company, and repeat the role in London and Paris: there, the *Revue Britannique* (March 1877) singled out for special praise her treatment of the sleepwalking scene, in which '*la salle toute entière était suspendre à ses lèvres et frissonait avec elle*' [the whole house hung from her lips, and shuddered with her]. Others compared her performances as Volumnia and Queen Margaret with the style and presence of Sarah Siddons.

Nor were women unusual in managerial roles. Earlier paragraphs have mentioned the importance of Mme Vestris as actor-manager, and the financial role of Mary Hudart Warner in the management of Sadler's Wells. Remarkably, it is still unusual to find reference to the fact that Marie Wilton was already managing the Prince of Wales' theatre for two years before she met, employed, and finally married Squire Bancroft, yet it is always he who is credited for the theatre's success. That her many highly successful performances on stage were in roles from contemporary plays now completely forgotten presumably accounts for her neglect as an actor.

Victorian Shakespeare was a rich—sometimes excessively rich— tapestry, in which the performance text was only one thread, but which gained greater prominence as the years passed. The most popular plays were those that reflected contemporary tastes, surprisingly similar and surprisingly unfamiliar. The second tetralogy and the great tragedies were frequent, as were the so-called happy comedies. *King John* was remarkably consistent. Macready's production was highly regarded, no less a figure than Queen Victoria placing it firmly among her favourite plays, and it was also frequently given by Phelps, Kean, and Irving. Many plays long unperformed were brought back to the stage, notably *Antony and Cleopatra*, *Timon of Athens*, and *Julius Caesar*, although what came to be known as the 'problem plays' were, perhaps unsurprisingly, rarely given. Extensive claims were made about the restoration of plays to their original texts; but, just as Victorian restoration of medieval churches often added elements to make the buildings appear more genuine, so Victorian actor-managers were selective in their use of the word authentic. Madame Vestris certainly used the original text of *A Midsummer Night's Dream*, but cut and rearranged the scenes; Charles Kean's historical authenticity extended to cutting scenes and interposing visual 'Episodes' to make their events more convincing; Squire Bancroft used the full text of *The Merchant of Venice*, but shuffled the scenes to avoid complex changes on the tiny stage of the Prince of Wales. Yet before feeling too superior, present-day readers should consider more recent practice. The Royal Shakespeare Company's *Wars of the Roses* season, praised by many as the finest contemporary production of the history cycles when it appeared on stage in 1963–4 and television in 1965, contained well over a thousand lines of pseudo-Shakespeare composed by John Barton as linking dialogue. When in 2004 Shakespeare's Globe acted *Romeo and Juliet* in something approaching sixteenth-century pronunciation, with the aid of the linguistic historian David Crystal, the play began with a short introduction to the new sounds and then went straight on to the first scene, entirely omitting the opening sonnet which contributes so much to the theme and structure of the play. Authenticity, it seems, is in the eye of the beholder, and here as in so many other ways Victorian performances were very much the product of their age.

Music and Visual Art

Any discussion of Victorian music related to Shakespeare is beset with problems. Perhaps the most immediate is the competition it faces from music in the rest of the world, and the expectations that this sets up. The musicologist or Shakespearian who looks for English operas to balance against Verdi's opera *Otello* or programme-overtures the equal of Tchaikovsky's *Romeo and Juliet*, let alone more structurally explorative works like the choral symphony on the same play by Hector Berlioz, will look in vain. The conditions necessary to produce these works, regardless of the musicians—both composers and performers—who would produce them simply did not exist until the very end of the period. The independent states that made up the emerging German nation each had its court orchestra, and each Italian city-state its opera company. Neither of these applied in Britain, and for most of the period there were only two full-time orchestras, the Crystal Palace Orchestra, founded by August Manns in 1854, and the Hallé in Manchester, established in 1858. Even the Henry Wood Promenade Concerts, begun in 1895, at first made do with a group of professional musicians hired separately for each performance. Italian opera performances at Drury Lane were similarly organized, and the same was true for every theatre where Shakespeare was performed. This did not mean that there were no musicians: rather, that there were very few permanent employment prospects for them. One of the consequences of this was that it was quite common to train as a pianist or violinist and make a living by taking private pupils, playing in or conducting orchestras for specific performances, training a choir, playing the organ in one or more churches and later, perhaps, taking a post at one of the larger teaching institutions such as the Royal Academy of Music founded in 1822.

Professional musicians were outnumbered by a large number of amateur, but often highly skilled, music-makers, most notably singers. They would sing not only in church choirs but in the local music festivals, usually held annually and lasting two or three weeks, that became increasingly fashionable throughout the century. Many followed the model of the Handel festivals held in London in the earlier century, held regularly to perform works by the anglicized German composer whose oratorios, for chorus and soloists, especially *Messiah*, remained very popular. Norwich, Leeds, Manchester, Birmingham, Edinburgh, and many other cities mounted such events, and as they grew in size they began to commission works from the composers who increasingly began to emerge from the Academy or its rival the Royal College of Music, now a teaching institution. At the same time, learning the piano became an essential element of cultural maturity, and the composition and sale of songs grew rapidly as the century developed and prosperity increased. Throughout the period, too, music did not mean only English music. Franz Liszt visited England in 1840; operas by Verdi and Wagner—the complete *Ring* cycle, conducted by Gustav Mahler in 1892—were produced in London; and Felix Mendelssohn came to occupy a position second only to Handel in the repertoires of provincial choirs. In all, the common gibe, coined after the title of a German volume, that Britain was *Das Land ohne Musik* is palpably untrue, unless *Musik* is taken to mean symphonic and operatic composition in the manner of Liszt, Wagner, and Richard Strauss. Traditional music history has seen all these forces working together to produce the English Musical Renaissance, a process in which England grew towards international stature in composition as well as performance. While the completion of this narrative occurred in the twentieth century with the works of Sir Edward Elgar (1857–1934) and Ralph Vaughan Williams (1872–1958), the ground was laid by Sir Charles Villiers Stanford (1852–1924) and Sir Charles Hubert Parry (1848–1918), with other figures in the world of light opera, Sir Arthur Sullivan (1842–1900) and Sir Edward German (1862–1936). That most of these figures were rewarded with knighthoods reveals that composition had finally become a recognized part of the nation's cultural identity.

Woven within the diverse and developing pattern of musical activity was the nation's concern for the works of Shakespeare. Its forms embraced orchestral overtures and concert suites, and songs for choirs or solo singers, but far and away the greatest amount of music was that composed for performance in theatres. In this, the pattern was set at the beginning of Victoria's reign by a composer-conductor who, because of his practice of drastically cutting and rearranging the works of Mozart and others, has been almost universally vilified by twentieth-century writers: Henry Rowley Bishop (1786–1855), musical director for Covent Garden between 1810 and 1824. His work also included music, mainly in the form of songs, for performances of Shakespeare's plays. In style, his songs imitate the melodic structures of Mozart's arias yet offer nothing of their harmonic intensity, structural development, or insight into the words they set. By the mid-1820s, Bishop had provided incidental music for six of the plays, including *2 Henry IV* and *Two Gentlemen of Verona* as well as an operatic treatment combining spoken text with separate songs of *The Comedy of Errors* and music to some of the better known comedies. That many of the songs are taken from one play and inserted into another reinforces the lack of seriousness with which the productions were approached. This and their invariably light tone revealed Georgian and early Victorian performance as concerned more with pleasing entertainment than subtle critical reading, mirroring the habit of performing a farce or short comedy before or after a full Shakespeare play.

Incidental music to *Love's Labour's Lost* (1839) is Bishop's only Shakespearian composition during the Victorian period, since his role as Professor of Music first at Edinburgh and then at Cambridge moved his energies in other directions. His music has been dismissed by subsequent critics as slight or negligible, a judgment which in absolute terms is probably valid, as are attacks on the savage cuts and revisions he inflicted on the work of earlier composers. But in Bishop's defence it should be remembered that, in adapting the music of Thomas Arne, Mozart, Rossini, or the French operatic composer Rodolphe Kreutzer, he was responding as a practical working musician to the demands of contemporary theatre. The vastness of his output suggests that it met popular tastes, and thus must be taken seriously in any discussion of the Shakespearian theatre of his times.

His career is also revealing, embracing conducting and arranging as well as composing, using players hired for specific performances, with no regular employment, and then moving towards teaching and administration. The pattern is repeated throughout the period, suggesting both the vigour and variety of musical production in the period and the sheer difficulty of economic survival for professional musicians, whether performers or composers.

In the early years of Victoria's reign, much of Bishop's work remained in the repertoire. For her revival of *A Midsummer Night's Dream* in the 1840–41 season, Madame Vestris used songs from the Bishop semi-operatic version: 'Over hill, over dale', Titania's lullaby, and the final 'Through the house give glimmering light'. To these were added new material that would favourably display her own singing voice, notably a duet between Vestris and the First Fairy setting 'I know a bank where the wild thyme blows'. Composed by Edward Horn, musical director for Vestris, its insertion was not welcomed by all: Queen Victoria found the performance marred by 'the introduction of stupid duets and songs'. The audience disagreed; the song was enthusiastically received and given again as an encore. In itself this is revealing about contemporary performance practice, something that strangely remains current in performances of opera, where applause will often greet a particularly favoured aria, which on special occasions, when sung by an especially celebrated performer, may well be repeated—something unlikely to occur in a concert performance of, say, Richard Strauss's *Four Last Songs*. Such events suggest an approach to performance emphasizing transient entertainment rather than anything seriously reflective of its ideas and larger movement. The song continued to be performed in productions of the play throughout the century.

Throughout the period the major form of Shakespearian music was that composed for presentation at specific productions. This would generally consist of a series of different pieces, all driven by the desire to present the mood of the action. An overture or prelude would be played first, followed at suitable moments by passages known as *entr'actes* that were played between scenes, offering a tonal meditation on the action or modulating between events past and forthcoming and, in later productions, concealing the sound of changes of scenery. More direct participation in stage events would be supplied by other pieces such as marches for processions and fanfares, sennets or tuckets to greet the arrival of kings and armies, reflecting the use of music, though of course not the styles, of their counterparts in Shakespeare's own theatres.

Throughout the period, actor-managers engaged their own musical directors, who in turn hired instrumentalists to play music that they either composed themselves or arranged from repertoire favourites or earlier pieces judged appropriate to the period of the play's action. Few of the composers are familiar today, and very little of their work has survived. John Hatton (1808–86) was director-composer for Charles Kean at the Princess's Theatre between 1853 and 1859, writing or arranging music for *Macbeth*, *King Lear*, *Richard II*, and other plays. His *Henry VIII* music included an overture, entr'actes, dances, and songs, that for *The Winter's Tale* had a 'Satyrs' dance' and the 'celebrated Pyrrhic Dance', with help acknowledged in the printed edition of the play on sale in the theatre from 'James A. Davies Esq., Lecturer on Ancient music'. Robert Stoepel (dates unknown) worked first with Kean, and then at the Lyceum before Irving's tenure; James Hamilton Clarke (1840–1912) left a post as organist of Queen's College Oxford to work as arranger-composer for Irving; John St. A. Johnson (dates unknown) composed music for Henry Irving's *Macbeth* at Her Majesty's in 1888.

At the period's close, Henry Irving transformed the use of music in the theatre by employing a regular orchestra of around thirty musicians and employing some of the major composers of his time. In 1878 he appointed Clarke, who composed music for *The Merchant of Venice* and *Hamlet*, the latter being particularly well received, and in the 1890s scored *Cymbeline* and, in collaboration with John Meredith Ball, *King Lear*. In 1882 Irving commissioned Sir Julius Benedict (1804–85), renowned as conductor and composer in Germany as well as England, to provide music to *Romeo and Juliet*. Six years later he approached Sir Arthur Sullivan, then at the height of his popularity for his comic, satirical operas written to the libretti of W. S. Gilbert, for the music to *Macbeth*, the overture to which later became an independent concert piece, discussed below. Sir Edward German's extensive suite of music for Irving's 1891 *Henry VIII* also took on a larger identity. Of its eight movements, the three dances, written in an imitation of old English folk songs, were published as an orchestral suite; the coronation march was so effective that it was used in the coronation of King George V in 1911. German went on to provide music for *Romeo and Juliet* (1895), *As You Like It* (1896), and *Much Ado about Nothing* (1898), but without the success of the earlier work. In 1901 Irving even approached the principal of the Royal College of Music, Sir Alexander Mackenzie (1847–1936), to provide music for his 1901 *Coriolanus*. All this suggests the importance of music in Irving's productions. Yet, just as he regarded other actors as supporting players in his own performance, so music was for him an enabling device, a narrative and emotional amplification and support for the movement and mood of the action, and it was he who made decisions on the length and nature of the music being played within his productions, not the composers themselves. Audiences and reviewers also held music in low esteem compared with performance and scenography: the set designs for *Coriolanus*, by the celebrated artist Sir Lawrence Alma-Tadema, gained far more extensive public attention than Mackenzie's music—and, in some circles, than the play itself.

Throughout the period, songs in the performances of the plays might be those of the text itself, or others borrowed from different sources to increase the intensity of the moment. Sometimes these make surprising combinations: Tree's 1898 production of *Julius Caesar* contained a setting of 'Orpheus with his lute' from *Henry VIII*, and the song also featured in productions of *The Taming of the Shrew*. The use of song settings traditionally associated with the original, where they were known to survive, was as yet rare, largely reserved to performances aiming at authenticity to the period of the plays' composition rather than their setting. In this regard the work of the musicologist and harpsichordist Arnold Dolmetsch was fundamental, aiding William Poel in the return to bare-stage productions. William Chappell's two volume *Popular Music of the Olden Time* (1855–9) and the publication of collections of early keyboard pieces such as the *Fitzwilliam Virginal Book* (1899) made available some of the music possibly used in the original productions of the plays, most notably that for *Twelfth Night*. But their use was dependent upon the style of the production as a whole and the availability of singers suitable for the roles involved, and remained largely the preserve of musicians and music historians.

Music for the Victorians did not, of course, mean only that by English composers. Verdi's *Otello* and *Macbeth* were both performed in Covent Garden to critical acclaim. Ambroise Thomas's opera *Hamlet* was performed more frequently, and attained much wider popularity; the scene depicting Ophelia's madness was often presented as a separate item, featuring in the early Promenade Concerts. Again, though, the division between popular taste and critical opinion is evident. Of its 1869 London performance *The Musical Times*, founded in 1844 as the voice of informed, professional musical opinion, questioned the very validity of treating the play as an opera and went on to attack passages in detail, condemning the encounter with the ghost as 'mere melodramatic "hurry"'. For many Victorians, however, Mendelssohn was the great ideal, and his overture to *A Midsummer Night's Dream*, beginning with four chords to suggest the mystery of the forest, moving to the braying ass and concluding with the serene richness of the lovers' theme, all of which are combined and interlaced before returning with triumphant clarity at the close, was greatly admired and much performed. Interestingly, though, it was the overture that was most performed, and most often as a concert piece. The much more experimental, and theatrically integrative, passages where the words of the play were spoken above an orchestral accompaniment, a Romantic reinvention of ancient Greek melodrama, were far less popular: the Victorians were interested in melodrama of a very different kind. The popularity of the incidental music to the play was extended by two very different occurrences which, taken together, reveal something about Victorian tastes. The first was the performance of the wedding march at the marriage of the Princess Royal in 1858, after which it achieved a near-permanent place in the nuptials of the nation. The second was a performance of the complete score, accompanied by a reading of the whole text of the play by no less than Fanny Kemble, at a concert in the Norwich Festival of 1852. This met with far less success, the audience put off by the sheer length of the concert—it did, after all, occupy only its second half— and the novelty of the evening's form in combining concert with a declaimed text.

Alongside music written for the theatre ran another genre, the programme overture that was one of the main forms of continental European composition. Growing from the eighteenth-century sonata form, it takes as its structural basis the presentation of two contrasting musical themes or groups of themes stated in an opening exposition. The development section that follows allows them to be fragmented, extended, combined, and generally explored in any musically valid manner—suggestively often referred to as 'dialogues'—and the piece ends with a recapitulation of the initial themes, with perhaps a coda adding further material at the close. A moment's reflection suggests this as an ideal, albeit challenging, armature for the presentation of dramatic processes. Tchaikovsky, for example, uses the two groups of themes to present the Montague-Capulet feud and the lovers' ecstasy, the development section suggesting the confusions and conflicts of the play before the recapitulation brings together the lovers in serene conclusion. The earliest English composer to explore this form was William Sterndale Bennett (1816–75), friend of Mendelssohn and Schumann and a leading figure in the early Victorian period. His overtures to *The Tempest* and *The Merry Wives of Windsor* both date from the early 1830s, the latter given its premiere by an orchestra formed by the British Society of Musicians in 1834. Yet, while the composer's piano concertos and symphonies were widely praised, the Shakespearian works were largely ignored. This may have been because of audience preferences, or the sheer difficulty of this kind of writing for most listeners.

Examining some of these compositions is helpful in revealing the ways in which English composers used one of the major international musical genres of the time to interpret the plays of Shakespeare. Henry Hugo Pierson (1815–73) studied in Germany and later became Reid Professor of Music at Edinburgh. His music for Shakespeare includes concert overtures to *Julius Caesar*, *Macbeth*, *As You Like It*, and *Romeo and Juliet*, and a funeral march to *Hamlet*. His *Romeo and Juliet* was first performed at a Crystal Palace Saturday concert and subsequently published in Leipzig, revealing a difference in the approach to symphonic music in the two countries. The overture is vigorous and forceful in its use of the programme-sonata form, with separate themes reflecting the two major characters, the ball at the Capulets' house, the fight, and many other episodes. There is a rhythmic energy that, in its syncopation, suggests Schumann; but whereas the German composer harnesses and develops this, Pierson's writing sounds breathless in its constant shifting of small melodic motifs, lacking the apparent ease of Shakespearian music in continental European tone poems. Mendelssohn reduces *A Midsummer Night's Dream* to a few readily identifiable themes. Tchaikovsky builds to a triumphant statement of the lovers' theme in double octaves in his *Romeo and Juliet* overture. Pierson's overture, while making full and competent use of formal structure and orchestral resources, seems always to be trying too hard: there are too many brief sections, never the fluency and breadth of continental versions that can present both a critical reading and an aesthetic transmediation of the plays.

While best-known for his operatic work with Gilbert, Arthur Sullivan also produced orchestral music treating Shakespearian themes. Among his earliest compositions was a suite based on *The Tempest*, performed like Pierson's work at Leipzig and then Covent Garden, but only given as part of a theatrical performance in Manchester in 1864. Yet, perhaps because of its uncertain identity as neither fully within or beyond the theatre, it has had only occasional revivals. Sullivan's overture to Irving's *Macbeth* was later presented as a self-contained concert piece. More extensive in duration and the use of orchestral forces, it employs a series of themes presenting the encounter with the witches, the murder of Duncan, and the final, redemptive appearance of Malcolm. The problem for most listeners, then as now, is that it is always heard with the knowledge of Sullivan's comic operas. The style is not so different as to prevent the constant feeling that not Malcolm's forces but the Yeomen of the Guard will form the final triumphant theme, and the piece lacks the independent strength to dispel such reactions. In 1877 Sir Edward German composed a symphonic poem *Hamlet*. This is much more assured than Pierson's or Sullivan's work, presenting main areas of the play's action through a series of contrasting themes and orchestral colours. Fragments of melody repeated at higher pitch, with frequent suspensions—notes from one chord held over above another, so that the ear demands that they resolve downwards—are used to suggest yearning. Tremolando chords in the strings above muted chords from wind and brass suggest threat and suspense; often these lead to rapid, chromatic scales above loud, brass chords, emphasized with drums and cymbals to present moments of conflict. Simple, slowly-moving melodies suggest dignity and resolution at the close. Yet, striking though much of this is, overall the piece again reflects the difficulty of using a symphonic structure to present something as complex as a Shakespeare tragedy: there is simply too much going on to be stated in musical terms, and even Tchaikovsky's programme overture to *Hamlet* is less successful than that to the *Dream*. Another difficulty in German's work is implicit in its musical vocabulary: the devices and techniques it uses had already, by the end of the century, become standard methods of presenting different kinds of mood and action, and would soon become clichéd in the extreme in music for silent film. It is not insignificant that many passages are given directions that reflect aspects of performance—*Pomposo* for the theme depicting Claudius, *Marcato* (emphatically) to present Hamlet's final decisive mood.

Later composers moved away from overtures attempting to present the sequence of a whole play. Parry's *Overture to an Unwritten Tragedy* (1893), perhaps written in the shadow of Brahms's *Tragic Overture*, is musically far more successful. While making no explicit allusion to Shakespeare, it must surely reflect the composer's ideas of the structure and progression of the major tragedies and the conflicts they represent, and in this acts as a kind of abstract meditation on tragedic form and mood. Other composers reflected the broader interest in character study, the little-known Frederick Corder writing his *Prospero* overture in 1888, moving across a range of moods with sure-footed Wagnerian style and orchestral power. Sir Edward Elgar's overture *Froissart* (1890) is concerned not with the *Chronicles* as the sources of Shakespeare's histories but with a much freer reading of the age of chivalry. Perhaps for this reason, it is far more assured as a concert piece. Or perhaps it is just, well, better. Not until 1913 did anything of major international stature appear that treated Shakespearian ideas with genuine force and originality, when Elgar's *Falstaff*, significantly described as a 'Symphonic Study', was given its first performance at the Leeds Festival.

As with orchestral music, there was a strong and almost insuperable division between songs composed for performance within a production and settings intended for solo singing, either as recital pieces or for amateur enjoyment at home. It is perhaps not too simplistic to say that, like larger symphonic music, the solo song in England moves towards maturity in the period by achieving the self-confidence of greater simplicity. The earliest songs, such as those from Bishop's semi-operas, follow a simple strophic, hymn-tune like pattern where the music is the same for each verse, so that no sense of dramatic growth or change is possible to reflect that of the words, all of which are set to simple melodies in regular musical phrases. By the end of the period, song had achieved greater sophistication in reflecting the quality of the words through greater variety, though not necessarily complexity, of structure. Parry and Stanford are today best known for their church music and choral-orchestral pieces, but their solo songs are perhaps the most valuable musical treatments of Shakespeare's words from this period. Parry's 'O mistress mine' uses a rushing piano figuration that propels the solo line towards the climax of 'Then come kiss me, sweet and twenty', capturing a sense of amorous excitement without any of the cloying sentiment of more popular vocal music of its time. By contrast, his setting of Desdemona's willow song is dark and hesitant, the vocal line chromatically jagged, reflecting a knowledge of Bach's use of such devices for extreme emotional presences yet without in any way burlesquing them. These are songs worthy of any international recital, as well as subtle and emotionally intelligent transmediations of the texts that, through their own integrity, suggest much about the verbal richness of the words in their dramatic settings. Parry also composed settings of two of the sonnets, 'Farewell, thou art too dear for my possessing', and 'If thou survive my well-contented day'. Both move beyond the strophic towards carefully constructed dramatic scenes in their own right by careful use of recollection and transformation of themes.

Stanford set only what were published as 'The Fool's Songs from *Twelfth Night*', but all show great skill and sensitivity. The final one, 'The rain it raineth every day' uses a recurrent chordal figure in the piano that suggests falling raindrops, but builds above this something much more sophisticated. Its strophic form is carefully manipulated so that, at the end, it moves from what seems a melancholy reflection, aided by the melisma on the word 'rain' (its setting to several notes to form a phrase on its own) to the use of a similar figure for 'strive' in the line 'And we'll strive to please you every day', after which the song ends with a very conventional cadence. The suggestion is that the singer has gone from an introspective melancholic reflecting on the passage of time to an extrovert performer trying to entertain, a subtle and complete presentation in musical terms of what goes on in the play. By contrast, Sullivan's setting of the same words is limited and superficial.

These songs, remarkable as they are, represent only a small fraction of those written by Parry and Stanford. Both composers also produced large-scale choral-orchestral works, Stanford setting Chaucer, Aeschylus, and Tennyson, Parry Tennyson and, most famously, three large works using texts from other English poets including Shelley's *Prometheus Unbound* (1880) and two Milton settings *L'Allegro and Il Penseroso* (1890) and *Blest Pair of Sirens* (1887), a work still performed by many professional and amateur choirs. Why, then, did neither compose more music—choral, vocal, orchestral, operatic—that set Shakespeare's words? The answer may be found in some much earlier English music. One of the finest, as well as the earliest, English operas, Henry Purcell's *Dido and Æneas* (1689), sets words by Nahum Tate once described as being so bad that the only thing to do was set them to music. By contrast, Purcell's *The Fairy Queen* (1692, rev. 1693) was designed as a series of masques to be performed in the intervals between the five acts of *A Midsummer Night's Dream* and, while treating mythic and folkloric themes related to the play, sets only a tiny fraction of its words. Perhaps this is the answer to the rarity of large-scale Shakespeare music in England, then and now: there is simply so much music in the words that adding any more would be superfluous. Benjamin Britten's *A Midsummer Night's Dream* (1960), to a libretto constructed by the composer and Peter Pears using only Shakespeare's text, but heavily cut, succeeds because it consists in no small part of recitative, much unaccompanied, perhaps for the same reason.

Throughout Victoria's reign a great stream of music was composed and performed that reflected a concern with Shakespeare's works, the greater part of it conceived and performed as a secondary complement to performance. With the important exceptions already noted, little survives of these scores, but this should not cause much surprise. The songs and incidental music composed by Guy Woolfenden, award-winning composer for the Royal Shakespeare Company from 1963 to 1998, were almost universally praised at the time but are now known only to a tiny number of musicologists and theatre historians. Yet the immediate appeal of music of the stage, and even its musical quality, are not the only reasons for the poor survival rate of Victorian compositions, especially those scored for a reasonably sized orchestra. Printing a large score and its associated instrumental parts was very expensive, demanding hand-engraving of copper or steel plates, an intensely specialized and labour-intensive business that has only recently, with the aid of computerized notation, become more practicable. Then as now, it was comparatively easy to secure a first performance for a new piece of concert music, when orchestral parts could be copied in manuscript, and the full score probably the composer's only copy; finding second or subsequent hearings was much harder.

Yet there is a more positive reason for the disappearance of these scores. Music for the theatre depends for its effectiveness on its relation to the action, staging, and performance style; the logical consequence of this is that it has little validity or appeal without such a location. That is the great irony surrounding Victorian Shakespeare music: it was so much a part of contemporary performance, popular in its own time because reflecting contemporary tastes, that it could have no independent, or longer-term, existence of its own, so that in a very significant way it has become the victim of its own immediate, and not inconsiderable, success.

* * * * *

While music was intricately connected with performance for most of Victoria's reign, visual art had separated itself from the theatre at its very beginning and, with some significant exceptions, remained so for the whole period. While paintings of stage action, often called 'theatrical conversation pieces', were popular in the eighteenth century, Victorian painting increasingly concerned itself with naturalistic depictions of scenes as if occurring outside the theatre. One reason for this was the popularity of the history painting, a category that included any powerful narrative, whether factual or invented; another was a single event that, in its aim to include images of all of the plays, including those rarely if ever performed, often made stage depictions impossible. This was the Shakespeare Gallery, devised by the print-publisher John Boydell, which spanned the end of the eighteenth and the opening of the nineteenth centuries, and included paintings related to all of the plays in the canon, which were also widely reproduced as engravings. The intersections of these forces made painting of the plays as actual events within naturalistic settings an almost inevitable practice.

This did not mean that the force and range of the Boydell collection was continued by the next generation of artists. Additionally, by the late 1830s the Romantic preoccupation with varieties of the sublime that defined many of its finest images had given way to much gentler modes of presentation, and the fashion for 'genre paintings' that celebrated moments of slight social interaction, often between rural figures in mildly picturesque landscapes or interiors, that were also part of the Boydell project, dominate Shakespeare painting at the beginning of the period. Instead of pivotal moments of decision or action, such paintings selected events of soft sentiment or mild humour and, even when venturing into more dangerous territory, presented the scenes in similarly temperate fashion. A major figure at this time was the American-born academician C. R. Leslie. His two scenes from *The Winter's Tale*, *Florizel and Perdita* (1837), and *Autolycus* (1823–36) selected moments from the fourth act that, while attractive enough as decorative pieces, make little comment on the symbolic nature of the sheep-shearing or the larger events that it foreshadows. The same is true of his treatments of *The Merry Wives of Windsor* and *The Taming of the Shrew*, understandably in the former, but for the latter avoiding both the severity of the theme and the comedy many Victorian readers and audiences saw within it. Even his image of the two Princes in *Richard III* is more concerned with sentiment than threat. That all these paintings were purchased for the collection of the Victoria and Albert Museum, in whose collection they remain, reveals the respect with which they were regarded by Victorian critics.

These are attractive compositions very much in the style of contemporary artists who delighted in rural scenes, but they lack the edge of social criticism of, say, George Morland, or the narrative implications of David Wilkie. William Mulready's version of 'The Seven Ages of Man' from *As You Like It* (1835–8: Victoria and Albert Museum) is at first sight very similar, showing figures that together represent all the ages within a softly lit medieval Italian city. There is little of intellectual import in these loosely linked portraits, but the painting marks an important change: instead of a single instant, the image combines elements held separate, albeit very slightly, in the play's verbal current. Many of the finest paintings of the eighteenth century had used this approach to telling interpretive effect, as would many from the decades to follow; within its apparent sentimental stillness, Mulready's painting marks an important move towards this greater depth. Others at the same time followed similar paths: Daniel Maclise's paintings of the letter scene in *Twelfth Night* (1840) and the play scene in *Hamlet* (1842: both Tate Britain, London) concentrated sequential action and character portrayal into a single image, freezing a moment of action to generate suspense and concentrate the reader's attention on past events and their potential future development.

While the foundation of the Pre-Raphaelite Brotherhood in 1848 was perhaps not quite such an abrupt change of style and structure as often suggested—there are similarities between their work and that of Maclise, for example—it did much to reinvigorate narrative painting of all kinds. That a great deal of their first work treated, with meticulous attention to detail of composition and narrative, subjects from Shakespeare or the Bible reveals both the seriousness of their approach and the degree to which the two literary subjects would increasingly be linked in the artistic, and perhaps the wider public, imagination of the period. There are similarities in tone, too, the Shakespeare images frequently having strong moral thrusts in subject and treatment. John Everett Millais's *Ophelia* (1851–2: Tate Britain, London) wholly rejected the theatre both through its extreme naturalistic presentation of the brook and its flowered banks and in showing a scene narrated, not enacted, in the play. Like all of the group's most successful paintings, it worked on several levels in its engagement with the play. Freezing the moment of recorded action, it offered a visual equivalent of Gertrude's speech; presenting the body of Ophelia it gave a moment of emotional concentration for the viewer to contemplate; and in the contrast between the vibrant colours of the flowers and foliage and the blank whiteness of Ophelia it emphasized her unfulfilled youth. More recent critics have taken this further, arguing that the suffering caused in the play by the character Hamlet has been extended in the depiction of Ophelia as victim, revealing the power of male control and, in the painting, the male gaze. Whether this was a view held by Victorian viewers is a complex, fugitive question: early reviewers concentrated more on the pathos of the scene, and the beauty of the painting. What is more certain is that its use of new techniques of painting in translucent washes over a white ground gave all these qualities an energy and immediacy quite absent in earlier paintings, emphasizing its own aesthetic identity to balance its function as a work of Shakespearian interpretation.

These elements are also apparent in Millais's *Ferdinand Lured by Ariel* (1850: Makins Collection, Washington, DC). This uses multiple depictions of the fairies accompanying the spirit to show other-worldly movement and ethereal temptation, their sickly translucent greens in stark contrast to the bright red of Ferdinand's tunic and the far more vibrant green of the foliage, a highly original reversal of the two worlds that are brought together in the scene. That at this time Ariel was presented on stage by an elegant young woman probably accounted for the painting's poor reception; even today the painting has not lost its power to disturb as a reading of the play. It also shows the artist's insight into the uncertainty of the moment within the play's movement, reminding the viewer that the positive outcome of Ferdinand's entry is by no means certain.

William Holman Hunt, another founding member of the group, adopted a more strongly moralistic tone in his paintings. *Claudio and Isabella* (1853: Tate Britain) shows the two characters from *Measure for Measure*. The precise location of the painting in the play, and the moral question that it raises—should Isabella sleep with the corrupt Angelo and so secure her brother Claudio's pardon—is precisely identified by the inscription on the original frame:

> CLAUDIO: Death is a frightful thing
> ISABELLA: And shamed life a hateful

Light is here used with great power to show, in the contrast between the flowering bush seen in spring sunlight outside the prison walls and the dark, solid textures within, the extremities offered in the play. Part of the painting's effect lies in the combination of this contrast, the radically different poses of the two characters and the moral statement of the caption: it is a highly skilled translation of the play's central issue. Not until 1896 would F. S. Boas coin the term 'problem plays', but it is hard to think of a better definition of the term than the painting's presentation of a moral question which has no clear answer. In this, the painting reveals a close grasp of the play and a strong independent moral thrust within its own painterly identity. The same insights are shown in *The Hireling Shepherd* (1852: Manchester City Art Galleries) which illustrates a verse of the Fool's song from *King Lear* to present both a literal and a metaphoric reading:

> Sleepest or wakest thou, jolly shepherd?
> Thy sheep are in the corn;
> And for one blast of thy minikin mouth
> Thy sheep shall take no harm

(Q1:3.6.23–6)

Hunt's moral concern here is as much with the state of the Church of England as with illustrating the lines from Shakespeare, harnessing the link between the two in a manner highly original in its use of symbol and dependent on the close relation between Shakespearian text and religious belief, a link especially pertinent at the time of the painting when the Oxford Movement was striving to reform the established church, which it felt had lost moral direction.

Hunt's *Valentine Rescuing Silvia from Proteus* (1851: Birmingham Museum and Art Gallery) from *The Two Gentlemen of Verona* rejects the earlier visual tradition of showing the intervention of Valentine to save Silvia from her attempted rape by Proteus and instead shows the moment that follows. The immediate resolution, and its larger uncertainty in terms of the exact significance of Valentine's apparent presentation of Silvia to Proteus, again throws the moral question back to the viewer. These are paintings of immense technical skill in their own right, but they also function as subtly provocative readings of the plays they present.

The third founder of the group, Dante Gabriel Rossetti, worked in a different manner and on a different scale in his Shakespeare images—wash drawings and engravings of Hamlet and Ophelia and two versions of the death of Lady Macbeth. These last are striking compositions, presenting the character not as a figure abandoned in her madness but as a woman of forceful sensuality—a reading that redefines her place in the play, emphasizing a role as both ambitious mortal and, as in some popular views at the time, the fourth witch. It also engages silently with a question raised by many contemporary readers of the play—why is Lady Macbeth's death apparently treated with so little significance? Other painters, not strictly part of the brotherhood but closely related to them in style, included Charles Allston Collins and William Dyce. Collins' *Convent Thoughts* (1851: Ashmolean Museum, Oxford) offers a surprising reading of some lines from *A Midsummer Night's Dream*; Dyce's *Henry VI at Towton* (late 1850s: Guildhall Art Gallery, London), in borrowing the composition used in his earlier paintings of Christ in the wilderness, inflects the moment of the play with religious intensity.

Painting after the initial impact of the Pre-Raphaelite Brotherhood (PRB) in many ways continued their concern for symbolic narrative and moral statement, although few matched their concentration of idea and execution. The main move was towards narrative and character-presentation through symbolic detail or allusion to other paintings, in this manner merging with major forms in paintings of the period (see Illustrations 4.1, 4.2, and 4.3). George Cattermole and Sir John Gilbert, best known as illustrators, produced a few images of individual scenes from the plays, and in the 1850s and 60s

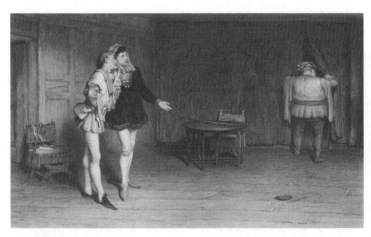

4.1 William Quiller Orchardson: *Falstaff, Hal and Poins*. Here the artist uses one of his favourite compositional devices, a large gap between characters, here to suggest the coming rejection of Falstaff.

4.2 Marcus Stone: *Lear and Cordelia.* In combining the elegant figure of the attentive daughter with attempts at historical accuracy in the archetype of the patriarch—he looks remarkably like Tennyson—the painting reveals itself as eminently Victorian.

the work of Robert Braithwaite Martineau and Alfred Elmore took their approach further through references to their other works with more contemporary social themes. Their paintings of the plays closely resemble their earlier canvases of families ruined by drink or gambling, blunting the moral force of the early PRB paintings at the same time as thickening their textures and colours. In the 1860s and 70s Philip Hermogenes Calderon painted some versions of the plays that place their events firmly within the style and structure of contemporary Victorian narrative, with little direct concern for interpretive statement. Lawrence Alma-Tadema extended his treatment of classical events to include an image of Antony and Cleopatra; as mentioned in Chapter 1, Edwin Landseer produced an image of Bottom and Titania that is uniquely disturbing in presenting Bottom as half naturalistic ass, half Victorian burgher. *A Midsummer Night's*

4.3 Frank Dicksee, engraved by J. M. Johnstone: *Othello and Desdemona*, 1890–1.
That this wood-engraving appeared in a popular newspaper reveals the social
breadth of interest in visual treatments of the plays; in treatment it continues one
of the most frequently depicted scenes.
© Trustees of the British Museum

Dream was also an important part of the fashion for fairy paintings in
the second half of the century. They range from disturbing imaginative treatments of the play's supernatural elements, through render-
ings as colossal in size and specific in detail as those of stagings of the
play at the century's end, to images that appear to seize on Shakespeare as a respectable justification for fleshy nudes. The three are
exemplified respectively in the work of Richard Dadd, Sir Joseph
Noel Paton, and John Simmons.

All the images so far discussed take as their basis moments from
the plays and show within them an awareness at some level of their
larger movement and ideas. They were matched by other styles that
operated very differently, in most cases rejecting the formal rhetoric of
large oil paintings and moving towards drawings or works intended

for reproduction—in this aided by the rapid advances in engraving on wood or steel, lithography and other techniques of printing. The main concern of such images was portraiture, using the styles of contemporary figurative art to present characters from the play as real people, instancing again the movement of separation in which the roles of the plays come increasingly to be seen as convincing human individuals that will be discussed in Chapter 6. Charles Heath's *The Shakespeare Gallery*, first published in 1837, was a volume containing engravings of nearly all the female characters, each prefaced by a short quotation from the relevant play. Its reissue in the 1840s with new images more contemporary in style and costume developed the movement of character beyond play. The 1847 version, under the title *Shakespeare's Heroines*, marked a change of focus that was matched by a change of style. The fragile prettiness of the earlier volume, suggesting late Georgian portraiture, is replaced by the more naturalistic style favoured in contemporary paintings that attempted greater psychological depth (see Illustration 4.4). The culmination of this movement came with *The Graphic Gallery of the Heroines of Shakespeare* from 1887 to 1888. The proprietor of *The Graphic* journal commissioned the leading artists of the day to paint a series of character portraits, which were displayed in a fashionable London gallery. Reproductions by one of the most advanced colour processes were presented with the journal, and they were also printed in monochrome to ensure their availability through several layers of Victorian society, a process matched by the reproduction of many other images of the plays during the period. Such fragmentation of the plays also extended to visual treatment of the songs, paralleling their musical settings with etchings and engravings that illustrate their content in ways quite separate from their larger dramatic functions.

Only one of the portraits in the Graphic Gallery, that of Queen Katherine from *Henry VIII*, was painted by a woman artist, Laura Alma-Tadema, a proportion representative of Shakespeare paintings of the period. It is not that women artists were not important at this time, although few attained the prominence of their male counterparts. Laura Alma-Tadema is matched in the earlier period by Elizabeth Siddal and Georgina Burne-Jones and in later years by many others, including Eleanor Fortescue-Brickdale, Mrs Blair Leighton,

4.4 C. R. Leslie: *Olivia*, from Charles Heath's *Shakespeare's Heroines*, 1848. Here the artist uses the classical column, a common motif in earlier portraiture, to emphasize the character's nobility.

Jane Morris, Louisa Starr, Evelyn de Morgan and Elizabeth Forbes. Louisa Starr's painting of Imogen inside the cave of Belarius (1873: untraced, reproduced in the *Illustrated London News*, 27 September 1873) and Elizabeth Forbes' painting of the same character in *Imogen Lying among the Flowers* (1898: Plymouth City Museum and Art Gallery) are important images, but there are very few Shakespeare paintings by women artists, who were more prolific in landscapes, genre pieces, or medieval subjects.

As the century moved on, interest in Shakespeare painting in general diminished, replaced by a concern for medieval history and legend or the depiction of meticulously researched scenes from classical Rome. Yet some important works were produced. In the 1880s and 1890s, Millais returned to Shakespeare, but treated the plays in much more distant, reflective manner. *'Blow, Blow thou Winter Wind'* (1892: Auckland Art Gallery Poi o Tamaki, New Zealand) shows a woman abandoned in a snowbound landscape, an image that comes close to a parody of the banishment of the daughter who brought disgrace on the family; a view of an autumn scene, titled *'Bare ruined choirs, where once [sic] the sweet birds sang'* (1873: Manchester City Art Galleries), is rare in basing itself on one of the sonnets. What is striking about both is that they present their texts by visualizing or reinventing their symbols: this is something quite new, and perhaps suggests a far deeper knowledge of the plays as aesthetic objects rather than narratives or moral fables. Some themes retained their attraction: the death of Ophelia was painted by, among others, Arthur Hughes and, in three quite separate compositions, William Waterhouse. Throughout the period, too, there were paintings of the dramatist himself, part of the concern for biography that is explored in Chapter 7.

Visual treatments of the plays were not restricted to the traditional media of paint, print, or book illustration. From the early 1850s, photography was employed in a variety of ways to record, interpret, and present the plays. The earliest instances were wood-engravings made as copies of daguerreotypes, inserted as images of actors in the 'Tallis Shakespeare', edited by Halliwell in 1850–51. When various processes made possible the production of prints on paper, photographic studios multiplied and actors began to commission their 'likenesses' for publicity purposes, in various sizes from the 'carte-de-visite' visiting card format to the large cabinet images that were used as 'house cards' placed in the foyers of theatres with, between them, quarto-sized prints intended to be signed and given to admiring audience members. The degree to which these actually recorded performance remains open to question. Images of the Keans and some of their company (see Illustration 4.5) seem accurately to present aspects of performance, and in some cases even the stage sets, but as the studio of Martin Laroche in which they were taken was close to the Princess's Theatre in Oxford Street there is no firm evidence of this, and the best that can be said is

4.5 Martin Laroche: Photograph of Ellen Tree and Drinkwater Meadows in the garden scene from *Richard II*, c. 1857. The hastily unrolled groundsheet, backdrop, and potted tree reveal this as an early studio shot, as do the fixed poses and direct frontal perspective.
© Victoria and Albert Museum, London

that they may represent actors in costume. Not until the end of the century was it possible to take photographs in the theatre, and because such images were taken after rehearsal with casts arranged to make full use of short-lived magnesium flares there is no guarantee that they present the action as it was in performance. By the 1880s, procedures for printing photographs—half tones or photographic blocks—were available, and photographs appeared frequently in the illustrated journals. The first edition of the plays to be illustrated with photographs appeared in 1900, using images of individual actors in character.

Not all photographs were intended as simple records. What came to be known as art photography, although the preserve of a few, was a major new development, the work of pioneers such as Henry Peach Robinson and Julia Margaret Cameron being especially important. Robinson assembled compositions from several separate exposures to create complex effects of lighting, or used lines from the plays as titles of otherwise naturalistic images. '*The beached margent of the sea*' (1870) uses this technique to combine a foreground beach, breaking waves and some seagulls, the whole enriched by the title quotation from *A Midsummer Night's Dream* perhaps functioning to add cultural weight, the image serving to give visual immediacy to what seems little more than a passing topical reference in the play. Cameron produced several portrait photographs of well-known figures of her time but made them ambiguous by naming them after Shakespearian characters, offering a teasing reflection on the nature of identity in the theatre and in actuality beyond it. Striking in a different way is her portrait photograph titled simply *Mariana*. Rather than presenting the figure as a model of sensuous indolence, as in Millais's celebrated painting from 1851, an image based as much on Tennyson's poem as on Shakespeare's play, Cameron shows her with head resting on hand, an allusion to the traditional posture of melancholy. Used in much earlier paintings to suggest a quality of mature, reflective independence, this suggests something far more positive than earlier readings of the character, a force enhanced by its appropriation of a posture hitherto shown exclusively in male subjects. Images of this kind were, however, rare in these photographers' work and exceptional outside it. For most Victorians, photographs were absolute, complete documentations of external reality—and for many critics and readers, especially those concerned with theatre history, they remain so today.

At the height of the Victorian period, more paintings related to Shakespeare were submitted to the Summer Exhibition of the Royal Academy than on any other subject, such was the interest in presenting the author, his characters, and his plays in visual terms. Artists ranged from enthusiastic amateurs to celebrated Academicians, approaches from watercolours of the flowers mentioned in the plays to allegorical presentations of the action and themes of the most complex plays, with portraits of characters, depictions of scenes, and invented episodes from the life of the dramatist among those between these extremes. In the Burlington House gallery these were seen and discussed by art lovers and members of fashionable society; in reproductions in magazines of specialist and general interest they reached a far larger readership. Some were engraved and printed with later editions of illustrated versions of the plays. In these ways, images of the plays, their characters and their leading actors became an essential part of the aesthetic, intellectual, and social fabric of the age. These paragraphs offer only a survey of the most outstanding artists and their works, and much research remains to be done in exploring and discussing the approaches taken by artists of all kinds during Victoria's reign. But the sheer volume of work produced, and its close relationship to the styles and subject matter of other contemporary painting reveal that, here as in so many other areas of endeavour, Shakespeare was at the centre of the Victorian imagination.

Shakespeare, the Novel, and Poetry

Given that—with the possible exception of poetry at some times and under specific circumstances—the novel was the dominant literary form of the period, and that Shakespeare's texts were increasingly seen as the embodiment of national and cultural identity, it would appear inevitable that both serious and popular fiction would make frequent and various allusion to the plays. What is particularly striking, however, is the variety of ways in which this allusion is manifest, often becoming most forceful when it is apparently least evident. There are, of course, strands of fiction that do not engage with the plays, even in the most oblique manner. Novels of sensation, detective fiction, and popular romance rarely allude to the plays, and where they do it is through a desire to elevate the tone of discussion or define a character; where verbal references occur it is often through using a phrase that by sheer frequency of use has ceased to be a conscious quotation. Yet, even within these genres, there are individual works that take on Shakespearian themes, albeit more often with reference to the life and the cult than the writings.

The novels that make the most striking use of the plays are those that employ elements of structure and movement that, while adapted to themes of insistent contemporary concern, and often without direct allusion to Shakespeare's writing, nonetheless show subtle and complex development and interweaving of many of the structures and patterns of the plays. For this reason, the novels are best discussed individually rather than by the themes and forms they use; the integration of these is, in no small measure, one of the striking ways in which they demonstrate their appropriation and modification of Shakespearian elements. There is, however, one writer whose use of the plays stands out for its sheer range of quotation, and for what it reveals about the writer and to no little extent his readers: Charles Dickens.

In her exhaustive study *Shakespeare and Dickens* (1996), Valerie Gager lists around a thousand Shakespearian references in Dickens' writing. Thirteen pages of this catalogue quote references to the man; the remaining one hundred present quotations from or references to individual works, presented play by play, that occur in the novels, and of these roughly a quarter are from *Hamlet*. Given Dickens' own love of the theatre, friendship with Macready, and his own performances, it is perhaps no surprise that the plays should figure prominently: what is perhaps more surprising is the form that references take, the effects they have, and what they imply about the novels' readers. A high proportion of the allusions are there to clarify an aspect of character by comparison, often in a way that generates humour through incongruity. Some of the most successful uses of quotations occur when they are made by characters in the novels in ways that reveal their own natures. In *David Copperfield* (1849–50) Mr Micawber quotes from the plays' more celebrated soliloquies and thus reveals his own pomposity to comic effect—a comedy often enhanced by misquotation. Often such resonances are carefully wrapped in the speaker's own words. In *Our Mutual Friend* (1864–5) Jenny Wren speaks with resigned sadness about her drunken father in saying 'He'd be sharper than a serpent's tooth if he wasn't as dull as ditch water', quoting Lear's line 'How sharper than a serpent's tooth it is/ To have a thankless child' (1.4.251–2). The pathos here results from the child speaking about the father, reversing the relationship of the original lines, and thus softening the situation in a manner enhanced by the character's repeated references to her father as if he were the child. Similarly misdirected quotations appear as chapter titles: one part of *The Pickwick Papers* (1836–7) includes the assertion 'the Course of True Love is not a railway', echoing lines from *A Midsummer Night's Dream*, again for comic effect through incongruity. That *Pickwick* is one of the earliest of his writings and *Our Mutual Friend* the last completed novel suggests what is borne out by detailed reading of the novels, that such use of quotation is a recurrent feature throughout Dickens' fiction.

As well as revealing a detailed and extensive knowledge of the plays in the writer himself, such prevalence of quotation would suggest a similar knowledge among his readers. The incongruity, and hence comedy and pathos, would after all not be understood without an understanding both of the fact that the words are quotations and of their significance in their original appearance. If this is indeed the case, the references offer invaluable evidence of the extent to which a knowledge of Shakespeare permeated Victorian society. Dickens' works, especially the earlier ones, had an immense readership that scythed through boundaries of class and income; that Shakespearian allusions could be made to such an extent suggests that a knowledge of the plays was similarly widespread—a notion amply supported by the work of Andrew Murphy in *Shakespeare for the People* (2003) and by that of many theatre historians. Yet perhaps there is another explanation. Many expressions from the plays had entered the language to the extent that they were used without any awareness of their being quotations. One does not have to see the relation to *Shakespeare* in the *Pickwick* title to appreciate its comic absurdity. When characters quote or misquote, or use language from the plays in a comically inappropriate way, another level of significance is suggested. Is Dickens the novelist satirizing the habit of misquotation prevalent among many of his own readers? Any or all of these possibilities remain implicit, but what is perhaps most revealing is the degree to which Dickens recalled and used the language of the plays, an example of the most extreme kind of a phenomenon that was widespread throughout the period.

Dickens' own love of the theatre and his own dramatized readings offer another focus of Shakespearian allusion in the novels. This is most keenly apparent in *Nicholas Nickleby* (1839), where the episode with the touring actors of Vincent Crummles offers a sharply detailed insight into the practices of an early Victorian touring company. The novel also offers some possible similarities with the plays in its larger structure. The discovery, near the novel's end, that Smike is the son of Newman Noggs recalls revelatory moments at the close of the comedies; the Cheeryble twins and the pastoralism of the visit to the 'sweetest little village' of Bow both suggest elements from these plays. Yet the comic elements are given a sharper edge. The scenes at the Saracen's Head, recalling the Eastcheap scenes from *Henry IV*, are intensified by the attempted seduction of Kate Nickleby that is revealed there, and the duel scene that might at first recall that between Aguecheek and Viola/Cesario has a darker ending in the death of Lord Frederick Verisopht. The novel is also an early satire of the Shakespeare cult, with Kate Nickleby's employer Julia Wititterly's claim 'I'm always ill after Shakespeare' and the account by Nicholas's mother of her visit to Stratford and the Birthplace. It is as if, in the novel's overall progression, separate elements from the plays have been drawn together and transformed by the demands of a popular serial novel set in a period just far enough in the past to allow a sense of gentle nostalgia and moral superiority in the reader.

Relationships between the sexes in Dickens might be seen as in some ways rekindling elements of their treatment by Shakespeare. Situations arise in the novels which superficially resemble those of the plays, as for example when Newman Noggs appears carrying Madeleine Bray; but here the suggestion of Lear carrying Cordelia is not sustained, the mood being one of popular melodrama rather than that of Shakespearian catastrophe. Dickens' second use of this trope, where Em'ly is carried by her father in *David Copperfield*, is emotionally more powerful, but in a manner wholly within Victorian sentimentality, and again lacking the cosmic resonance of *King Lear*. The networks of power relations between fathers, guardians, and uncles and the young women in their care are similarly remote from the movement from father to husband undertaken by the young women of the comedies, and are often wrapped in plot complications of self-interest and financial greed, or infused with sentimentality. The relationship of care, already mentioned with relation to Jenny Wren in *Our Mutual Friend*, is quite different from the vigorous plot-direction of Viola or Rosalind. Further, the movement towards marriage in Dickens is either unfulfilled or, where complete, as in Copperfield's marriage to Dora, rests on a traditional notion of male courtship that denies the vigorous action of the female partner and the move to self-knowledge that this implies. And to think of Dickens' female characters in any frame of sexual fulfilment is beyond probability: young women are the objects of sexual predation, as shown with Little Em'ly and Steerforth in *David Copperfield*, or Kate Nickleby and Sir Mulberry Hawk, or are perpetually infantilized, like *Copper-field*'s Dora or Little Em'ly. Where an individual voice is heard, in the powerful and innovative separate 'Esther's Narrative' of *Bleak House* (1852–3) it is that of the caring female who puts aside hopes of emotional fulfilment. Overall, the impression is that, while quotation, comic misquotation, and passing reference are profuse, there is never any sense of the larger structures or concerns of the plays within the novels. Rather than the trajectory of the comedies, or still less the tragedies, Dickens' novels rest structurally on the demands imposed by their serial composition. Ironically, that which has most to do with the theatre, and hence of the performance of Shakespeare in the 1830s, is that which is most clearly episodic: *Nicholas Nickleby*.

Such differences in characterization and structure are matched in differences in the use of figurative language. Dickens' use of metaphor is either restricted to single moments for comedy, or developed in extended passages of extreme exaggeration. The passages describing industrial Coketown in *Hard Times* (1854) are perhaps the most immediate example of the latter; of the former, details of physical appearance of character, compared with animal or inanimate elements, are frequent. Both lack the more complex associative patterns of Shakespeare's imagery, where one comparison leads on to another, and their deeper and often darker moral and psychological force. Where larger allusions or structural forms seem feasible, Dickens rejects them: the fog in *Bleak House* is constructed quite differently from the moral obfuscation generated by the recurrent, heavily patterned images of contagion in *Macbeth*. What remains of the relation between Dickens and Shakespeare is a quality that secured the place of both in the popular imagination: the ability to create characters with whom readers and viewers could sympathize, and moral issues with which they could identify. The means are quite different, but the pairing was strong in the popular imagination; and, as a later chapter will explore, was closely related to Victorian ideas of authorship that produced the lionizing of Dickens and the adulation of Shakespeare as ideals of human understanding.

Novelists who began writing in the second half of the Victorian period, and produced their mature works in its later decades, demonstrate rather different relationships with the plays of Shakespeare, suggesting difference between the major social concerns of the two periods in which they were produced. Many such novels appear to draw upon plays of all genres to explore social and psychological issues of their own times. Within this larger conspectus, a group of interrelated concerns is particularly striking. The relations of power between different social groups, reminiscent of the court-country antithesis that drives many of the comedies, are often expressed topographically in the oppositions between an already deeply threatened rural community and the economically far stronger industrial complex. In this they echo the idealized, and often satirized, Arcadian landscapes of the earlier comedies that are held in tension against the educated higher orders from the metropolitan centres. These tensions are often concentrated in situations where female identity and independence are both constructed and contested; and these in turn are often presented as part of conflicts related to love relationships. While for many theatregoers, readers, and performers, the movement of the comedies was seen—and in many cases is still seen—as a progress, albeit irregular, towards romantic fulfilment, it should not surprise us that the most intellectually perceptive and socially aware novelists of the period should seize on their structures as a way of discussing complex issues of gender, especially those concerning sexual and emotional fulfilment as they relate to economic and intellectual independence for women.

It is, of course, dangerous to draw parallels between periods so different in time and identity: but given the knowledge of the plays that pervaded Victorian society, extending far beyond the power and influence of any other literary form, it does not seem surprising that the plays should hang heavy in the minds of novelists. To this should perhaps be added the many apparently similar sociopolitical circumstances of the two periods. Both coupled a woman head of state with an overwhelmingly male power system; both saw a rapidly changing structure of aristocracy, nobility, and gentry; and both evidenced that phenomenon beloved of all social historians, a rapidly developing urban middle class, a change concerned as much with definition of these terms as with mobility within and between strata. By the 1840s, the novel had become far more than a form of literary entertainment: Scott's historical novels and Dickens' engagements with social reform had in the 1830s established the genre as the major forum for the debate of insistent contemporary issues within forms more immediately accessible than the limitations of pamphleteering and political party, the former practical and the latter ideological. In the next decade, the 'condition of England' writers explored immediate, and often regional, issues. By the second half of the century, these elements had been extensively mined, and something new was needed. The Brontës and others found it in the world of emotion, reflected in turbulent scenes and events in the natural world. But for the serious novelist from the 1860s onwards, Shakespeare was arguably the only formal model available that allowed the combination of character development and plot construction. Among these writers, two stand out for their imaginative appropriation of Shakespearian forms in plots engaging with contemporary issues: George Eliot and Thomas Hardy.

Before considering these, however, a novel from much earlier in the period needs mention: Charlotte Brontë's *Shirley* (1849). Brontë's earlier *Jane Eyre* (1847) has, since its publication, been much more popular because of its mixture of romance, mystery, and social advancement, and the later novel is in many ways less successfully constructed. But it is an intriguing experiment in bringing together the discussion of insistent social themes with the love interest demanded by most novel readers, and in doing so it can be seen as a transformation of themes and techniques recurrent in Shakespeare's comedies. The driving conflict is that between the reformist mill-owner Robert Gérard Moore and the wealthy heiress Shirley Keeldar. What in many ways takes on the intellectual, if not the circumstantial, identity of the love conflict of *Much Ado About Nothing* and *The Taming of the Shrew*, sharpened by financial difficulties caused by the Napoleonic war, is resolved by the introduction of Moore's brother Louis and his marriage to Shirley, a plot direction that superficially recalls the return of Sebastian at the end of *Twelfth Night*. As the war ends and the cloth trade is once again profitable, Robert's fortunes are restored, and he marries Shirley's bosom friend Caroline Helstone, a figure who acts as Celia to Shirley's Rosalind, and perhaps also, given the male roles that both take on, Aliena to her Ganymede. Love interest, a discussion of social unrest caused by new manufacturing processes—set in an earlier period but metaphoric of later industrialization—are thus drawn together through adoption and adaptation of familiar Shakespearian patterns of character and plot.

George Eliot is generally regarded as the most intellectually demanding Victorian novelist, a quality that reveals itself in the discussion of contemporary issues as well as the complex structures within which they are presented. In the earlier novels there are elements that seem to draw directly on Shakespeare—the scenes in the public house in *Adam Bede* (1859), for example, which are often compared to the tavern scenes in *1* and *2 Henry IV.* The earlier *Scenes of Clerical Life* (1858), largely concerned with issues of changing rural life, resembles the comedies in setting and in some of its characterization. But it is the later novels that embody most fully the combination of affairs of the heart, vigorous plot events, and dramatized moral debate that reveals the deepest resemblance to the plays of Shakespeare. Put simply, they combine the structural patterns and human relationships of the comedies with the mood and tone of the tragedies. *The Mill on the Floss* (1860), still the most popular of the novels, has in Maggie Tulliver a character who bears comparison with Shakespeare's young women in identity and situation. Her delineation is aided by the contrast to her ailing father and weak brother, so that she becomes the directing agent of the plot while also seeking her own emotional fulfilment. This duality is repeated in greater depth, and with far greater success in terms of narrative balance, in the later *Middlemarch*, published serially between 1870 and 1872 and generally regarded as the most finely achieved of Eliot's novels. A pattern of two pairs of lovers and the conflicting natures and aspirations of the members of each is presented in relation to spiritual, ethical, and scientific concerns of the age, so that concept and character are seamlessly united. The setting within the changing processes of rural and metropolitan life, and the use of characters from carefully demarcated but by no means impermeably bounded social strata, makes contemporary key elements of many of the comedies. The resemblances are never openly stated; but the echoes that most Victorians would have heard implicitly created a common ground between reader and text, a shared body of knowledge that both clarifies the events through giving them a sense of pre-existing familiarity, and endows them with the resonance of literary tradition. It is perhaps these qualities, as much as the insight and depth of characterization, that led to Eliot's work being frequently described as the most Shakespearian of English novels. Such judgments went beyond English reviewers: the French journal *La Nature* in 1879 called Eliot '*le plus Shakespearien, peut-à-dire, des romanciers anglais*'.

Reduced to its basic elements, such a structure of character and idea sounds mechanistic. The provincial location of *Middlemarch* is close enough to the countryside in both landscape and manners to reveal itself as a parallel to the forests of Shakespeare's comedies in opposition to the court, suggested in the novel by the gentry and lesser aristocracy of London. The two worlds overlap in the dynamics of Victorian self-advancement in a moral site where Sir Andrew Aguecheek's descendants would be quite familiar. Driven by her desire for spiritual and moral fulfilment, Dorothea Brooke marries Mr Casaubon, a scholar who is searching for the secret of universal mythology. Impelled by a desire for social advancement, Rosamund marries Lydgate, a scientist working to find the universal 'basic tissue' uniting all living forms. Casaubon's scheme fails because he lacks contact with current academic research, and Lydgate rejects his aristocratic family connections in favour of his scholarship. The balance is, if anything, too exact; but the pairing of character and situation is something that is inevitably enriched by the Shakespearian echoes audible within it. Reversal of love and the exchange of partners reflect the comedies; the failure of the relationships moves towards the tone of tragedy, if not its violent ending.

Much of this chapter has suggested similarities between Victorian novels and the comedies of Shakespeare, though in many cases their formal patterns are darkened by their relation to contemporary issues. The idea, and the structure, of tragedy assumes greater importance in the work of Thomas Hardy; but here, again, the comedies are significant, and even in the later, darker novels, Shakespeare's comedic forms are important formal principles. Hardy's knowledge of Shakespeare was extensive: he read the plays in Charles Knight's *Pictorial Shakspere* and saw many of the productions of Samuel Phelps, and the novels contain around 150 quotations from the plays. Again, the early novels seem intent to echo or develop Shakespeare's concerns with rural matters within a more contemporary setting. *Under the Greenwood Tree* (1872) takes its title from one of the songs in *As You Like It*, and its rural setting has led to many comparisons with that play. It is not that the novel imitates Shakespeare's rustic characters, or that both share a naturalistic presentation of them: both invent their own rustic worlds, and people them in different ways. But the fact that Shakespeare has already done this establishes a rhetoric and vocabulary of setting that, although different, offers itself as something directly recognizable to Victorian readers familiar with the plays, and thus becomes a stable footing on which comparisons can be built. *Far From the Madding Crowd* (1874) seems in some ways closest to the plays, presenting a version of Dorsetshire country life that, in its close observation of the natural world, seems to continue the strong influence of Shakespeare's language that a little earlier was apparent in the poetry of John Keats. The description of an ancient barn in Chapter 22, often cited as evidence of Hardy's closeness to the actualities of rural life, has overshadowed the sheep-shearing taking place within it, an episode that inevitably recalls the lengthy scene in *The Winter's Tale* that both celebrates ritual and order and reveals their dissolution, and it is hard to think that this parallel was not apparent to many of the novel's first readers.

There are, of course, episodes of loss in the novel—the hayrick fire, the sheep falling over the ridge—which perhaps owe something to the demands of maintaining interest in a serial novel. Yet they do little to reflect the larger social concerns of the 1870s, when the agricultural depression was at its height and farming communities banded together to form trade unions and, in the most extreme cases, to find money to send the youngest sons to Australia to find work. The rural world is among the closest of those presented in serious Victorian novels to Shakespeare's Arcadias in *Love's Labour's Lost* and *As You Like It*, although the novel lacks their engagement with the artifice of the convention coupled with their elements of strong threat. If these are present in Hardy's novel, they are held at some distance from the main plot and the presentation of a love relationship that, above all, presents the main female character, Bathsheba Everdene, as a woman of individuality and power who balances the management of her farm with, and in places against, her own desires. The resemblance to Viola/Cesario is clear; yet it is far from simple parody, the character being wholly immersed in the detail of event and circumstance—financial, social, sexual—of the period. The courtship scene, in which Sergeant Troy dazzles Bathsheba with a demonstration of his swordsmanship, is a powerful piece of sexual sublimation that must have been darkly troubling in pre-Freudian England. Against this play of gender and power, which moves towards a successful resolution in a manner apparently fractured, yet given more completion than any of the so-called happy comedies, is set the darker treatment of Fanny Robin. That she awaits Troy at the wrong church for their wedding, and thus initiates her final decline to abandonment, poverty, and death, is typical of Hardy's sombre misdirections; but it also has echoes of the incompletenesses, the small misalignments, that drive some of the tragedies, most forcefully the failure of the letter to arrive in time and so secure Cordelia's release.

From *The Woodlanders* (1887) on, the novels take this darkness much further, revealing what in many ways can be considered a reworking of the dramatist's concerns and structural techniques within an immediate address to what Hardy saw as the exigencies of his own time—which were not always the same as those seen by others, nor was their treatment expected. In this novel Shakespeare's Arden becomes much more sombre, and the result is to make its presentation of actuality, especially in the plotting, far more forceful in comparison with the earlier novels. Like *Far from the Madding Crowd*, and much of Hardy's major fiction, *The Woodlanders* rests on a complex pattern of misdirected and unreturned affection complicated by imbalances of rank and location. The farm worker Marty South loves the cider-maker Giles Winterbourne, but he is attracted to Grace Melbury. Her parents, wealthy merchants, insist on her marriage to Edred Fitzpiers who, as a doctor, represents social advancement; yet Fitzpiers is attracted to the aristocrat Felice Charmond. The network together presents in almost geometrical precision the social layers of mid-Victorian society as it moves from an agrarian to a mercantile system. When her marriage fails Grace goes to live in the woods, the puritanical Giles giving her his house and living in a hut, where he sickens and dies. Grace returns to the metropolitan Fitzpiers, and Marty is left to grieve, the concluding paragraphs of the novel suggesting that she is in mourning for the lost rural community as much as in despair over a lost loved one. To see this only as a continuation of the complexities of the early comedies, in which the Forest of Arden is displaced by Hardy's Wessex, is only a part of the resemblance to Shakespeare: it involves social and economic forces, and patterns as much mythic as naturalistic that are developed in the later novels. The ending leaves the reader predictably puzzled in the same way as the works subsequently christened 'problem comedies'—there are no solutions, only uncertainties and moral dilemmas.

In Hardy's mature novels the quality that is most evidently Shakespearian is the fine balance between the creation of characters that seem genuinely human, and with whom the reader is instinctively drawn to sympathize, and a formality of plot design and an engagement with issues of contemporary morality and its socio-economic bases that constantly reminds one of its literary constructedness. In *Tess of the D'Urbervilles* (1891, revised 1892) the confrontation between social orders is formidable. The central character, Tess Durbeyfield, from a poor country family, considers herself related to the aristocratic d'Urberville clan. Seduced by Alec Stoke-d'Urberville, who himself has no claim to the ancient lineage, and bearing by him a child—named Sorrow—who dies, she marries Angel Clare, a clergyman's son, who rejects her when learning of the earlier relationship. The pattern of exploitation, rejection, and brutality continues until Tess murders d'Urberville and is hanged. Tess is presented in many ways as a child of the natural world, beyond both the systems of authority that the male characters demand, in d'Urberville's rough uncaring sensuality and Clare's unbending morality. This is no simple clash of worlds: despite the novel's setting and recurrent natural imagery, and a powerful scene where a steam threshing machine is presented as a diabolic intruder in the natural order of harvest, Tess's seduction, taking place in the woods, is presented as an event from feral nature, almost beyond human feeling. In many ways the novel takes Shakespeare's green world, with its own conflicts of desire, and inflects it with insistent contemporary questions, the vanishing rural order and the uncaring standards of both male desire and uncompromising morality acting as powerful metaphors of each other. Shakespearian patterns and Shakespearian settings are forcefully, and to many original readers unacceptably, presented in a manner that at the same time takes to its extremes many of the concerns of the Victorian novel.

Such features are given most direct statement in Hardy's final novel, *Jude the Obscure* (1895). Hardy himself acknowledged that it was designed on principles of rectangular geometry, in which characters and events are presented in pairs that mirror each other and so ultimately hold the reader apart from full empathy. Yet despite this the novel is one of great emotional power. Again there is the complex relation of four people, again the conflict between high morality and erotic love; the antithesis between town and country is modified by Jude's desire for education at the university in Christminster, Hardy's version of Oxford. That Sue Bridehead, Jude's cousin, is married to the schoolteacher who first inspired Jude with the love of learning and herself is training to be a teacher adds to the complexity. This could be a pre-Shavian debate about changing moral standards, and there are many passages where Jude and Sue discuss their relationship in these terms. But there are also moments of extreme feeling, far deeper than Dickens's sentimentality. Jude's son, by his estranged wife Arabella Donn, is cared for by Jude and Sue, herself having left a failed marriage and unwilling to marry again despite her love for Jude. Hearing the couple's despairing discussion of their extreme poverty, the boy hangs himself and his two siblings, leaving a note saying '*Done because we are too menny*'. While clearly part of the novel's downward trajectory, the horror of the event is still strongly affecting, aided by the simplicity of the boy's note. Yet such immediacy is repeatedly offset by the use of symbolism. Courtship takes place through an open window, or while the two partners are on opposing sides of a hedge, for example. Towards the end of the novel, it seems that the characters, as well as the readers, are aware of the literariness of the symbolism as a means of reflection upon events. After failing to gain admission to Christminster, Jude tries to make a living by baking and selling cakes in the form of the Gothic windows of the colleges to which he has been denied admission.

While some of the patterns of Hardy's novels are related to the plays, the quality most often compared with Shakespeare is their approach to tragedic structure and tragic event. Famously, he prefaced a part of *Tess of the D'Urbervilles* with lines from *King Lear*, 'As flies to wanton boys are we to the Gods, / They kill us for their sport'. Taken with one of Hardy's most celebrated poems, 'The Convergence of the Twain', in which fate is seen constructing the iceberg in parallel to the building of the *R. M. S. Titanic*, this has caused some to see the novels as tragedies directed by a malign Fate. Yet this is both too limited and far too specific a reading. The characters' falls are not controlled by dark forces; their own actions, those of others, and chance misalignments offer a much bleaker progression, showing in Hardy an awareness of human frailty that echoes John Ruskin's idea that it is their own folly that causes the downfall of Shakespeare's tragic protagonists. In using such elements to direct their plots, the novels rise above earlier notions of tragedy in the same way as do those of Shakespeare; not specific character faults, a single action, or any larger force causes the downfall of figures in both forms, but instead complex interweavings of these and other forces. Nor should we forget that the serial form in which all of Hardy's major novels first appeared demanded a fair amount of rapid action, and the time in which he wrote had a strong taste for sensation. Again, there are similarities which reveal themselves as modified by the different periods in which each was written. Shakespearian tragedy built on fashions of Senecan violence and the public execution, manipulating them to powerful aesthetic effect, most remarkably in *Titus Androni-cus*: Hardy wrote at a time when sensational events in high society were popular both in novels and plays and as the subject of trials at the Old Bailey. Something of the same tastes is apparent in the fact that when Hardy rented fashionable accommodation in the capital for the London season he attended both police court trials and society balls. Court versus country, extreme violence versus powerful human feeling: the antitheses, in different rhetorical registers and contrasted forms and settings, are arguably present in the work of both writers.

All of Hardy's major novels were attacked in their time for apparent immorality, and more recently because of their complex and unclear symbolism. Yet perhaps they are better understood in terms of Shakespeare's problem plays, in which issues are raised but not resolved. The unanswered questions of *Love's Labour's*, the apparently unsatisfactory conclusions to *Measure for Measure*, and some of the darker relationships of *Pericles* and *The Two Noble Kinsmen* all seem close to the issues raised in these novels. All revolve in some way around questions of resolving desire in human relationships in a manner that satisfies both men and women, within a society that is governed by status and the force of economics. The marriage of Mariana at the close of *Measure for Measure* is only one example of this. Imposed by the Duke on his return, the marriage secures her economic security and reputation, but also denies her any possibility of finding a partner for herself. At the same time, of course, it offers itself as a parody of the romance convention that demands a marriage in closure. All these problems, in Hardy as in Shakespeare, have no direct solution, either in literature or as moral issues: instead they are propositions for debate, in which the sheer artifice of the construction of the plays and novels is essential in reminding readers and viewers of their philosophical nature.

* * * * *

If the Victorian novel is ingenious and inventive in the ways that it assimilates and develops patterns and structures from the plays of Shakespeare, Victorian poetry is perhaps more concentrated in its concern with the absorption and development of their linguistic forms in its engagement with contemporary issues. Two major paths are apparent, both of which continue and extend the directions taken in the eighteenth century and the Romantic period. One is the development of the unrhymed iambic pentameter line, through verse paragraphs of various lengths, as a way of exploring character and narrative. Growing from the plays themselves, these elements are re-shaped by the period's interests in narrative of all kinds, and the form itself is modified by its use in the intervening years, most remarkably by Milton in *Paradise Lost* and Wordsworth in *The Prelude*. That Wordsworth revised the poem in 1851 suggests his continuing concern with its structure and ideas—as well, of course, as making it in some measure Victorian. Whereas Milton used the form for Biblical moral narrative 'to justify the ways of God to man,' Wordsworth adopted it as a form of spiritual autobiography and political reflection. Conscious of the tradition thus established, Victorian poets modified and extended the form to present a range of contemporary ideas and uncertainties, often with greater rhythmic experimentation. The second development of Shakespearian form and idea was the use of the sonnet—as a personal statement, within sequences building on Shakespeare's, occasionally as a political utterance, and rarely without a reflexive awareness of the form itself and its tradition.

Many of the most powerful uses of the Shakespearian line come in a genre commonly known as the 'dramatic monologue', in which words are spoken by a character within a specific situation, in a sense extending the rhetorical tradition of ethopoeia which Shakespeare learnt from the classical instruction manuals at Stratford Grammar

School. Robert Browning is often regarded as the most skilful expo-
nent of the form. His 'Caliban upon Setebos' (*Dramatis Personae*,
1864) uses the line within tightly structured verse paragraphs to present a meditation by Shakespeare's character about his moral situation—'Letting the rank tongue blossom into speech', in the closing
words of its prefatory paragraph. Browning was not the first to give
new words to a Shakespearian character—Shelley had adopted the
persona of Ariel in 'With a Guitar. To Jane' in 1822, for example. But
the force of Browning's poem lies in its address to the moral position
of Caliban at the end of the play, and its attempt to present some
degree of insight into the character's place within creation, as well as
acting as a powerful satire on Victorian religious thought. Speakers in
Browning's other poems are often drawn from an imagined Italian
renaissance peopled by poisoning counts and clerics. All invest the
form with a colloquial force and rhythmic vigour, making them
among the most popular of his works; yet they have a quality of ironic
detachment that, coupled with the intellectualism of their referential
frames, keeps them at a distance from their readers in a manner quite
absent from formally similar works by Tennyson.

Of these 'Ulysses' (written 1833; first published 1842), while actually
written just before Victoria's reign, was and remains the most popular,
spoken by the aged hero on his return from the Odyssey and moving
from immobility to resolution in a manner that foresaw the conflict
between indolence and action beneath much Victorian thought. With
this is matched an authority and resonance of tone that made it one of
the most read and most quoted of his poems. The poem's conclusion,
the result of the speaker's inner debate, reveals his resolution:

> That which we are, we are
> One equal temper of heroic hearts,
> Made weak by time and fate, but strong in will
> To strive, to seek, to find, and not to yield.

The sentiments are a fine expression of Victorian manly duty; but the
verse form and movement derives from Shakespeare, perhaps particularly from the simpler diction of the last plays. That the final line
was inscribed on the cross erected at the graves of Captain Scott's
explorers in the Antarctic in 1913 suggests its lasting power, and that

of the world view it presents; the Shakespearian echoes are surely part of that. Tennyson's engagement with Shakespeare did not end with his use of the iambic pentameter: his 'Mariana' (1830) and 'Mariana in the South' (1832) are lyric monologues spoken by the woman abandoned by Angelo in *Measure for Measure*. The first is an early essay in the richly sombre sonorities and melancholic moods for which the poet would later be famed; the painting by John Everett Millais (1851: private collection) powerfully transforms the sonorities and moods into rich tonal values within compositional stillness. The second adopts the form of something approaching a medieval ballad, and is an early foray into the presentation of mental disturbances later fulfilled in Tennyson's *Maud*. In presenting characters beyond the plays in which they appear, the two poems are early examples of a move that will become increasingly fashionable, as Chapter 7 will make clear.

Not all poems that use Shakespeare's line share this confidence. Matthew Arnold's 'Dover Beach' (written *c.* 1851; first published 1867), one of the most direct expressions of the crisis in faith brought about by the debate about evolution, audible even before the *Origin of Species* appeared in 1859, reaches a different conclusion, and offers another kind of Victorian feeling. The poem ends with a plea 'Love, let us be true to one another' in the face of a world that

> Hath really neither joy, nor love, nor light,
> Nor certitude, nor peace, nor help for pain;
> And we are here as on a darkling plain
> Swept with confused alarms of struggle and flight
> Where ignorant armies clash by night.

That the same verse form can convey such different modes of feeling, and use logical and syntactic structures so disparate, reveals its strength. Again this comes from the deep knowledge of the movement and force of the Shakespearian line with which so much Victorian poetry was infused, and that Arnold had made explicit in his sonnet to Shakespeare quoted in Chapter 1.

Along with monologues of this kind, the Shakespearian iambic pentameter was employed for many much longer poems. Elizabeth Barrett Browning's *Aurora Leigh* (1856) is in some ways the closest, and in others the most distant, parallel to Wordsworth's *Prelude*. Both are autobiographical in recording the growth of the individual as well as the growth of the artist; but to these qualities Browning adds the struggles of the eponymous central figure for identity and fulfilment, through the emotions as a woman as well as through art as a poet. The plot involves reversals and crossings in love familiar from both popular and serious novels; the text itself, in its swift changes of speaker and setting, employs the Shakespearian line with great flexibility and assurance. It stands as a voice in opposition to Coventry Patmore's *The Angel in the House* (1862), a poem celebrating the joys of domestic married life. While today much derided for its parochialism and the apparently subservient role of the wifely character after whom it is titled, it does offer another view of amorous fulfilment. Perhaps the difficulty present-day readers have with it results in no small measure from its presentation of an ideology widespread in Victorian suburbia, of the kind later satirized in *The Diary of A Nobody* (1892) by George and Weedon Grossmith. What is striking about this work is precisely that it does not use the Shakespearian line; instead, its form is a much more colloquial pattern that, narrowly avoiding the insistence of the old fourteener, nonetheless moves in three-line segments that give it a limping, halting movement. This reveals by contrast the extreme flexibility of the iambic pentameter, and how much the more serious Victorian poets had learned from Shakespeare about its use.

Robert Browning extended the form further in more different, more self-reflective ways. *The Ring and the Book* (1868–9) is essentially a highly intellectualized detective novel in which a murder is recounted from the viewpoints of ten characters, in the Italian renaissance setting familiar from his shorter monologues. At the same time it is a virtuosic exercise in ethopoeia—speech by a specific character in a specific situation—that seems quite deliberately to engage with Shakespearian powers of narrative and character portrayal. Matthew Arnold's 'Sohrab and Rustum' (1853) and 'Balder Dead' (1855) take narratives from much earlier sources, presenting his classical scholarship within a Shakespearian line to engage with contemporary issues to offer a far bleaker answer to the question posed by Tennyson's 'Ulysses'. Arnold's *Thyrsis* (1867), a 'Monody' written in memory of Arthur Hugh Clough, also uses iambic pentameter, while his 'elegiac poem' 'The Scholar-Gipsy' (1853) is written in ten-line stanzas in which the sixth line has only three iambic feet, a pause or incompleteness that reflects the melancholy and remoteness of the poem's subject, an adaptation of the Shakespearian form to match a mood and tone dominant throughout Arnold's poetic output.

Tennyson's most outstanding use of the line is the lengthy collection of poems together known as the *Idylls of the King*, which appeared in a number of forms between 1842 and 1885. The first part, sharing the title *Morte D'Arthur* with the late-fifteenth-century poem by Thomas Malory, achieved great popularity, its opening stating again the concern with time and loss recurrent through Tennyson's writing and the period in general:

> Then slowly answered Arthur from the barge
> 'The old order changeth, yielding place to new,
> And God fulfils himself in many ways,
> Lest one good custom should corrupt the world'.

Here the second line's much freer rhythmic form matches its idea of change; it is almost a further, contemporary extension of the greater structural flexibility found in the last plays by Furnivall and others. Overall, while the tone of magnificent gloom that suffuses much of the poem has made it unfashionable, for the Victorians it offered much that was attractive. The use of an earlier English source, revived in terms that reflected concerns of the present about government, the state of the nation, and the role of the educated man, along with a story rich in battle, conflict, and the search for national identity through the reinvention of the past was an approach bound to ensure success. All these features are of course essential to Shakespeare's history plays; and when to them is added the recurrent discussion of love and duty in the adulterous relationship of Launcelot and Guinevere, the link to both serious and popular novels of the poet's own time is clear, along with a subtle modification of Shakespeare's own love themes. William Morris used the medieval past in similar ways in *The Earthly Paradise* (1868–70) developing the Shakespearian line through his own voice to reflect his concerns with the relation between art and work seen throughout his life as artist, designer, poet, and socialist campaigner.

That all these writers use the Shakespearian line in poems that include monologue and dialogue between a range of characters reflects the power of the poet's influence, and also perhaps the continuing feeling in some, though by no means all, circles that the plays were best encountered through reading, not performance. It is as if the texture and structure of Shakespeare's writing is being used as the basis for variations of intellectual as well as aesthetic concerns. In 1910, the *Fantasia on a Theme of Thomas Tallis* by Ralph Vaughan Williams was first performed in Gloucester Cathedral, and hailed immediately as a statement of essential English identity in terms uniting tradition and innovation. Perhaps the same may be said of these historical epics in their use of Shakespearian forms to address the new through the old.

Shakespeare's presence is more obviously apparent, if not necessarily more significant, in Victorian poets' use of the sonnet. As much formal as thematic, again mingling patterns and concerns of the seventeenth and nineteenth centuries, the sonnet was for many Victorians a forum for reflection in isolation as well as the basis of meditative and narrative sequences. Almost always its use reveals a concern with its formal complexities, either by implication through structural decisions or explicitly through open discussion. Not all Victorian sonnets followed Shakespeare in examining the nature of love, however; the political thrust given it by the Romantic writers was also present. It is worth remembering that Shelley's 'England in 1819', one of the most passionate denunciations of Georgian social structure, was first published only in 1839. The poem is also Shakespearian in a different way, subtly alluding to John of Gaunt's 'This England' speech in *Richard II* by withholding its main verb to act as the climactic accusation after a long, increasingly despairing litany of state-directed atrocities and failings. In the year of Victoria's accession, Wordsworth wrote a series of sonnets on the subject of capital punishment which, while lacking Shelley's passion, make clear that the sonnet is a valid forum for political debate. Its use for this purpose continued through the century.

Another recurrent theme for the sonnet is ekphrastic, in response to actual or imagined paintings. The best known of these are by Dante Rossetti, the two sonnets that explain the iconography of his own painting *The Girlhood of Mary Virgin* (1848: Tate Britain, London) but there are also meditative poems on the work of Italian renaissance painters by Rossetti himself and Robert Browning. In these there is an echo of similar concerns and devices in Shakespeare which, although not addressing specific images, demonstrate familiarity with the workings of visual art and conventions of its use in verse, such as the blazon, where elements of the loved one's appearance are listed as a verbal parallel to the act of seeing and reading the image.

Three examples reveal something of the larger range of Victorian uses of the sonnet form, but there are many others. Charles Tennyson Turner, younger brother of the Poet Laureate, produced three volumes of sonnets (1864, 1868, 1873) that typify the form's more popular use in the wake of Romantic writing. With titles such as 'Wind on the Corn', 'On startling some Pigeons', and 'The Harvest Moon' these are delicate studies of transitory experiences with nature, resonant with sonnets of a slightly earlier generation, and alternating between the Shakespearian and Petrarchan forms according to their theme and movement. In 1855, Sidney Dobell and Alexander Smith published a pamphlet called *Sonnets on the War* which addressed some of the actualities of battle in the Crimea and their effects on those at home. They do not approach the bitterness of Wilfred Owen's 'Anthem for Doomed Youth,' itself an ironic appropriation of Shakespeare's love sonnets to the 'lovely boy'; but they are far removed from the complacent patriotism of the kind often associated with their period. Dobell's 'The Army Surgeon' talks of the wounded on the battlefield as 'a moving field of mangled worms' and ends with a Shakespearian couplet that rejects its frequent use to reverse the meaning of the earlier lines:

> —so, as he goes,
> Around his feet in clamorous agony
> They rise and fall; and the seething plain
> Bubbles a cauldron vast of many coloured pain.

The sonnets of Julian Fane, described in a contemporary note as 'close and masterly imitations of Shakespeare's', include several written in successive years on 13 March and titled 'Ad Matrem', using the Shakespearian form to compose love poems to his mother. These are much more direct in following the pattern and movement of Shakespeare's poems, developing a series of metaphors, using a recurrent rhetorical figure, and always ending with a concluding couplet of epigrammatic force that unites or completes the poem's argument. That dated 13 March 1862 hangs from the opening 'Oft in the afterdays, when thou and I/Have fallen from the scope of human view' a series of examples of how the mother's 'gracious presence' will be remembered. The couplet serves to draw them together, at the same time appropriating such later worship for his present relations with his mother:

> So shall I live with thee, and thy dear fame
> Shall link my love unto thine honoured name.

While to present-day readers the nature of this relationship is far from comfortable, it was common in Victorian thought and feeling; that it is stated in a carefully turned revision of a Shakespearian conclusion places Shakespeare at the foundation of this dimension of contemporary emotion.

By far the most important use of the sonnet, however, is in the sequence. Here as in other uses, it is clear that writers are not influenced by Shakespeare alone. Rossetti and many others are fully aware of the sonnets of Petrarch and Dante, and make use of their structural forms—the placing of the *volta*, or turn, in theme or treatment, earlier than in Shakespeare's poems, and the avoidance of the concluding couplet in which it is often located by Shakespeare. In this the period continued a debate, explicit in some cases and implicit in the choice of form, that had gone on through the Romantic period. Keats avoided the Shakespearian form, with its stress on the concluding couplet, in his sonnets, and many later writers considered that, while it was ideally suited to love poetry, its structure was less appropriate for political or moral statement. Some felt that the movement to closure, often achieved through a reversal of concept or attitude, presented by the final couplet was a rhetorical device too easily foreseen by the reader and, when used in a sequence, might break the narrative continuity. Possibly true; but we should remember that, except in some small groups of poems, Shakespeare was not mainly concerned with narrative or conceptual continuity in the *Sonnets* and that his handling of the form was, let us say, sophisticated enough to avoid the pitfalls of less skilful users.

Elizabeth Barrett Browning's *Sonnets from the Portuguese* (1850), probably the most widely read sequence of its time, demonstrates an awareness of the debate and quite clearly places itself within the tradition of the *Sonnets* of 1609. Its fifty sonnets are concerned with the directly autobiographical progress of the poet's own love for her future husband Robert, at the same time exploring an artistic growth in a coupling similar to that given fictional form in *Aurora Leigh*. What is immediately clear is the appropriation of a form hitherto associated with the expression of male passion, and at that largely unfulfilled, for a narrative of female affections eventually satisfied. This at once marks a change in the form because of the new voice it introduces, and affords to the subject a status often denied by its association with popular romance fiction; its serious discussion in a form inevitably associated with Shakespeare brings it a wholly new validation and dignity. Perhaps to establish their relationship with a much older tradition, or perhaps to ensure a more fluid progression, the sonnets do not use the Shakespearian form. Instead, the rhyme is structured in two quatrains and two tercets, with the volta variously located, or sometimes omitted, within a single continuous movement. The overall narrative moves from statements of complete unworthiness to expressions of joy in the discovery of shared love. The expression is immediately accessible, often using single word sentences; at times sonnets are paired in a debate between emotional extremes, perhaps recalling the groups of four in Shakespeare's sonnets. What accounted for its popularity, and perhaps also for the distaste with which it has often been regarded by male critics, is the openness with which it deals with feelings. The penultimate sonnet 'How do I love thee? Let me count the ways' is still very popular; while many find its open sentiment too direct, its formal quality should not be overlooked. It is in many ways a transformation of the blazon, changing it from a list of visual attributes to a series of statements of affection: that these are spoken by a woman instead of about one adds to the transformative power.

George Meredith's *Modern Love* (1862) offers an approach to the sonnet sequence wholly opposed to Browning's work in almost every way, rejecting both the form and tone of the Shakespearian sonnet and its more recent appropriations so completely that they become an essential part of its effect. A fractured, discontinuous narrative of a failed relationship, sometimes in the words of the betrayed husband, sometimes from a distanced and often ironic narrator, it uses its own version of the sonnet form, now with sixteen lines. The first of these changes intersects directly with the tradition of the lover complaining from afar at the disdain of the mistress, with the narratorial voice ironizing its absurdities; the second makes possible a greater narrative immediacy by removing the question of where the volta, the turn from subject to comment, the shift in metaphor or tone, should come. Both give the sequence the modernity claimed in the title—itself heavily ironic—but they are so pronounced as to make the qualities they reject constantly present. The same is true of the themes discussed. Time is a recurrent issue but, instead of Shakespeare's concern with perpetuation of beauty through verse, it is the agonies of memory that are presented. Imagery of nature and the animal world is frequent, but this is offset by the constant bitterness of tone. Sometimes the language comes so close to Shakespeare that it seems a failed attempt at quotation. Sonnet XLI, for example, ends with the lines:

> They waste the soul with spurious desire,
> That is not the ripe flame upon the bough.

It is hard not to read them in comparison with Shakespeare's 'expense of spirit in a waste of shame', and to feel their inadequacy as a result. But that, surely, is the point: as modern love is unattainable, its failure bitterly resented, so the form for its debate is tired and insufficient. In its bleak tone, though not its subject matter, the sequence offers something of a prevision of two much later works regarding the sonnets of Shakespeare, those of Samuel Butler and Oscar Wilde, both of which are discussed in Chapter 8.

Dante Rossetti's sequence *The House of Life* (1870–81) is a much more expansive work in both extent (102 sonnets as opposed to Browning's 50 and Meredith's 43) and theme, combining elements of courtship, mature love, and the grief of bereavement with elements of spiritual autobiography. It begins with a prefatory sonnet that discusses the suitability of the form for such a theme, and thus immediately locates itself within the debate, explicit and implied, that is carried on throughout the period. That it uses the Shakespearian form, going so far as to separate the octave and sestet with a line space, makes clear an allusiveness stated openly in its very opening line, 'A Sonnet is a moment's monument'. The poems themselves use a variety of sonnet forms and range over many topics, so that the autobiographical element is softened and expanded. Yet overall their main referential frame is Italian, especially Dantescan, and their thrust towards the praise of aesthetics rather than of love—'This is that Lady beauty, in whose praise/Thy voice and hand shake still', Sonnet LXXVII, 'Soul's Beauty', asserts. The work is built on the Victorian way of seeing the sonnets of 1609 as primarily autobiographical, mingled with Rossetti's love of Italian poetry and visual art to produce a very personal collection. Collection, not sequence; as the prefatory poem asserts, the sonnets here are each 'a moment's monument', and in this they continue something of the nature of Shakespeare's work. We might also see in them something of a culturally transformed version of the eroticism of their earlier counterpart, made much more open. Sonnet VIa, 'Nuptial Sleep', had to be withdrawn because of its sexual directness. Shakespeare's sexuality is wound more tightly into the textual fabric of the poems, and thus to many Victorian readers escaped recognition—although, as a later chapter will make clear, they did not escape censorship, and censure, in some places.

Although Rossetti's sequence engages with time, it is again memory and loss rather than the power of verse to overcome it that is the concern. Here, as in many other poems from the second half of the century, there are echoes of Tennyson's *In Memoriam A. H. H.* (1833–50), the period's central statement of bewilderment and recovery after a loss of faith as much of a loved one. The sequence has many similarities with Shakespeare's sonnets. Structurally, its three Christmases recall the three references to the month of April in the poems of 1609, although with a sense of personal growth not present in Shakespeare's poems because of their place within the strong narrative sequence of Tennyson's poem. More directly, the poet makes reference to Shakespeare when referring to his feelings for the dead man by claiming 'nor can/The soul of Shakespeare love thee more'. These elements, and the many references to reaching for and touching hands with the dead man, have led many to see the sequence as the most explicit later parallel to the homoeroticism of Shakespeare's poems. But the overall movement, from despair to some measure of reconciliation, and the verse form, quite different from the Shakespearian sonnet, or any other kind, mark it out as a quite different continuation of some of the emotional forces at work within the earlier collection. *Hermaphroditus* (1866), a group of four sonnets by Algernon Charles Swinburne, also comes close to the mood and object of some of Shakespeare's sonnets, in its concern with love within and across genders, one of them recalling Shakespeare's Sonnet 144.

While Shakespeare's verse was a major force in Victorian poetry, it was not the only one. The recovery of ancient ballad forms, the use of a wide variety of other metrical structures, and the address to wholly new subject matter reveal the period as one of great innovation and energy in its poetic output. Yet perhaps even this is evidence of a Shakespearian force; that poetry is written, published, and read in great profusion testifies to an awareness of its force and value in confronting, as well as escaping, contemporary concerns, and the prevalence of reading and seeing Shakespeare's language surely has a great deal to do with the poetic activity of the period at all levels.

That Tennyson, Morris, and others set their large-scale epics in the more remote past is often linked to the revival of interest in the Middle Ages as a retreat from what Morris, in *The Earthly Paradise*, called 'the six counties overhung with smoke', or as a way of reinvigorating Christian belief. These are certainly valid views; but it may also be that, as in other fields, many writers carefully avoided treating the periods most directly covered by Shakespeare in the history plays, just as did Walter Scott in his historical novels. The same is true of historical drama of the period. Often considered an age where playwriting was concerned either with farce or, increasingly in the later decades, social issues, the Victorian period also saw something of a revival in verse drama, often with historical subjects. John Westland Marston was popular in this field at the beginning of the period with *The Patrician's Daughter* (1841), an attempt at tragedy resting on class divisions. Some decades later, Tennyson made quite explicit his desire, in the verse plays *Queen Mary* (1875), *Harold* (1876), and *Becket* (1884), to produce an epic on 'the making of England' that would 'complete' the periods covered by Shakespeare. *Queen Mary* presents the life of Mary Tudor, using Shakespearian blank verse for the noble characters and prose for the commoners, following contemporary understanding of Shakespeare's divisions. Yet the play cannot be said to succeed. The combination of approaching 50 speaking parts and large numbers of mutes and supernumeraries, frequent and complex expository passages, and the absence of the tonal sensitivity found in his poetry did not make for theatrical success. The later *Becket* was more effective, but only when Henry Irving had cut it by something approaching a third. Both are interesting for another reason: in their demands for complex built-up scenes, spectacles of battle, and ornate processions they imitate more a mid-Victorian notion of what Shakespeare would have done with the resources of the Victorian theatre; thus, in their own inadequacy, they demonstrate a very Victorian approach to the dramatist's works.

Searching for Shakespeare:
Poems, Lives, and Portraits

Writing in 1827, Wordsworth advised his readers 'Scorn not the sonnet's little room' and continued 'With this key/Shakespeare unlocked his heart'. With these two statements, he seemingly restored the sonnets of Shakespeare to critical and public attention and directed the main way in which they would be read until the very end of Victoria's reign. Yet although at the century's end there were notable efforts to explore them as complex literary structures, far more attention was given to sonnets as autobiographical statements, concerned with the dates of composition and their addressee, most particularly in identifying the Dark Lady and attempting variously to explain, justify, or simply reject those addressed to the 'lovely boy' or 'fair youth'. In a sense, the Victorian development of the sonnet form, discussed in the preceding chapter, could be read as much as a movement in spite of Shakespeare as because of him, attempting both to recover the form employed for objects thought proper in the time of Petrarch and Sidney, and redirect it to the concerns of mid-nineteenth century writers and readers. This is not to exclude the work of some critics and anthologists in exploring the poems in themselves; but it is certainly the case that, for the great majority of readers, the sonnets were part of a larger approach to 'Shakespeare' which saw the writings themselves as intentional codes or instinctive revelations of the life and mind of the greatest Englishman. In this they were matched by an outpouring of biographical writings and the search for the true likeness of the artist in portraits; and these three related areas are the subject of this chapter.

At times it is not necessary to read beyond the titles of works discussing the sonnets for their aims to become clear: *Autobiographical poems. Being his sonnets clearly developed; with his character drawn chiefly from his works*, by Charles Armitage Brown (1838); *Shakespeare's sonnets solved, and the mystery of his friendship, love, and rivalry revealed*, by J. R. Smith (1870); *Sonnets never before interpreted; his private friends identified; together with a recovered likeness of himself*, by Gerald Massey (1865, reprinted 1872, 1886, and 1888). Set against these are the editions and writings that attempted more scholarly readings. Important in this was the re-establishment of the text of 1609 and the rejection of earlier attempts to revise and re-order them, notably that of John Benson in 1640, which changed the genders of some of the pronouns in sonnets addressed to the lovely boy so that they were apparently addressed to a woman, altered the order, gave the poems descriptive titles, combined some into longer poems and altogether omitted eight sonnets. Edmond Malone's edition of the late eighteenth century was important in restoring the text of 1609 and the original order, and serious Victorian editions built on this work. At the beginning of the period, Charles Knight and, in later years, Edward Dowden and George Wyndham, produced scholarly editions. Some of the sonnets were made more widely available by Francis Turner Palgrave, whose *Golden Treasury* (1861) was the most read single collection of short poems from its publication until the end of the century. A different kind of readership was attracted by *Shakspere's Songs and Sonnets* (1862), a selection of lyrics from the plays and of the sonnets, with designs by Sir John Gilbert and a very short introduction by Howard Staunton. Most of these were original inventions rather than borrowings from his edition of the *Works*; some bear comparison with work of Millais, Rossetti, Hughes, and others of the more detailed 'sixties school' of wood-engraving.

David Main's extensive anthology *A Treasury of English Sonnets* (1880) included 57 of Shakespeare's poems, with 22 pages of annotation and comment from the most recent scholarly texts. Its choice of sonnets, and the comments made on them, offer interesting insights into the reception of the poems. Taken with the selection in the *Golden Treasury*, this provides as good an account as any of the larger awareness of, and approach to, the sonnets during the middle years of the century. 'Taken with', because all the sonnets included by Palgrave also appear in Main, suggesting a marked sharing of taste in the basis of their selections. The difference is that Palgrave arranges all the poems according to subject, breaking the order of the *Sonnets*, whereas Main presents them in their original order. That said, the selections reveal a shared liking between critical and popular readers, and the list includes many of the sonnets that are still best known. Palgrave follows the precedent set much earlier by Benson, presenting the 20 sonnets individually or in twos and threes related by subject and given appropriate titles, but interspersed with short poems by Shakespeare's contemporaries. Thus 64 and 65, headed 'Time and love' come first, followed by 57 and 97, headed 'Absence'. Further groupings include 109 and 104, 'The Unchangeable'; 18 and 106, 'Shall I compare thee to a summer's day?' and 'When in the chronicle of wasted time' headed 'To his Love'; and 60 and 87 as 'Revelations'. Of the individual sonnets 29, 'When in disgrace with fortune and men's eyes' is headed 'A Consolation', and 73, 'That time of year thou mayst in me behold' appears after the song 'When icicles hang by the wall' from *Love's Labour's Lost* under the heading 'Winter'. Sonnet 30, 'When to the sessions of sweet silent thought' follows under the title 'Remembrance' and then immediately come 60, 'Like as the waves make toward the pebbled shore' and 87, 'Farewell thou art too dear for my possessing', both headed 'Revolutions'. Other sonnets included individually are 'Let me not to the marriage of true minds/admit impediment' (116: 'True Love'); 'No longer mourn for me when I am dead' (71: 'The Triumph of Death'); and 'They that have power to hurt' (94: 'The life without passion'). None of the first 17, the poems most directly addressed to the lovely boy and read by recent critics as among the most explicitly erotic, is included; only 148, 'O me! What eyes hath love put in my head' is taken from the final 27, the 'Dark Lady' group.

Essentially, the result is that the collection has been heavily edited and rearranged, with many of the darker or more complex sonnets omitted and only those that can be categorized with relative ease included. No 'Th'expense of spirit in a waste of shame', none of the group discussing complicated ideas of visual representation, none of those identified by later editors as existing in groups of four that discuss related themes. This is Shakespeare chopped and shuffled, the power of individual poems still strong but given explicit emotional direction through titles, and the cumulative, perplexing power of the whole quite lacking.

In 1865 Palgrave edited a volume titled *Shakespeare's Songs and Sonnets* which, as well as including songs from the plays and the sonnets appearing in *Love's Labour's Lost*, carefully avoided including some of the 1609 poems by giving those included titles rather than numbers, so that their absence is not immediately apparent. Thus 'A woman's face, with Nature's own hand painted' (20), 'Let those who are in favour with their stars' (25), 'Lord of my love, to whom in vassalage' (26), and the two last sonnets, with their allusions to the sweating baths as cures for syphilis, are all banished. Sonnet 135 is titled 'William Shakespeare' to de-fuse the sexual significances of the repeated puns on 'will,' and 151, 'Love is too young', is similarly absent, presumably because of the allusion to erection in the line 'Her love for whose dear love I rise and fall'. 'Crabbed age and youth' is, however, added. This would suggest that editors assumed that the wider readership intended for these editions was not ready for explicitness, although curiously this rests on the assumption that readers would have understood the double meanings from which they were being protected. Meanwhile, the complete editions of the works included all the sonnets, albeit in most cases without direct comment, save for the rearrangements offered, especially by Charles Knight, to place them in a biographical frame.

One of the curious consequences of literary fame, apparent for many important writers but perhaps first manifest with Shakespeare, is that the work itself is progressively ignored as the life and personality of the writer takes over. Sometimes the two are successfully combined, as in Dowden's *William Shakespeare: His Mind and Art* discussed in Chapter 2; more often in the Victorian period the works are regarded as a series of coded autobiographical references, and nowhere is this more evident than with Shakespeare's sonnets. The process has three main points of focus, which sometimes merge together. The first is establishing the identity of the 'Onlie Begetter' identified in the dedication as Mr W. H., and the signatory of the dedication, T. T. The second concerns the identity of the 'Dark Lady', and the third, that of the 'better spirit' of Sonnet 80 and of other references in the sonnets around that number, generally referred to as the 'rival poet'. Of these, the last attracted the least attention. Eighteenth-century suggestions included Edmund Spenser and Samuel Daniel, whose sonnet sequence *Delia* appeared in 1592 and is often seen as a major influence on Shakespeare's sonnets, many of which were probably written and privately circulated in manuscript in the middle of that decade. Christopher Marlowe and Ben Jonson were both Victorian proposals, but William Minto's *Characteristics of English Poets* in 1874 suggested Chapman, a suggestion still seen as the most credible. That the mention of a poet regarded as a rival by the most significant writer of the period now attracts less interest than the identities of figures within the poem itself has much to reveal about the way the *Sonnets* as a whole were and are by many still regarded: it is not for their place in the growth of English poetry, but for what they reveal about amorous intrigues of the late sixteenth century that they have been analysed and debated.

Victorians found the dedication difficult to decipher first because of the complexity of its wording and typography. T. T. has been identified as Thomas Thorpe, the stationer who commissioned George Eld to print and William Aspley to sell the 1609 quarto book of poems. But the identity of W. H. has been the subject of far greater speculation. One of the problems here is the exact significance of 'onlie begetter'. Charles Knight discussed this in some depth in his notes to the *Sonnets*, offering various alternatives. Building on the triple relationship of stationer-printer-bookseller he argues that W. H. could refer to a stationer's assistant who purloined the manuscript poems and gave them to Thorpe—and in that sense is the 'onlie begetter'. He then used this shady provenance to argue that the 1609 volume failed to adopt a coherent sequence, and so suggested his own. Others have taken an approach that links to the romantic idea of the poet as creator, the 'onlie begetter' thus being Shakespeare himself; but the approach that has attracted most attention has been to interpret W. H. as the person to whom the sonnets themselves were addressed.

During the period two main candidates were advanced. In 1837 James Boaden suggested William Herbert, later third Earl of Pembroke, relating his apparent reluctance to marry to the advice given in Sonnets 1–17. The second major contender is Henry Wriothesley, Third Earl of Southampton, Shakespeare's patron and the dedicatee of *Venus and Adonis* and *Lucrece*, both published before the *Sonnets*. Again the reluctance to marry is suggestive, and added to this is his vanity, which chimes well with the *Sonnets'* references to the lovely boy's appearance. The disadvantage here is the reversal of his initials—W. H. instead of H. W.—in the dedication, for which various explanations have been advanced, the simplest being that initials often were reversed in literary dedications. Both of these identifications rest on the assumption that the dedicatee of the poems is also their addressee, an idea by no means universally accepted by earlier Victorian critics, who preferred to see them as addressed to a variety of the poet's friends, or simply as dramatic inventions spoken through a range of unnamed characters. These issues are still under debate, though the identification of Southampton is currently the most strongly supported.

Victorian attempts to identify the Dark Lady took ingenuity of textual reading to its extreme borders. Gerald Massey's approach is perhaps the most convoluted. Sonnet CXLVI, advising the Lady to stop investing her powers on outward display of face and body, ends with these lines:

> Buy terms divine in selling hours of dross;
> Within be fed, without be rich no more:
>> So shalt thou feed on Death, that feeds on men,
>> And Death once dead, there's no more dying them.

Massey sees in this an allusion to Lady Penelope Rich, the object of Philip Sidney's sonnet sequence *Astrophil and Stella*. This would at least have the advantage of placing Shakespeare's sonnets, or one of them, in something of a self-conscious literary convention, although the single appearance late in the collection would seem to make this less than likely as an explanation of the whole. However, Massey takes the allusion much further. He argues that this sonnet, and hence most of the others concerning the Dark Lady, was written to express the jealousy of Elizabeth Vernon, who in 1598 married Henry Wriothesley, third Earl of Southampton and thought by many to be the W. H. of the *Sonnets'* dedication. Others, meanwhile, are written in the character of William Herbert, Third Earl of Pembroke and another candidate as W. H., to express his love for Lady Rich. This at least allows for the earlier notion that the sonnets as a whole are written through various characters, the dramatist adopting different voices through the collection; yet Massey goes further, suggesting that such sonnets were actually written by these individuals. As well as resting on the flimsiest of connections, the suggestion makes little sense in wider terms, given the difference in ages between the various figures involved. But it does move the sonnets into the arena of a complex Tudor love triangle, offering both a remote explanation for the imprecision of names and relationships in the sonnets themselves and giving them an appeal worthy of a Victorian sensation novel. Another notion, that these sonnets were written by the Earl of Southampton and addressed to Elizabeth Vernon, had been made much earlier, by Anna Brownell Jameson in her *Memoirs of the Loves of the Poets* (1829). The link continues: much more recently it has been claimed that Shakespeare was Elizabeth Vernon's lover, and the father of her daughter Penelope. Along with the suggestion that, in consequence, Lady Diana Spencer, Princess of Wales, would have been a descendant of the poet, this makes clear that the extremities of identity-hunting were not exclusive to the Victorians.

A similar desire to unravel a pun gave rise to another identification, that of Mary Fitton, dedicatee of William Kempe's *Nine daies Wonder*, the pamphlet written by the clown in Shakespeare's company recording the jig he danced from London to Norwich. Here the pun is implied rather than stated, a suggestion that Fitton is the 'fit one' in sonnet 151—a strange reading, which also goes out of its way to ignore the wordplay on erection and detumescence that permeates the sonnet. That Fitton was the Mistress of the Earl of Pembroke supplies another triangular relationship; that she was thought to have a dark complexion offered further support. At the end of the century the discovery of her portrait, showing her fair skin and brown hair, effectively cancelled the theory. None of these apparent solutions really explains why the identity of a character, who may or may not be based on an actual living person, would actually matter to a reading of the sonnets.

These issues of identity and order were much debated during the period, and the fact that they took place in academic journals such as *Notes & Queries* and more general ones such as the *Athenaeum* suggests their pervasiveness. What is also striking is the way in

6.1 An engraving of W. E. Frost's *Disarming of Cupid* (sonnet CLIV). Here the final sonnet, today often read as a cynical reference to the 'sweating baths' used to cure syphilis, is presented as a classical fulfilment to the narrative most Victorians looked for in the collection.

which they reflect larger preoccupations of the time. The desire to rearrange the poems suggests both the desire for classification and order, seen in the botanical sciences and growing administrative structures on the one hand, and the obsession with narrative progression seen in the novel and genre painting on the other (see Illustration 6.1). The search for the identities of many of the figures implied in the poems has resonances in the popular novels of Mary Elizabeth Braddon and others, perhaps recalling historical accounts of the complex intersections of the Elizabethan court and its secret service. And clearly the yearning to explain the sonnets to the lovely boy as allusions to Queen Elizabeth combines the notion of Shakespeare the supreme patriot and a fear and hatred of homosexuality—at a time before the coinage of that word, when expressions such as 'sexual inversion' and 'Hellenism' were employed. A more explicit approach to this theme, going to the very edge of a direct suggestion of a homosexual relationship, was taken by Samuel Butler; this and Oscar Wilde's writing, forming as they both do a quite new departure, are discussed in Chapter 8.

The search for biographical information also extended to Shakespeare's other narrative poems, *Venus and Adonis* and *The Rape of Lucrece*. Neither of these was popular during the period, perhaps because of the more openly erotic qualities they display. They are important in being dedicated to Southampton, adding support to claims of his being the addressee of the sonnets and for the detail, sparse though it be, they offer about Shakespeare's life. A similar importance was given to *The Passionate Pilgrim*, the collection that included pirated texts of two of the sonnets in 1599. This supported the comment of Francis Meres in *Palladis Tamia* (1598) that the 'sugred sonnets' were circulated among Shakespeare's friends. Taken together, all of these suggest Shakespeare's output of poetry being concentrated in the last decade of the sixteenth century; taken with work on the dating of the plays, this allows cross comparisons between the two genres, to the clarification of both. Yet the subject matter of the poems largely excluded them from consideration during the Victorian period. Whereas Knight devotes nearly 35 double-column pages to discussing the sonnets in terms of order and biography, he gives less than half a column to 'A Lover's Complaint', claiming that 'there can be no doubt of its genuineness', despite its being 'sometimes obscure' and on occasion using metaphors 'strange and forced'. His discussion of *Venus and Adonis* and *Lucrece* rests largely on eighteenth-century predecessors, and makes large but unsupported claims for the greatness of the poems and their place in the hearts of the people: the silence of his embarrassment makes it especially audible.

* * * * *

The *Sonnets* were only one of the materials used in the construction of Shakespeare's life, and in this represent one aspect of the move towards reliance on documents—some actual, some invented—and away from recollections and legends that were the basis of eighteenth-century writings, in the model of the 'Life' that prefaced Nicholas Rowe's edition of 1709. Charles Knight is again a pivotal figure, his biography appearing in the final volume of his *Pictorial Shakspere* in 1842 and as a considerably revised and enlarged separate book in 1865. Knight's first writing on Shakespeare's life had appeared in the *Penny Magazine*, its first number including a very short biographical note to mark the birthday, as well as two of the sonnets. Short references to biography also occur scattered throughout the 'Illustrations' sections of his edition of the plays. One of these, in *Twelfth Night*, was the first to make clear that Anne Hathaway may well have inherited far more than the infamous 'second-best bed' mentioned in the will, her inheritance perhaps including a share of the Stratford properties.

That this rested on research into Jacobean legal practices rather than hearsay suggests a major difference between Knight's work and those of his predecessors, most apparent in the final version of his *Life*. Whereas Rowe visited Stratford in search of anecdote, Knight used the journey to visit all the buildings associated with the dramatist and to consult as many records as he could find, before complementing this work with research at the Bodleian Library in Oxford. This gave the work a new authority of origin, even if some of the documents he used were those later proven to be Collier's forgeries. But such rigour was balanced by the kind of speculation also found in many later, more popular biographical writings, suggesting Shakespeare's response to particular places and events, and also to make the dramatist seem real to the reader by presenting what Knight termed 'the circumstances around him'. Many of the suggestions about Shakespeare's experiences are woven into a discussion of his dramatic practice. The suggestion that he saw the Coventry cycle plays is possibly more credible than that he saw the royal progress of Queen Elizabeth at nearby Kenilworth Castle—an idea made fashionable in fictional terms by Walter Scott's *Kenilworth* of 1821—but both are suggestive additions to the range of sources and resemblances that are apparent in the plays, and which remain the subject of academic study.

In other passages, Knight tries to subsume Shakespeare into early Victorian respectability, his home life first with parents and then with wife and children being presented as prosperous, comfortable, and conventional. He rejects the deer-stealing episode and asserts that Shakespeare visited Italy, in both areas going against convention and, in the latter, making an assertion still controversial. Today, Knight's biography stands as deeply flawed through its reliance on the documents forged by John Payne Collier, but it should be remembered that these were not exposed until somewhat later: in mingling forms of detailed, source-based life-writing with episodes of imaginative invention—never presented as anything less—it bears curious resemblances to kinds of fiction and biography popular at the end of the twentieth century.

Among the first of Knight's detractors was the much younger James Orchard Halliwell, whose *Life* appeared in 1848. Comparison with Knight reveals the two poles between which almost every later Shakespeare biography has been constructed. Whereas Knight, for all his research, wove the information he found, and sometimes misinterpreted, into a continuous, engaging narrative, Halliwell's book consisted principally of 89 documents, 57 of them previously unpublished, that his preface claimed presented 'an unprejudiced and complete view of every known fact respecting the poet'. Many are reproduced in full, giving the volume the appearance of a heavily annotated anthology. There are texts of legal documents, records of fines incurred, letters about financial transactions, parish registers—the whole seems more a kit of parts from which an armature may be assembled than a completely sculpted likeness. The approach bears the impress of an earlier generation and different profession, that of the antiquaries of the later eighteenth century; yet, like Knight's text, it is not without pollution from Collier's forgeries, reproducing as it does a letter from the Earl of Southampton that was already under suspicion. Himself still mistrusted because of the Trinity College thefts, and the suspicion of similar offences against Phillips, Halliwell attracted suspicion and open hostility from some reviewers. In the establishment journal the *Athenaeum* Peter Cunningham claimed to find no more than 'three new facts in the thick octavo volume', listed errors of transcription and rejected the claim that the deed to the Blackfriars Gatehouse was now lost, pointing to its display at a recent meeting of the Shakespeare Society. Such levels of vituperation between scholars, in and beyond the pages of learned journals, are common throughout the period; Halliwell had been similarly outspoken about Knight, and in the highly specialized, and highly competitive, world of antiquarian research they are especially forceful.

Perhaps in consequence of these attacks, in 1850 Halliwell produced another volume, *A New Boke about Shakespeare and Stratford-on-Avon*, aiming to introduce the facsimile publication of every document of value about Shakespeare and the Shakespeare family. A revised version of the *Life* appeared in 1853; a decade later Halliwell produced *A Descriptive Calendar of Ancient Manuscripts and Records in the Possession of the Corporation of Stratford-upon-Avon*, moving still further back into earlier antiquarian practice by publishing at his own expense, writing as one specialist to others. These publications were followed in 1874 by his *Illustrations of the Life of Shakespeare*, a collection of documents arranged seemingly at random that had been amassed during his earlier researches. Many are of great importance: proof that the Globe theatre was built in 1599 and not, as Malone had asserted, 1594, and a memorandum registering payment to Kempe, Shakespeare, and Burbage for two comedies acted the same year for the Queen at Greenwich. All these works came together in 1881 in his *Outlines of the Life of Shakespeare*, at first a volume of under 200 pages and finally, in the seventh edition, of well over eight hundred, of which only one hundred are concerned with the life. The remainder present the author's final collection of documents, more as a miscellany than an ordered sequence, but again containing essential material for the construction of an academic account of the life.

In 1832 Alexander Dyce had produced a short 'Memoir of Shakespeare', which had no new material but achieved extended exposure when reprinted in the 1868 Tauchnitz edition of the plays, and was consequently read by English émigrés in Europe. For his Moxon edition of 1857, however, Dyce wrote a more extensive biography. It covers the familiar ground without making any claim to originality or completeness, refusing to become involved with the Collier debate by including some of his material but enclosing it in square brackets to show its unreliable nature. Accepting some earlier claims, such as the deer-stealing story, and the idea of Shakespeare meeting his friends at the Mermaid, he rejects others, such as the claimed identity of the *Sonnets*' W. H. as Pembroke. His Shakespeare is a solid workman, concerned to make his way in the world; there is no hint of the personality presented through the imaginative speculations of Knight, nor are documents presented with such remorseless intensity as in Halliwell's volumes. Yet these qualities clearly appealed to many readers for their avoidance of controversy, and Dyce's version was widely read until almost the end of the century when a more vigorous rival appeared. This was the biography by Sidney Lee. That it was begun as an entry for the *Dictionary of National Biography* testifies to its importance; it marks the apotheosis of Shakespeare into the ranks of the great and good. A curious parallel exists with Lee's own identity. Born Simon Lazarus, he was advised by Benjamin Jowett to change his name when an exhibitioner at Balliol College, Oxford. It is a curious reflection on the prejudices of Victorian England that a Jewish Prime Minister was quite acceptable, but for an aspiring young scholar such an identity was thought a hindrance. And thus Lee, in his own assumed identity, did more than any other single figure to construct and propagate the identity of the great English dramatist. The final version of the biography appeared in 1896, and will be discussed in Chapter 8.

For some, the search for Shakespeare went far beyond biographies, in the endeavour to prove that the plays and poems had a quite different author. Such efforts were a complex mixture of class prejudice, literary detective fiction, and in places a concern for cryptography that would, at the very least, have earned in the 1940s a preliminary interview at Bletchley Park. The idea that, either alone or with suitable collaborators, Francis Bacon had written the works of Shakespeare was forcefully proposed by Delia Bacon in an article in *Putnam's Magazine* of 1856 and developed the next year in *The Philosophy of the Plays of Shakespeare Unfolded*. Although Delia Bacon moved first to St Albans, the burial place of Francis Bacon, and then to Stratford, she failed to convince anyone, her attempts to persuade Carlyle inducing alternate bouts of rage and hysterical laughter. The idea was developed by others including Ignatius Donnelly and Orville Ward Owen, who devised a machine to unlock the cryptographic secrets of Bacon's authorship.

That all these enthusiasts were American adds a further layer of irony: presumably it was acceptable for the dramatist to be English if he were an English nobleman, such as Francis Bacon. During the nineteenth century the idea was almost wholly restricted to transatlantic writers, and only in 1918 did a comparable theory arise in England, when Thomas Looney (mercifully, pronounced 'Loney') advanced Edward de Vere, seventeenth Earl of Oxford, as the author. But for the main part, concerns in the British Isles were more with finding, and in some cases inventing, evidence of the life of the more widely acknowledged author.

One event of considerable significance in this regard occurred in 1856: the presentation of the Chandos portrait of Shakespeare as the first donation to the newly founded National Portrait Gallery, an institution important in national culture both because and in spite of its nature. Including work by many of the most outstanding artists, it is clearly a major aesthetic institution; offering a visual index to the people who have constructed the nation's identity it has a status above the vagaries of aesthetic style. This ambivalence goes to the root of the concern for portraits of Shakespeare that developed alongside the interest in the life of the artist during the later Victorian period. What mattered was not the artistic perfection of the work, or at best not that alone: it was the ways in which the image offered a glimpse into the mind, the personality and the whole character of the individual portrayed. In this, the cult of portraiture mirrored and extended the interest in the life, and the countryside where Shakespeare grew up: it is an extension of interest that goes beyond the fundamental reason why the object provokes it, a concern with the producer not the product or, to use terms more fitting for the period and the relationship, the creator not the creations.

Remarkable among paintings advanced as portraits of Shakespeare, the Chandos portrait has strong claims to having been painted from the life. Named after the Third Duke of Chandos, who briefly owned it in the late eighteenth century, it was bought in 1848 by the Earl of Ellesmere, who donated it to the Portrait Gallery on his appointment as one of its first trustees. Its ownership could be traced back first to William Davenant, the godson—and, according to legend, the natural son—of Shakespeare, and thence less securely to John Taylor, a painter and actor reputed to have known Shakespeare. James Boaden's *Inquiry into the Authenticity of Various Pictures and Prints* (1824), the first sustained attempt to list and discuss claimants to authenticity, commented:

The eyes have great expression, and the compression of the lips indicates the earnest employment of the mind—it is a rare combination of penetration and placid composure.

Like many later accounts of the portrait, this approaches the image not as a painting but as a real figure, and invests it with characteristics thought fit for Shakespeare. As the sonnets have vanished under the search for identities, so the portrait has become a lens through which the expected nature of the Bard is seen. Not all writers found it so perfect a presentation. In his 1864 survey *Life Portraits of William Shakespeare*, J. Hain Friswell complained:

One cannot readily imagine our essentially English Shakespeare to have been a dark, heavy man, with a foreign expression, of decidedly Jewish physiognomy, thin curly hair, a somewhat lubricious mouth, red-edged eyes, wanton lips, with a coarse expression and his ears tricked out with earrings.

Clearly Friswell had a very precise notion of the Bard, with which the painting did not accord. His anti-Semitism is typical of a certain strand of English thought at the time, and the discomfort at the presence of the earring displays ignorance of the fact that many wore earrings as a source of money to pay for burial. Most important of all is the complaint about darkness: had Friswell looked a little more closely and considered the image as a painting, he might have noticed the heavy varnish to which it had been subjected and seen this as the cause of discoloration.

A similar approach is perhaps evident in the reception of what became known as the Flower portrait, an image reputedly discovered in Potters Bar and purchased by Edgar Flower, scion of the Stratford brewing family that generously supported the development of Stratford-upon-Avon as the centre of the Shakespeare cult. Convinced that the painting was genuine by its strong similarity to the Droeshout engraving in the First Folio, Flower presented the painting to the Shakespeare Memorial Theatre in 1895. The close resemblance to the Droeshout in itself makes the image suspect, since very few frontispiece engravings of the period were produced after oil paintings; and the 'William Shakespeare 1609' inscribed at the top left bears little resemblance to texts on other paintings of that time. Again, the desire to see displaced what was seen, and the painting was long regarded as authentic, until detailed examination at the end of the twentieth century revealed that it had been painted, using early nineteenth-century pigments, over an earlier image showing the Madonna and Child. In this there is a wonderful appropriateness: that the central icon of the Catholic faith is displaced by a face purporting to be the essential expression of English identity is a perfect, tangible embodiment of the way Shakespeare was regarded by many at the end of the nineteenth century. The desire to see the portraits in this very specific manner is also clear in the treatment of the so-called Janssen portrait. One of a group of paintings showing the same figure, it was repainted at some time in the nineteenth century to displace the full head of hair by the powerfully intellectual domed forehead thought to be essential to Shakespeare's genius. As Chapter 1 made clear, the so-called 'Stratford Portrait' had long been discounted, the resemblance to an inn sign making it suspect on grounds both of aesthetics and social propriety.

Other paintings united the Droeshout engraving with fictional narratives of Shakespeare's life and influence, all showing in different ways the integration of the Shakespeare legend into contemporary life. *Sir Walter Scott at Shakespeare's Tomb* (*c.* 1840–45, Shakespeare Birthplace Trust), generally attributed to David Roberts, brought together the two writers who did more than any others to construct the English idea of history in the early-Victorian period. John Faed's *Shakespeare and His Friends at the Mermaid Tavern* (1850: Private Collection) shows another version of the Droeshout engraving at the centre of a group of men in a mock-Tudor interior. All are dressed in appropriate historical costume, but their positioning and body language is wholly Victorian, the picture effectively presenting a Victorian gentlemen's club in costume. In *A Sculptor's Workshop, Stratford-upon-Avon, 1617* (1857: Royal Shakespeare Company), Henry Wallis shows a figure kneeling before a bust of the dramatist, while a companion holds Shakespeare's death mask, young children play and an older child looks on. Outside, the tower of Holy Trinity and the River Avon are visible. Already, Stratford has become a shrine and place of pilgrimage. The bust shown in two of these paintings, made in the seventeenth century by Gerard Janssen, had already been reconfigured according to later taste when, near the end of the eighteenth century, at the instigation of Edmond Malone, its bright colours were painted over in tones suggesting bare stone, thought more fitting to the dignity of the Bard as he was then conceived.

The Roberts painting is important in revealing another element of Victorian Shakespeare activity: the visit to Stratford as a secular pilgrimage. At least since the celebrations of 1769, when David Garrick organized celebrations of the bicentenary and slightly overshot the date, Stratford had become an essential destination for those professing any cultural stature. In his *Remarks on Shakespeare, his Birthplace, Etc.* (1877), C. Roach Smith noted the profuse, if today somewhat alarming, evidence of this:

Many succeed in performing this national pilgrimage, as the walls of his birthplace and of Anne Hathaway's cottage testify; for they are covered with thousands upon thousands of signatures of noble as well as gentle, of eminent as well as of obscure, regardless alike of the questionable good taste of their scribbling, and of the perishable material.

Some were more ingenious: Walter Scott scratched his name on the window, Dickens on the wall and Thackeray on the ceiling. William Winter, best known for his three volumes on the performance histories of the plays, was one of many Americans who made the trip to Stratford in the later nineteenth century. In *Shakespeare's England* (1886; revised and illustrated edition, 1893), he described as 'The Actor's Pillar' a section of the chimney piece of the Birthplace that had become the province of performers, and which bore the signatures of, among others, Edmund Kean. All of the signatures were whitewashed over in the 1940s, after careful photographic records had been made.

Shakespeare's Birthplace had been a tourist destination since the middle of the eighteenth century, but in the early Victorian years the building and its contents were in very poor repair. A visit by the American author Washington Irving, and its description in his *Sketch-Book* (1819–20), perhaps fanned rumours that the impresario Phineas T. Barnum was planning to buy the building and transfer it in parts for reassembly and display in America. In 1847 the Birthplace was purchased by public subscription, and the Shakespeare Birthplace Trust founded, and in 1856 a gift from John Shakespeare, from Ashby-de-la-Zouche, made possible the extensive restoration then urgently necessary. The need to restore was matched by the need to mythologize: the outer walls of brick that had been added when part of the house was used as an inn were removed, to reveal the original, though largely rebuilt, façade of wooden beams and plaster infill, and new gables were built to replicate those shown in the earliest surviving drawings (see Illustration 6.2). The houses forming a terrace on either side were demolished: the house was now in a fit state for its role as national shrine. It also had a more scholarly purpose, part of the building housing a library that was open to visitors.

6.2 A photograph of Shakespeare's Birthplace by William Russell Sedgefield for use in a stereoscope, a wooden frame which held two slightly different images that, when viewed through the frame's lenses, produced a three-dimensional view. The image dates from before the removal of the brick facade visible at the right, or the addition of the gable windows.
© Victoria and Albert Museum, London

In 1857 the railway reached Stratford-upon-Avon—although, as in Oxford and Cambridge, it was kept at a little distance from the centre of the town itself. Now more easily accomplished, visits were further stimulated by the tercentenary celebrations, and became an almost mandatory element of social advancement. By the final decades of the century all their components were laid out in what would now be termed a 'heritage trail', offering carefully choreographed minglings of historical continuity and mythic re-creation. Anne Hathaway's cottage, privately owned until purchased by the Birthplace Trust in 1892, had been divided into two parts in 1836, one of which was open to the public. Its location at about a mile from the town itself offered an attractive, if often muddy, recreational walk through countryside typical of the region; its naming as a cottage belies its fairly considerable size, but adds to the air of rustic originality and true old Englishness suggested by its approaches. Visits to the town also featured in popular fiction. 'A Startling Confession' by J. Hollingshead (*Train: A First Class Magazine*, September 1857) tells how an envious dramatist sets fire to the Birthplace out of anger and jealousy; in *Asphodel* (1881), the 'sensation novelist' Mary Elizabeth Braddon presents a character who claims to hate Shakespeare because of the ceaseless paeans addressed to him by visitors to the town.

In October 1861 Halliwell and others set up a Shakespeare Fund. One of its aims was the purchase, restoration, and opening of the gardens and remaining foundations of New Place, Shakespeare's Stratford home from 1597—although the dates and durations of his visits there remain uncertain. In 1891 its management was taken over by the Birthplace Trust. Halliwell's *Historical Account of New Place* (1864) was a part of his campaign, further evidencing his extraordinary combination of antiquarianism, scholarly zeal, and overactive imagination: but the work was certainly important in drawing attention to the buildings and gardens, and the town itself in Shakespeare's day. New Place had fared badly in the eighteenth century. In the ownership of the Reverend Francis Gastrell it had been the resort of tourists wishing to take parts of the mulberry tree apparently planted by Shakespeare. Gastrell found this intolerable, and so in 1756 he cut down the tree and sold it to Thomas Sharp, who made boxes, cups, toys, and pieces of furniture from this seemingly inexhaustible organism. Three years later, angered by high tax demands, Gastrell demolished the house and left Stratford, thus completing a narrative that reveals the darker side of the Shakespeare pilgrimage trade. But the gardens, once restored, were an important place of quiet for Victorian tourists, who found flowers mentioned in the plays and a newly-planted mulberry tree. Other buildings remained closed to the public. Stratford Grammar School, still in use then as now, was not open to visitors, but its location on the corner of Church Street and Chapel Lane made it another essential component of the pilgrim's itinerary. Hall's Croft, the large, detached building that was the home of Shakespeare's daughter Susanna after her marriage to Dr John Hall, was still in private occupation, remaining so until bought by the Birthplace Trust in 1949 and made public two years later.

Another beneficiary of the Shakespeare Fund was the Shakespeare Museum, which opened in 1868 in a building adjacent to New Place. Its contents largely consisted of the collection put together by Robert Bell Wheler, a local solicitor-turned-antiquary who had made the discovery of local documents and other materials his life's work. A great deal of the material is of strictly local interest, and of that related to Shakespeare much lacks clear authenticity. A ring engraved with the letters 'W. S.' offers little to support Wheler's claim of its being a love token presented to Anne Hathaway; a manuscript account of Shakespeare sleeping beneath a crab tree before leaving for London perpetuates an earlier legend; and a box made from the mulberry tree in New Place gardens and presented to the Prince of Wales in 1806 all represent different limbs of the contemporary Shakespeare cult. Some items are of greater value: the title deeds of the properties owned by Shakespeare are foremost among these, and of more recent interest are Wheler's own unpublished works, including a manuscript account of the Shakespeare Tercentenary and a volume published in 1853 to commemorate the tercentenary of the award of a royal charter to Stratford Grammar School. The collection, now part of the holdings of the Birthplace Trust, also included the material on which Wheler based his 1824 history of the Birthplace; that Halliwell reprinted the text of this in a thirteen-page brochure in 1863 reveals the high opinion in which he held it, and also reveals the nascent tradition of the guide book. F. W. Fairholt published *The Home of Shakespeare Illustrated and Described* in 1843, and in the next decade J. C. M. Bellew's *Shakespeare's Home in New Place* appeared. Guides to the town as a whole were also popular, notably *Ward & Lock's illustrated guide to, and popular history of Stratford-upon-Avon, the home of Shakespeare, with excursions in the neighbourhood* (1881). More serious tastes were catered for by Sidney Lee and Edward Hull in *Stratford-on-Avon from the Earliest Times to the Death of Shakespeare* (1885).

Further important sites of veneration were the Guild Chapel and Holy Trinity Church. The connection between Shakespeare and the former was tenuous, resting on his father's period as Chamberlain of Stratford Corporation and the possibility that he may have been taught there while a pupil at the Grammar School, and possibly saw the wall paintings narrating the story of the Holy Cross before they were whitewashed over. Their rediscovery and restoration in 1804, however, made them available to later visitors. Holy Trinity Church, as suggested by the painting of Scott in the chancel, was the essential climax of any Victorian visit, and the centre of celebrations of Shakespeare's birthday which included placing a fresh quill pen in the sculpted hand of the bust every year. The procession of townspeople and visitors, including diplomatic representatives and other worthies, is a more recent tradition, having begun in 1916.

These were the buildings that the visitor would have seen: what responses did they evoke? C. Roach Smith offers some insights into what the more literary-minded might have gained from such a trip, suggesting that, 'in the streets of Stratford' and 'the fields, meadows, and villages', the onlooker will see things that Shakespeare himself saw and that 'the impress of many of these objects is reflected most vividly throughout his works'. The idea of the setting as some kind of visible, tangible work of literary close-reading is attractive; later in the pamphlet he gives some instances of this kind of connection, citing the plants growing around the path to Anne Hathaway's cottage to the description of the mad Lear:

> Crown'd with rank fumiter, and furrow weeds,
> With harlocks, hemlock, nettles, cuckoo-flowers
> Darnel, and all the idle weeds that grow
> In our sustaining corn.

Roach Smith goes on to mention seeing a 'hedge-pig', relating it to the animal mentioned in *Macbeth*, and in later pages refers to the closing song of *Love's Labour's Lost* and the sheep-shearing scene of *The Winter's Tale* as resting on Shakespeare's close observation of 'the whole vegetable kingdom' in and around Stratford. The writer had begun this discussion in *The Rural life of Shakespeare, as Illustrated by his Works* (1870). As well as reflecting the Victorian concern for the language of flowers—seen for example in an illustrated dictionary produced by Kate Greenaway in 1884—such writing is heavy with symbolic import about the status of Shakespeare and the plays. The references surely go beyond alluding to what Shakespeare saw, to present the flowers as metaphors of the innate Englishness, and the lack of continental discipline or order, that typify the plays in the national consciousness.

Similar references to the rural nature of Stratford are frequent in William Winter's book mentioned earlier, and the volume also contains further factual information and a brief biography of Shakespeare; but its main value lies in its detail. Winter writes of the furniture in the Birthplace, including the desk from the Grammar

School at which Shakespeare supposedly sat; the enthusiasm with which he is greeted by Mrs Baker, descendant of the Hathaway family; and her parting gift of roses and woodbine from the cottage porch. Again there is lengthy description of the wild flowers and weeds in the gardens of the houses, and beside the path to Shottery and Anne Hathaway's cottage. Another aspect of Winter's account is its combination of forthright doubt about the authenticity of some of the objects on display and the stories that surround them, and the genuine emotion that the writer feels about being in Stratford. The comments are personal, and by a visitor from overseas, but they appear in one of the most popular books to describe such a visit, so presumably hint at the responses of many visitors. Here is Winter describing the experience of standing in the chancel of Holy Trinity church:

Once again there is sound of organ music, very low and soft, in Stratford Church, and the dim light, broken by the richly stained windows, streams across the dusky chancel, filling the still air with opal haze and flooding those gray gravestones with its mellow radiance. Not a word is spoken; but, at intervals, the rustle of leaves is audible in a sighing wind. What visions are these, that suddenly fill the region! What royal faces of monarchs, proud with power, or pallid with anguish! What sweet, imperial women, gleeful with happy youth and love, or wide-eyed and rigid in tearless woe! What warriors, with serpent diadems, defiant of death and hell! The mournful eyes of Hamlet, the wild countenance of Lear; Ariel with his harp, and Prospero with his wand!

The passage conveys powerfully the idea that being in Stratford transforms and intensifies the experience of the plays and their characters, uniting author, text, characters, and place.

Not all visitors were similarly euphoric. In July 1848 George Eliot visited Stratford with Edward Flower, Ralph Waldo Emerson, and Charles Bray, ribbon manufacturer, phrenologist and philosopher—a group that goes some way towards embracing every area of Victorian life, albeit lacking the church and the army. Mrs Bray recorded that the journey in an open carriage 'was the pleasantest part of the day'. Thomas Hardy visited the town in 1896; his *Life*, written by his second wife Florence Hardy, records nothing of the visit and quickly passes on to their continuing tour to Dover, where he read *King Lear*. The most forceful rebuff came a little after the Victorian age. In 1903

Henry James, whose theatre criticism was perhaps the most intellectually incisive of the period, published a short story called 'The Birthplace'. Morris and Isabel Gedge, a couple with greater cultural aspirations than means to support them, are offered the post of curators of a national shrine that, although unidentified, is quite clearly the house in Henley Street. Disillusioned by the banality of the visitors' questions and encouraged by a more perceptive couple who come to the building, the husband begins to extend his commentaries into what he considers to be absurd parodies. The climax is reached when, visited unexpectedly by Mr Grant-Jackson, the head of 'the Body' that owns the building, Gedge fully expects dismissal from the post and the loss of the accommodation that goes with it. Instead, he is given a rise in salary and told to continue his elaborate fictions, so popular have they become with the visiting pilgrims, who take them with deadly seriousness. Throughout the tone is typical of James at his most subtly satirical, and the story as a whole is an important comment on one aspect of the Victorian Shakespeare religion.

The most remarkable coming together of antiquarian document-hunting, fictional characterization, and Shakespearian identities, and the one with perhaps the least expected consequences in its pervasive effect on Victorian culture, was to appear near the end of Victoria's reign, as the final chapter will make clear: Oscar Wilde's 'The Portrait of Mr W. H.' (1889). The sonnets, the hunger to construct a life for both Shakespeare and those who read and wrote about him, come together here as throughout the period in the reading of the works, most especially the sonnets. A little later, W. B. Yeats was to assert that 'The intellect of man is forced to choose/Perfection of the life, or of the work' ('The Choice', 1931). Looking back, it might well seem that for the majority of Victorians, at least in their most seeming-confident, materially assertive phase, the life was what mattered, both in the construction of Shakespeare's identity and in the ways that it might help shape their own.

Shakespeare beyond Shakespeare

The search for Shakespeare the man through the poems, portraits, and shards of biography examined in the preceding chapter is balanced by another direction: that in which Shakespearian activity moved beyond the plays to examine Shakespeare as a moral, exemplary force. The word 'Shakespeare' here is used as it was employed in much Victorian writing, as an undefined but clearly understood entity embracing the works and the larger principles on which they are founded, interpreted, and presented in the language of critics writing for a range of audiences, but always with an assumed and generally unspoken truth that the works reveal the man, and the man is unparalleled in human understanding. 'Shakespeare', in short, had come to define the essence of moral and intellectual excellence, a model for all to follow.

The nature and value of this wider significance was established early in the period by Thomas Carlyle, whose lecture 'The Poet as Hero' was delivered in May 1840 and published shortly afterwards. Throughout the lecture it is clear that the dramatic force of the works is not being considered: instead, it is the larger truths of human identity in its most ideal form that are analysed. Or rather, asserted: there is no direct analysis of the texts as such. The moral importance of the works is presented as inseparable from their intelligence and human understanding, which are regarded as an elemental drive that is divinely inspired. Shakespeare, in short, is a 'Force of Nature'. To this notion is related a stress on the peculiarly English nature of

Shakespeare's identity. That the same essay discusses Dante is important, as repeatedly the national differences between the two poets are emphasized. Whereas Dante provides the 'Faith or soul', Shakespeare gives 'the Practice or body' through an understanding wholly instinctive. The English identity as essentially pragmatic is important here, and although Carlyle sees 'a kind of sacredness' in Shakespeare's existence it is something clearly defined in national terms: 'A true English heart breathes, calm and strong, through the whole business'. The full title of the volume in which the lecture appeared is important: *On Heroes and Hero-Worship*. Most present-day readers would be uncomfortable with such a concept, preferring the idea of a role-model; but given the Victorian notion of self-advancement it is one wholly consistent with the ethics of the time, and seems to echo a public-school notion of a growth to maturity, with Shakespeare as the nation's house master or captain of rugger. But if this sounds too far from Shakespeare the dramatist, an earlier comment of Carlyle's is an important corrective. The plays are 'truer than reality itself, since the essence of unmixed reality is bodied forth in them under more expressive symbols' (*The State of German Literature*, 1827).

A different approach to Shakespeare's moral stature and example is found in the works of a later Victorian, John Ruskin. Early experience of the plays read aloud by his father produced a deep knowledge of the texts, and his writings contain profuse references and quotations. Ruskin's faith in the importance of the theatre as a means of both entertainment and education for people of all conditions, especially working craftsmen and artisans, rests firmly on this. Sometimes, though, Ruskin's approach can be puzzling. An extensive passage in the fourth volume of his *Modern Painters* (1856) sees Shakespeare's shortcomings largely as the result of his not living in a mountainous area, and thus not developing the strong characteristics typical of those who do. The discussion is best understood as metaphorical, part of Ruskin's continual striving to understand the nature of human existence within the natural world, and inflected by his concern for the stature of men who work by physical labour. Yet to see it wholly in this way is to limit it: the pages reveal both his desire to relate the actuality of the natural world to their aesthetic representation in painting, and perhaps also as a contribution to the Victorian debate, implicit in many areas, of the nature of manhood in an industrial society. Additionally, the passage should be seen within the larger context of the book as a whole, in which the passage on 'The Mountain Glory' balances and offsets that on 'The Mountain Gloom'.

More immediately striking, and the subject of much more discussion by recent critics, is Ruskin's assertion that the female characters are the most genuinely heroic in the plays, advanced directly and by implication in many places, including the lecture 'Of Queens' Gardens' (published in *Sesame and Lilies*, 1864) and letters to Anna Brownell Jameson and Helen Faucit. This goes beyond an assertion that Shakespeare's female figures are 'infallibly faithful and wise counsellors', implying their secondary and supportive function: the women in the plays, with Virgilia from *Coriolanus* singled out for special mention as 'perhaps the loveliest', are 'conceived in the highest heroic type of humanity'. There are no heroic male figures in the plays, 'whereas there is hardly a play that has not a perfect woman in it, steadfast in grave hope, and errorless in purpose'. Some feminist critics have attacked this, seeing it as evidencing Victorian views of the place of women merely as one of support for their men. More recently, however, the lecture has been seen as advancing a system of values that are positive in opposing the unimaginative and exploitative forces of industrial capitalism. This larger view, it has been suggested, is also part of Ruskin's approach to *The Merchant of Venice*, in which the values of Shylock and Antonio represent respectively those of capitalist individualism and human compassion. Most particularly, David-Everett Blythe has argued in a 1981 article that Shylock represents the usury associated with the Venetian shift to paper money instead of gold, moving away from faith and true labour to a false standard that debases not merely commerce but the whole basis of human society.

Ruskin's later writings, however, move away from this position and the larger adulation of the plays. Now their major characters are seen as ineffectual, failing to overcome the difficulties they themselves have created—'folly' is a key term here, both for human errors and their consequences, all by implication the result of the male, industrial value-systems. Ruskin's passionate rejection of the commercialism of later Victorian society, and his equally passionate championing of the dignity of the individual working man, lies at the essence of his address to Shakespeare. The absence of this quality in the figures traditionally seen as Shakespeare's heroes is marked by the fact that ultimately they all fail, and thus offer no kind of example of decency for working men and women, a group for whom Ruskin increasingly had respect through his advocacy of artistic design and manufacture that would have such a strong influence on William Morris and the Arts and Crafts Movement. Shakespeare's failure to offer examples of this kind of everyday heroism was ultimately, for Ruskin, a major flaw. Towards the end of his life he wrote of the way in which the actions of major characters annulled 'every happy scene in the loveliest plays' and doubted whether anyone in contemporary life had learnt anything from Shakespeare. Ultimately, perhaps, for Ruskin what matters is the worth of the plays' exemplary force within his own political and social struggle, which is strikingly different from the values found in the plays by most of his contemporaries.

Walter Bagehot is perhaps less likely as a Shakespeare critic, his major work concerning parliamentary procedure, but this evidences again the ways in which the moral force of the plays permeated every aspect of Victorian activity. In an essay on Dickens, he engages with the old concept of Shakespeare's irregularity, his lack of 'definite proportion of faculties', but attributes this to his 'overteeming imagination' that causes 'a great feeling of irregularity'. In the same piece he compares some of Dickens' grotesques to Falstaff, and argues that both are the product of a different kind of imagination from that of 'the real painters of essential human nature'. Discussing some contemporary poetry, he voices the familiar idea of Shakespeare's imagination being so full—'an inexhaustible fountain of human nature'—that it sometimes overflowed, producing 'erroneous conceits and superfluous images'. In another essay he seems to conclude this debate with the invention of a quality called 'animated moderation', claiming that Shakespeare and Homer had 'this union of life with measure, of spirit with reasonableness'. Elsewhere, discussing Hartley Coleridge, Bagehot diagnoses Hamlet's inactivity as the result of his 'forever speculating on the reality of existence', and goes on to link the quality with Kant as something that runs counter to Shakespeare's own nature.

Bagehot expounds this idea most fully in his essay 'Shakespeare—the Man', a title that, in reflecting the general concern with the dramatist rather than the drama, would be forcefully rejected at century's end. The greatness of Shakespeare certainly lies in the writing, Bagehot stresses, but also in the 'great experience' from which it derived—a quality demonstrated by contrast to Milton, Scott, and Goethe. In this, Shakespeare is a 'common man', his works accessible to all because of their innate understanding. Shakespeare's power of creating women characters is unequalled, resulting from his observational power; that he lacks obvious religious affiliations or the earnestness they often beget is further testimony to his individual humanity, the greatness of his work. In many ways, Bagehot is repeating ideas from his own period and before; but that he does so at all again reveals the centrality of the idea of Shakespeare as the great, and greatly pragmatic, English moralist to much Victorian thought.

A more immediate source of Shakespeare as a moral example was provided by the Reverend Aaron Augustus Morgan in *The Mind of Shakespeare, as Exhibited in His Works*, which first appeared in 1860 and was reprinted, with illustrations taken from Sir John Gilbert's edition, in 1867. That this predates Dowden's *Mind and Art* volume by nearly two decades is suggestive not of its influence, but of the prevalence of the approach that sees the plays as evidence of psychological, intellectual, or moral qualities, and it is with the last of these that Morgan is concerned. The preface is suggestive of a larger uncertainty towards the dramatist, hinting at vestigial Victorian concerns about the propriety of the drama. Shakespeare, it asserts, was 'at once dramatist, Poet, Philosopher, Humourist, and critical delineator of Human Nature'. That the categories are arranged in ascending order of importance is confirmed by later assertions, in which concern for the plays themselves as dramatic entities, always slight, dwindles and finally collapses completely. It was 'greatly due to accidental circumstances that the chief emanations of his mind were embodied in the form of Dramas'; writing a play is 'not perhaps the best field for the free exhibition of a lofty intellect'. These claims justify the book's organization, in which short passages from the plays are presented for the 'system of Morality and Virtue' they present, all organized under subject headings in alphabetical order. As a result, 'the reader may without fear conform to them himself, and adopt them for his own', enabling him to master the moral obstacles that are 'a frequent theme with our great dramatist'.

This is made more achievable by the presentation of the moral statements 'untrammelled by dramatic appendage'—and it is also more convenient for those who don't have time to see the plays. Opening the book at random at the letter C reveals passages listed under the headings Conscience (two full pages), Conspiracy, Contentment, Contrast, Conversation ('Dull, before dinner', with only one quotation of four words), Courage, and Courtiers ('A Model One'). It is easy to make fun of this approach—we should remember our own age's concern for reductive self-help books and websites—but the volume suggests much about mid-Victorian approaches to Shakespeare, morality, social advancement, and the organization of knowledge. The first three are taken as self-evident in the very existence of the book; the last reflects a preoccupation with order, system, and listing, essentials for the major engineering works of the time, in forms related to transport, social structures, and the building of empire. But at the same time this order, and the moral principles and forms on which it rested, would soon come under question, and the involvement of Shakespearian criticism, performance, and wider application reflected this, too, as the final chapter will make clear.

Morgan's collection of lines and passages of moral or intellectual value is extended far more widely in the Victorian practice of learning passages by heart, either for ethical purposes or to assist in elocution. Sometimes these two purposes were combined in the practice of learning key speeches in isolation; sometimes individual lines were adopted and accorded the status of proverbs or statements of traditional wisdom, to the extent that their being quotations was quite forgotten. A minor branch of this was the use of quotations for comic purposes, where their sheer absurdity and deliberate misplacement was the basis of comedy—a use that itself depended on the reader's grasp, however limited, of their original place and meaning. But the main function was overwhelmingly educational, either in the formal setting of the schoolroom or in larger settings of moral discourse in everyday life, in which Shakespeare was seen as a guide, philosopher, and friend second only to the Bible in depth and force.

The study of Shakespeare at school had, by the later years of Victoria's reign, been part of the curriculum at most public schools, aided by the preparation of special editions discussed in Chapter 2. For most children, however, there were the National Schools, run by charitable organizations, at which attendance was voluntary, and where instead of being studied as complete entities the plays were put to a different use. By the 1860s, passages from the plays, taken from anthologies, were used to test reading aloud or recitation by heart. Later, particularly after the Education Act of 1870, elementary education became first available and then compulsory for all. Its cornerstone was literacy, and essential to this was reading Shakespeare. In 1882 'Standards' were introduced to test and certify levels of achievement. Pupils who, in the terminology of the day, 'presented themselves for inspection at Standard VI', were expected to 'Read a passage from one of Shakespeare's historical plays, or from a history of England'. Standard VII required 'a passage from Shakespeare or Milton, or from some other standard author, or from a history of England'. Popular among these were Portia's 'Quality of Mercy' speech from *The Merchant of Venice* and the 'Seven Ages of Man' from *As You Like It*, along with patriotic passages from the history plays. What is striking here is not simply the appropriation of Shakespeare's texts as a source for reading exercises; that they are offered as alternatives to passages from writings on English history reveals the depth to which they have become integrated within ideas of national identity. Additionally, that Shakespeare stands at the head of the list of 'standard authors' also reveals the dramatist's place at the very foundation of the idea of a canon of national literature.

English literature came late to academic study, it being thought that classical literature was the proper concern of those attending universities. At first it was offered as a subject in the university colleges founded in the north of England during the last quarter of the century, for those who had not learned Latin and Greek at school. Intriguingly, the link between history and literature is again strong. When chairs of literature were established at Oxford and Cambridge, they were held by men (of course) who were known as writers rather than critics. A powerful exception was A. C. Bradley, who placed Shakespeare at the centre of his curricula at the Universities of Liverpool and Glasgow before moving to Oxford at the very end of the century. His work on Shakespeare will be discussed in the next chapter; for the moment, though, it is important to stress that the beginnings of serious study of the plays grew out of popular education, outside the older universities, and was thus related more to the movement for popular literacy, the desire for self-improvement and the interest in English history than to the scholarly work of editing and criticism outlined in Chapter 2—and that is in itself further evidence of the central position of Shakespeare in English society during Victoria's reign.

* * * * *

Related to the discussion of the plays as a source of moral guidance was a form of writing that had begun in the previous century and is in many circles still popular today: the discussion of characters as actual people. Resting on the truth, by now universally acknowledged, that Shakespeare's understanding of humanity was unequalled, this was often used as a way of furthering understanding of human nature. William Richardson had established the approach with his *A Philosophical Analysis and Illustration of Some of Shakespeare's Remarkable Characters* (1774) and two subsequent volumes. Here the characters were examined with the aim of offering some kind of moral—in the case of Macbeth for example, that 'naturally amiable' individuals may become ferocious and inhuman when they indulge a ruling passion. As Chapter 2 made clear, the discussion of character was a major thread of the critical exploration of the plays, and often figured in the introductions to scholarly editions. But generally it was woven into other ideas about the plays, most often their dating or the maturity of authorship they demonstrated. The more popular Victorian approaches to characters presented them as individuals, rarely mentioning their position within plays except insofar as they interacted with other characters who, like them, were seen as real people. There was also another major difference: the characters most often discussed were female, and so were the writers who discussed them.

The earliest of the Victorian character studies is Anna Brownell Jameson's *Characteristics of Women, Moral, Poetical and Historical*, which appeared 'with fifty vignette etchings' by the author in 1832 but remained popular throughout the century. The inclusion of images offers an important link to the tradition of character portraits discussed in Chapter 4; that subsequent editions appeared without them suggests a move towards seeing character studies in word and image as related, but essentially separate, forms, each offering its own kind of interpretation. Jameson's book was republished in 1840 as *Shakespeare's Heroines*, but not again until 1897 and 1901, on both occasions with profuse illustrations in the style of the decade. More important was the omission in subsequent editions of the Preface to the first publication, which significantly diluted its political force. The Preface took the form of a dialogue between 'Medon' and 'Alda', the latter the woman author justifying the book's aims and the former a male interrogator: the aims are clearly as much sociopolitical as literary-theatrical, yet in a manner particularly suited to explication through reference to the plays. Alda argues directly that women's education is 'founded in mistaken principles' and 'tends to increase fearfully the sum of misery and error in both sexes', but goes on to reject direct attack on these, choosing instead 'to illustrate certain positions by examples' and allow readers 'to deduce the moral themselves'. Shakespeare's characters are chosen for this as there are few historical equivalents: the ideals are 'those of which history never heard, or disdains to speak'. Once more, then, Shakespeare's writings are seen as something beyond dramatic literature: their choice rests on firm principles, and again illustrates the much broader function of Shakespeare in Victorian thought. That the Preface was dropped in all subsequent editions suggests an interesting trajectory, moving away from a philosophical positioning towards a decorative object, something reflecting changes in the approach to the subject as well as to the book, with aesthetic rather than social or intellectual concerns taking over at the end of the century.

These aims understood, the structure and content of the book become much clearer. Characters are organized into four groups. The first, 'Characters of Intellect', are Portia, Isabella, Beatrice, and Rosalind; yet the choice seems to reflect moral fortitude as well as logical insight, all being seen as able to make ethical choices and defend them with force—the fact that Portia's 'Quality of Mercy' speech was one of the most frequently learned and recited reveals the prominence of this view. Next come 'Characters of Passion and Imagination', with Juliet, Helena, Perdita, Viola, Ophelia, and Miranda— some of the choices seem inevitable, others less so. There follows a group of 'Characters of the Affections', Hermione, Desdemona,

Imogen, and Cordelia; and finally 'Historical Characters', including most of the female characters from the Roman plays and surprisingly few from the English histories, although the Victorian liking for *King John* is marked by the inclusion of Constance. Lady Macbeth is perhaps surprising in the group, but the justification is forceful: the character is 'not utterly depraved and hardened by the habit of crime', and her strength is greater than Macbeth's, as she is 'not a woman to start at shadows'. It is in the sleepwalking scene that her 'seared brain and broken heart' are laid bare, and in this lies the breadth of Shakespeare's human understanding, in presenting evil while making the audience aware of 'the opposite good which shall balance and relieve it'. Like so many books once very popular in the Victorian period, Jameson's has since suffered from being too often dismissed and too rarely read: the balance between the characters and the methods of their presentation is much more subtle than often asserted, and the frequent comparisons with Webster, Aeschylus, Sophocles, and Schiller reveal a breadth of approach that recalls Arnold's critical writing.

A different approach is taken by Helen Faucit, who wrote from her experience of playing the roles in *On Some of Shakespeare's Female Characters: Ophelia, Portia, Desdemona, Juliet, Imogen, Rosalind, Beatrice*. First published in 1885, the book went through another five editions by 1899. Reasons for this popularity are variously explained. Perhaps her stage reputation was the cause; perhaps the subtitle listing the roles most popular during the period also helped. Possibly, too, the fact that Helen Faucit was now Lady Martin, her husband Theodore having been knighted on the completion of his life of Prince Albert in 1880, would have appealed to those with social aspirations. All are valid, and eminently Victorian, motives. The subtitle of Faucit's book may have been a marketing ploy, naming as it does many of Faucit's most celebrated roles; but it also suggests a preference for the younger characters from the comedies and tragedies. Hermione and Lady Macbeth, roles for which Faucit was also much praised, are omitted, perhaps for reasons that give a clue to the writer's approach in the book and the actor's on the stage.

Faucit's writing is an unusual combination of character study and theatrical memoir, the two in places coming together in comments on Shakespeare's skill in character delineation. This range of thought is often given expression in language familiar from the popular novels of the time, especially in passages of authorial comment about events of emotional intensity or betrayal. Here, for example, is Faucit on Ophelia in the scene that she has earlier described as Laertes' 'lecturing her' on Hamlet:

Poor maiden! To have this treasured secret of her inner life, her very soul, a secret so sweet, so sacred, so covered over, as she thinks, from all eyes—thus dragged rudely to the light; discussed in the most commonplace tone, and her very maidenly modesty questioned!

Relationships are discussed in a similar way. Hamlet is:

so self-centred, so enwrapped in his own suffering, that he has no thought to waste on the delicate girl whom he had wooed with such a 'fire of love', and had taught to listen to his most honeyed vows.

Stylistic difference apart, many of Faucit's judgments echo those of Gervinus or Furnivall. Portia is 'a perfect piece of Nature's handiwork', and Imogen 'always occupied the largest place in my heart'. The passages of theatrical reminiscence are valuable as dramatic history, especially the accounts of her first appearance at Richmond and her recollections of Edmund Kean. They also suggest something of Faucit's approach to acting, almost approaching a Stanislavskian identification, and certainly anticipating Ellen Terry's writing about her own roles. Both writers are shown in a double process of character creation as they develop their own identities as women performers and those of the characters they perform. This is most marked in a passage from Faucit's discussion of Portia:

I could never part with my characters when the curtain fell and the audience departed. As I had lived with them through their early lives, so I also lived into their future.

Striking, too, are the passages where Faucit praises Shakespeare's care and understanding in delineating women characters. She claims never to have acted Juliet 'without finding fresh cause to marvel at the genius which created this child-woman' and later asserts 'Women are deeply in debt to Shakespeare for all the lovely noble things he has put into his women's hearts and mouths'. Only rarely does the writing discuss the plays as aesthetic entities, speaking for example of the 'harmony' of *Romeo and Juliet* and how the opening sonnet reveals its 'whole purpose'. Here, as elsewhere, Faucit follows the example of earlier male writers; that her writings were begun as letters addressed to Tennyson, Browning, and other celebrated figures, and that they were very widely read, suggests that they reflected ideas and feelings about the plays and their characters—the two are by no means the same thing—current in the middle of the century.

Other writers chose different ways to extend character beyond performance or printed text. At the beginning of the period, Charles and Mary Lamb's *Tales from Shakespeare*, first published in 1807, were already established as a series of prose re-tellings of some of the plays for children—mainly for girls, it being assumed that their brothers would have read the plays in their preparatory or public schools. They remained popular throughout the century, and have never been out of print since. In 1851 there appeared the first volume of *The Girlhood of Shakespeare's Heroines* by Mary Cowden Clarke. By then, Clarke had produced her edition of the plays and her Shakespeare concordance, so the book was clearly the product of a serious, established Shakespeare scholar. Unlike the Lambs' stories, this is not a collection in which the plays are re-told for children. Instead it invented narratives of the lives of the major women characters before the plays, each one ending, in a remarkable act of creative intelligence, with the first line each spoke in the play. This was a remarkable extension both of the plays themselves and of Jameson's practice of character analysis: to say that it anticipates Freud is confusing and ahistorical, but it certainly explores the ways in which events of childhood have a bearing on events in the plays themselves. Clearly, if the idea of characters having separate identities is not accepted at all then this is quite invalid; but if, as many readers then as now would assert, the characters can be seen as self-defining, then the value of the approach is considerable—and as an act of creative writing it is by no means negligible. This becomes especially significant when the book is regarded not as primarily directed towards children, an intended readership against which the vocabulary, syntax, and general structure constantly argue.

These elements come together to present character and event before the action of the plays through situations familiar from the nineteenth-century novel. Juliet is neglected by her jealous mother and spends more time with her nurse, or dreaming alone on the balcony, while Tybalt reveals a violent, vengeful temper. The story begins with an account of the towering storm on the night of Juliet's birth, recalling the use of climate to project character in the Brontës' novels; the plot includes a mysterious deaf, deformed character who is always masked, and an attempt to put poison in a pair of gloves, reflecting a taste for the Gothic in its conception of a Renaissance court. The future Lady Macbeth, called by her historical name Gruach, pities her father's lack of ambition yet looks kindly on him while he is asleep. She forces the young page Culan to retrieve a ball fallen over a cliff, after she has cruelly shot an arrow at a bird's nest to help him find it, but he lacks courage and has to be helped by Grym, a man-at-arms in the castle. References to 'the weird', and the prophecies of a mysterious figure called 'the Highlander' hint at the common view of Lady Macbeth as the fourth witch in the play. Desdemona's childhood is marred by bereavement and loss, and she is moved when her companion Barbara, rejected by her lover Paolo, who thinks she is Nina, who has earlier attempted to stab him in a fit of jealousy, sits quietly singing a willow song. The most extreme story is Ophelia's, with the deaths of two close friends, one of whom sings of 'bonny sweet Robin', dream visions of other deaths and graves, and a reference to a brook fringed with willows. Claudius is a dark, jealous figure, but the relationship with Gertrude is introduced when he clutches and tears at her dress, as close as any of the tales comes to sublimated eroticism. This and a passage of nearly a page describing Polonius speaking to his wife and family 'in manner of an oration' reveals an awareness of the ambivalence of character that escaped many Victorian critics, and those who made their young charges learn the speech giving advice to Laertes. These are remarkable pieces of writing, too easily dismissed as products of their age intended for children: in manner they approach the darker reaches of Victorian popular fiction, but in concept they are original and—perhaps as they were intended to be—thought-provoking about the plays and their figures.

All the above approaches to Shakespeare suggest the kind of moral earnestness that is invariably associated with the Victorians, but it should not be assumed that this was the only mood in which the plays were approached. Increasingly towards the end of the period, when popular publishing had become much cheaper and more widespread, lines from the plays were often given comically irreverent treatment in cartoons. These were different from those in *Punch* mentioned in Chapter 1; instead, they deliberately misread the lines, or used them with punning relevance to the scenes shown. Yet if these were perhaps regarded in some circles as disrespectful to the Bard, the larger impression they convey is of affectionate playfulness; it is as if, while still valued for his moral pronouncements, rich language, and moments of fancy, Shakespeare is being welcomed into the Victorian parlour like a rather remote, distinguished relative but someone who, as one of us, can still relax when off duty.

8.1 The opening of *Cymbeline*, prefaced by a photograph of Ellen Terry as Imogen in the Collins Shakespeare of 1900, showing the reading experience offered by this very popular late-Victorian edition

Last Years

The two closing decades of the nineteenth century saw radical changes in the way that the plays and poems of Shakespeare were presented on stage, in criticism, and in the public imagination. In part this was the result of a larger movement away from the insistent moral tone of high Victorianism provided by the so-called Aesthetic Movement, where art for art's sake displaced the idea of art as an adjunct to public and private morality; in part it was the result of styles and attitudes having reached as far as they could go without turning into self-parody. This did not mean that some of the older stances did not remain. Criticism centred on character was still prevalent, but was redefined and reinvigorated by the more rigorous intellectualism coming from the new university departments of English Literature, with far less emphasis on authorial biography. Productions of the plays in heavily cut form to allow for increasingly magnificent settings continued well into the new century; but they were increasingly threatened by others that sought to replicate the bare stages of Shakespeare's own time. While the sonnets began to be explored more thoroughly as poems, biographical readings appeared that emphasized as directly as the law and public taste allowed the relationship between the speaker and the 'fair youth' or 'lovely boy'. It was, then, a period of contrasts, in which the newer forms fought with those that had been established in the preceding decades but which began to seem increasingly outmoded as the new century approached.

At the beginning of his *Shakespearian Tragedy*, A. C. Bradley wrote:

In these lectures, at any rate for the most part, we are to be content with his *dramatic* view, and are not to ask whether it corresponded exactly with his opinions or creed outside his poetry—the opinions or creed of the being whom we sometimes oddly call 'Shakespeare the man'. It does not seem likely that outside his poetry he was a very simple-minded Catholic or protestant or Atheist, as some have maintained; but we cannot be sure, as with those other poets we can, that in his works he expressed his deepest and most cherished convictions on ultimate questions, or even that he had any. And in his dramatic conceptions there is enough to occupy us.

'Shakespeare the man' is in quotation marks for good reason. Not only does the figuration denote quotation from almost any of the serious writers of the preceding generation; it hints at the irrelevance of the concept to any discussion of the plays, aided in this by the disingenuous 'sometimes oddly' in the same sentence. Criticism will continue, it implies, but now it will be a serious academic endeavour, as denoted by the word 'lectures'. Although published in 1904, the lectures were given at Liverpool and Glasgow in the 1880s and 1890s. Rather than exploring the plays for evidence of the mind of a great philosopher, or mining the poems for evidence of a life, they proclaim their concern with the plays as 'dramatic conceptions'.

While the new approach rejected many earlier stances, it still rested firmly on the work of preceding scholars. The work of retrieving, editing, and making available the texts of the plays in reliable form was the essential prerequisite for Bradley's work, which enabled a new generation of readers to encounter the text without questions of authenticity or variant readings unless they chose to enter into discussions of this kind. Bradley's introduction makes clear the relationship between his work and that of his predecessors. He openly rejects biography and textual scholarship, instead explaining the need 'to compare, to analyse, to dissect'; but he also rejects *Titus Andronicus*, being written before Shakespeare's 'characteristic conception' had developed, and *Timon of Athens*, as a collaborative work, both statements resting clearly on earlier research. Clearly, issues of variant readings of Quartos versus Folio, original or modernized spelling, controversies over single or joint authorship and the other issues that had preoccupied earlier scholars are not Bradley's concern. That these have been resolved is never openly stated, but implicit within the address to a text that is now a matter of accepted, received scholarly opinion.

This relationship, and the aims of the study, emerge clearly in the first lecture. Bradley defines tragedy as a dramatic form or movement, distinct from the earlier *de casibus* tradition in that the tragic fact is much larger, and the direct consequence of the central character, so that personhood and event are inseparable. In short, 'deeds issue from character', the plays driven by the internal conflict, something closer to Hegel's idea of tragedy than Aristotle's. The main body of the book discusses the major tragedies in accord with this principle, but with repeated stress on the complexity of the tragic form: 'tragedy would not be tragedy if it were not a painful mystery'. As with many books of the period, Bradley's has suffered from reductive summaries seeing it as a simple presentation of the crucial flaw within each tragic protagonist. What is also remarkable about the book, especially in its discussion of *Macbeth*, is the presentation of the action in a manner approaching the immediacy of theatrical performance. Bradley presents character within action, discussing motivation and mood in each event almost as a presentation in the theatre, and always locating character within a much larger, more practical, analytic discussion of the play's workings than had been apparent in earlier critical writing.

Other writers adopted different stances. Walter Pater, whose studies of Italian Renaissance painting and literature were important in developing English awareness of European art, wrote three essays later collected in his *Appreciations* (1889) that with hindsight can be seen to demonstrate this newness of approach. *Love's Labour's Lost* is compared to painting, its structure regarded as a series of 'pictorial groups' arranged before an unchanging background, the whole structured through a rhythm of recurrence and change in which the slightness of sources and subject is transformed into poetry that recalls the sonnets. *Measure for Measure* is praised because its form overcomes the limitations of its subject, and is again compared to painting, this time an Italian fresco. The third essay, 'Shakespeare's English Kings', is the most extensive, claiming that Shakespeare's sympathies lay with the monarchs defeated in the struggle for Tudor primacy, again stressing the importance of formal structures, although here arguing that Shakespeare's plays are at their finest when they achieve a 'unity of lyrical effect' of the kind found in music. Pater's insistence elsewhere that all art 'aspires to the condition of music' in aiming for a perfect integration of form and content clearly underlies these essays, and this gives them a unique quality that emphasizes the structural force of the plays while retaining their distance as an aesthetic construction, offering comments about the design of character and the idea of historical nationalism through discussion of how these elements are achieved. The tone is relaxed, the writing consisting largely of general statements about the plays; but this rests on a thorough knowledge of their operations as aesthetic and intellectual objects. Unlike those in earlier writing, the generalizations are born of thoroughgoing exploration of the texts, rather than arising from a desire to place each within a particular period of the dramatist's work, show authorial maturity or demonstrate national identity. In none of the essays does Pater explore the moral issues raised in the plays.

The writer who moved farthest away from the reverential tone of earlier critics, with their stress on Shakespeare's moral power, was George Bernard Shaw. In 1895 he began writing theatre criticism for the *Saturday Review* under the pseudonym of Corno di Bassetto, reflecting an interest in music which is fundamental to his approach to Shakespeare's plays. Repeatedly in his reviews, letters, and other writing he stresses the importance of the sounds of Shakespeare's language rather than the moral power or human understanding of the plays. These he summarized in a letter to *The Daily News* in April 1905:

Shakespeare's power lies in his enormous command of word music, which gives fascination to his most blackguardly repartees and sublimity to his hollowest platitudes.

In part, this is polemical writing of a skilled self-publicist, but the shift of emphasis belongs to a larger change in attitude seen in other aspects of criticism and performance. It marks a move away from morality towards the immediate sensory aspects of dramatic poetry that are one aspect of the so-called aesthetic movement, where the precise identity of the art object is seen as its only value, and art for art's sake replaces art for the sake of moral improvement.

Treatment of the *Sonnets* at the period's close was dominated by three texts, which again reflect something of the paradoxes of the last years. A major development was the 1898 edition of *Shakespeare's Poems* by George Wyndham. By including *Venus and Adonis, Lucrece* and the *Sonnets*, although neither 'The Phoenix and the Turtle' nor *The Passionate Pilgrim*, it did much to establish the non-dramatic writings within the canon. Its substantial introduction engages with the themes and sources of the poems, placing them all within both English and European conventions and containing sections discussing imagery, 'verbal music', and 'eloquent discourse', approaches that lean towards methods of reading that would become prominent in the middle years of the next century. The texts themselves have full annotations and comments that are still valuable today—and in some cases are cited as authoritative in major present-day editions. The discussion of *Venus and Adonis* and *Lucrece* explores the poems' sources and their treatment and, here as with the *Sonnets*, the annotation is extensive, scholarly, and thoughtful. The edition is also important for what it omits. While accepting that the *Sonnets* come from a basis of human understanding, Wyndham makes no attempt at biographical reading; and he discusses the narrative poems in relation to Ovid, Chaucer, and poems on related themes by Shakespeare's immediate predecessors rather than in terms of their morality. Wyndham was a significant scholar in many fields, editing North's *Plutarch* and writing on Ronsard; the placement of the poems within this intellectual and aesthetic frame did much to enhance their status as something far beyond confessional autobiography.

Quite a different stance is taken by Samuel Butler in his *Shakespeare's Sonnets*, published a year after Wyndham's edition. Traditional in following the earlier pattern of establishing a chronology and new order for the collection through biographical conjecture, it was radically new in coming as close as was legally possible to arguing that the poems were the product of a relationship between Shakespeare and a young man identified only as William Hughes, 'more boy than man', in 1585. The sonnets were given to Hughes, who, angry at Shakespeare's cooling affections, gave them to Thorpe for publication—an event, Butler argues, that was 'exquisitely painful to Shakespeare'. Butler's rearrangement of the poems rests on the supposition that the final group of sonnets, addressed to the 'Dark Lady', were moved by Hughes from their original place after the first group, to avoid their being linked with those urging him to marry and unite 'his own mistress and his friend'. Butler's approach is far from what in present-day terms would be a triumphalist outing of the poet, however. He calls the encounter a 'grave indiscretion', revealing a 'leprous or cancerous trait' in the poet, and claims that the poems were intended only for Hughes' eyes, making their later readers 'receivers of stolen goods'. The volume's introduction concludes by saying that 'the love of the English poet for Mr W. H. was, though only for a short time, more Greek than English. I cannot explain this.' For present-day readers there is a curious contradiction here, given Butler's own bisexual nature. Seen within the time of the volume's publication, Butler's attitude is more easily understood, since he is essentially addressing two audiences. For those interested in the poems who retained a traditional view of Shakespeare as the English ideal, he is at pains to make clear that the episode with Hughes was a moral fault. For those with a more advanced attitude to what at the time was known as Hellenism or Greek love, following the work of Havelock Ellis and others, the edition becomes almost a celebratory statement of Shakespeare's sexuality. And the volume does achieve a certain academic stature by concluding with a typographic facsimile of the 1609 edition, something not easily available elsewhere.

Butler's edition also needs to be seen within the shadow of a major event of the 1890s, the trial and subsequent imprisonment of Oscar Wilde for indecency and sodomy in 1895. Some years before, Wilde had published his own approach to the *Sonnets*, 'The Portrait of Mr. W.H.', which appeared first in *Blackwood's Magazine* in 1889. In many ways a *roman à clef* about Wilde's own sexuality, it is also a very skilful engagement with many of the preoccupations of Victorian Bardolatry, couched in a careful, serious parody of the style of contemporary magazine fiction. The story hinges on the discovery of a portrait of a young man, in the style of 'François Clouet's later work', that a friend of the fictional narrator identifies as 'some wonderful boy actor of great beauty' named Will Hughes. Its discovery in an Elizabethan coffer in Warwickshire nicely parodies the discovery of portraits of Shakespeare himself, and the name of the subject explains the punning references to 'will' in some of the sonnets—both skilful appropriations of the methods of many critics who sought to explain or identify portraits or biographical allusions, genuine or forged, throughout the Victorian period. The story is much darker, however, ending with the death of the central figure when the painting is exposed as a forgery. This is the plot of the original story; but between its appearance and 1893 Wilde extended it to double its original 12,000 words, adding a lengthy passage on the order of the sonnets and arranging them in four main groups, developing an elaborate argument to justify W. H. as Hughes, and discussing the aesthetics of the Renaissance, which 'already touched Hellenism at so many points', complete with allusions to Montaigne, Ficino, and Pico della Mirandola. The extended version remained unpublished until 1920, when it appeared in a limited edition.

What makes the story's later version valuable in the history of Victorian Shakespeare activity is that the reader is never really certain whether it is an elaborate parody of the academic searches that surround the *Sonnets*, or a serious suggestion designed to replace those of Charles Knight and many others. Seen in this way, the relationship with Butler's edition becomes more complex: that work becomes almost a tribute to Wilde's writing, presenting a serious argument about a Will Hughes to balance the fictitious one invented by Wilde. When seen within the frame of Wilde's arrest, the complex relation between the two works places the *Sonnets* at the centre of another, much sadder, aspect of Victorian private life made brutally public, as perhaps the most sombre instance of Shakespeare's presence in every level of thought and feeling. There was also a longer-term consequence. In the early years of the new century, the writing of sonnets became an established code for homoerotic exchange; and during the First World War some of Wilfred Owen's finest poems, including the sonnet 'Anthem for Doomed Youth', are deeply enriched by associations of this kind.

Meanwhile, the establishment view of Shakespeare was confirmed by the appearance in 1898 of the revised, extended version of Sidney Lee's biography, modestly called *A Life of William Shakespeare*. The title's reticence was only partially confirmed by the work itself, which sought to clarify uncertainties and erase errors in earlier versions. In choosing to follow Knight's approach of offering a continuous narrative it lacked the immediacy of Halliwell's biographical anthologies, but for good reason: owing its origin to the account in the *Dictionary of National Biography*, it still carried something of the imprimatur of the official, establishment version. The text is progressive, detailed, and still readable today, balancing consideration of the plays and the events of Shakespeare's life, rejecting excessive circumstantial detail or speculation yet supporting all its statements with scrupulous annotation. Here, particularly in the discussion of dates of performance and publication, the sources of the plays or other works contemporary with them, it builds on the work of earlier Victorian scholars, especially the members of the Shakespeare Society and its successor, the latter with regard to metrical tests. While he is cautious about these, finding them 'often vague and conflicting', Lee generally follows their findings, rejecting *Titus* as largely the work of an earlier hand and claiming *Romeo and Juliet* as the first tragedy and *Love's Labour's Lost* as the first comedy. He is also careful to stress Shakespeare's indebtedness to both Marlowe and Lyly. By Victorian standards the book is fairly short, but it meets the goals set in such standards by presenting the figure as part of a national identity as much by tacit assumption as open statement, the sheer depth and detail offering itself as testimony both to the importance of its task and to the Victorian concern for method and order, despite its occasional errors, clarified by later research, and inconsistencies, apparent to diligent original readers. Its preface claims to avoid 'aesthetic studies' of the plays, yet there are points where it makes qualitative judgments in this field. Like earlier commentators it finds *Two Gentlemen of Verona* full of 'trifling and irritating conceits', but is more original about *The Merchant of Venice*, claiming that Shylock is the play's hero and complimenting the 'gentle and humorous incidents of the concluding act'. It is also at pains to restore accuracy wherever possible: one of its ten appendices contains a list of forged documents purporting to come from Shakespeare's life, mainly of Collier's invention. Ironically, given their location, the pages on the *Sonnets* argue that they cannot be read as autobiography, and instead Lee devotes many pages to the conventional forms and conceits they use, relating them not only to Daniel's *Delia* but to contemporary European sonnets. In this, like earlier assertions of Shakespeare's knowledge of European languages and literature, Lee moves further away from the idea of the independent native genius. He does, however, offer an identification for Mr W. H. as William Hall, a minor publishing functionary. There is more than a little poignancy in the fact that, just as Wilde was presenting his own reading of these cryptic letters as a way of metaphorically legitimizing his own identity through fiction, Lee, who had himself constructed a new identity through his change of name, was offering a reading far less contentious.

Towards the end of the century, before and around the time of Wilde's trial and the appearance of Lee's *Life*, theatrical performance was pursuing paths that again demonstrate the clash between convention and innovation. In 1888 Irving had produced a *Macbeth* that, complete with illusionistic flying witches, massive architectural forms, and armies of supernumeraries sweeping across rocky plains, perhaps marked the apogee of naturalistic scenography. In 1895, he turned to *Cymbeline* as his last new Shakespearian production of the century, himself playing Iachimo, with Ellen Terry as Imogen. Scenography was again elaborate, with seventeen separate sets including a vast built-up cave of Belisarius and an elaborate throne-room for the final judgment scene; to accommodate scene changes and to focus the play more fully on Iachimo, the text was heavily cut, losing about 2,000 lines from its original 3,750. Most contemporary reviewers commented on the youthful femininity and vigour of Terry, then aged forty-eight; others found her addition of interjections and asides distracting, and she herself complained that the production moved far too slowly. Irving's Iachimo was puzzling. Some saw his interpretation as turning the part into a tragic hero misled by his own evil actions, but moving towards final repentance in a scene that built on paintings of Christ before Pilate; after the production, Irving himself reputedly told William Winter, who had assisted in making the cuts, that '*Cymbeline*, except for Imogen, isn't worth a damn, for the stage'. The familiar Victorian pattern of actor-manager constructing text and scene around himself and his leading lady had continued, but the response of reviewers and audience showed something missing: that Terry was admired for the resemblance to her earlier triumphs suggests that the play was approached in a spirit of nostalgia, even melancholy. That, when it closed, it was succeeded by a revival of *The Bells*, Irving's first great success, again hints at a desire to recapture past glories.

Despite these backward glances, there were elements of the new in the production. A month before the play opened, George Bernard Shaw wrote to Terry, giving advice about which lines she should cut, how she should approach others, and what aspects of stage business she should retain. Terry responded by sending Irving's acting edition, and Shaw's response is worth quoting at length because it reveals the difference between the two men's approaches to Shakespeare:

Generally speaking, the cutting of the play is stupid to the last extremity. Even from the broadest popular view, the omission of the grandiose scene about England and Caesar for the queen, Cloten and the Roman, is a mistake. Cloten's part is spoiled. Every part is spoiled except 'the governor's; and he has actually damaged his own by wantonly cutting off your white and azure eyelids laced with blue of heaven's own tinct.

Shaw is not objecting to the cutting of the play as such, but rather to the way in which it has been done. The detailed objection reveals an approach to the play as a balanced unity, showing a concern for the overall rhythm of the production quite distinct from the tradition of giving the actor-manager an importance that distorts the whole. Although in his earlier correspondence Shaw had complained that much of the play is dull, he stresses at the end of the passage quoted above the importance of retaining Iachimo's own lines (2.2.22–3) spoken over the sleeping Imogen. Again, Shaw shows his concern for 'word music', something often overlooked by performers of an earlier generation. The confrontation between the old order and the new seen here is echoed in another detail of the performance. The relatively minor role of Arviragus was played by a figure who would become a major influence in European theatre in the next century, Terry's son, Edward Gordon Craig, whose concept of the *Übermarionett* would undermine the whole concept of acting as personation, instead moving the focus onto language and, at its most extreme, pure movement.

Contemporary with Irving's later productions was the work of a small group of performers concerned with approaching the plays quite differently, rejecting extreme naturalism and intensely felt characterization in favour of something approaching the conditions and style of Shakespeare's own time. In an article in the magazine *Theatre* William Poel, the leading figure in this new movement, spoke of realism as 'enervating and exhausting' and argued that his own production style would 'stimulate and fertilize'. In 1879 Poel founded The Elizabethans, a group meeting in schools and church halls to give readings of the plays in their earliest forms. In the next two years he worked as an instructor for the Shakespeare Reading Society, a group founded at University College London—the coming together of the worlds of theatre and academy should not be underestimated in its importance. In 1881 he directed a performance of the first Quarto *Hamlet* at St. George's Hall, a setting thought to be closer to Shakespeare's theatre than most professional playing-spaces in London. Poel himself took the title role, with Maud Holt, Lady Tree, as Ophelia; Bernard Partridge was Laertes. This led to the foundation of the Elizabethan Shakespeare Society, with the aim of performing the plays 'with only those stage appliances which were usually applied during the Elizabethan period'. It was not simply that the players acted on a bare stage: their performance attempted to return to sixteenth-century style, avoiding psychological or interactive effects and instead encouraging comparatively rapid delivery emphasizing the musical, rhythmic patterns of the verse. To reinforce this, Poel cast the plays partly according to the actors' vocal ranges, as if selecting the voices in a choral group. The involvement of Arnold Dolmetsch in providing music contemporary to the plays in place of the rich, post-Wagnerian scores of late-Victorian fashion was also important in generating a quite different relation between audience and performance, as well as suggesting the involvement of Shakespeare production with other leading areas of artistic activity.

On 7 December 1895, to mark what was thought to be the tercentenary of its first performance, Poel mounted *The Comedy of Errors* in the hall of Gray's Inn. There was no stage, and the actors performed before the screen wall of the hall, entering through the serving doors, with the audience arranged in a squared horseshoe configuration before them. The play ran without an interval, and at the close the Queen's Prayer from the Tudor comedy *Ralph Roister Doister* was spoken by the cast, and an ensemble led by Arnold Dolmetsch gave a recital of Elizabethan music. To Shaw it was 'a delectable entertainment which defies all description by the pen'. Two years later, *Twelfth Night* was given at Middle Temple Hall, again the conjectural site of its first performance. A raised platform stage was constructed, flanked by classical columns, with a roof and rear gallery, based on the de Witt sketch of the original Swan Theatre. Halberdiers stood on and beside the stage and in the approaching corridors, and Dolmetsch composed Elizabethan-style music, played on sixteenth century instruments. The authenticity was, however, moderated in one way, all the characters in Olivia's household being dressed in black and those from Duke Orsino's in red.

Poel's productions in the century's final years included *Measure for Measure*, *The Two Gentlemen of Verona* and *The Tempest*, as well as *Doctor Faustus*, *The Duchess of Malfi* and scenes from *Arden of Faversham* and *Edward III*. Yet the revival was not without irony. As early as 1844 *The Taming of the Shrew* had been performed in conditions designed to replicate those of Shakespeare's time: it was produced by James Robinson Planché, whose designs for the history plays were one of the major forces behind the growth of historical spectacular in Shakespearian theatre.

Performance of this kind, with its emphasis on verse speaking and the absence of any single star, was quite the opposite of the heavily scenographic, heavily cut star-vehicles of the Lyceum and Her Majesty's, and at first drew heavy criticism. William Archer dismissed it as the preserve of 'the dilettante and the enthusiast' and described it as 'acted after the manner of the Nineteenth Century Amateur'. The idea of performance without scenery was forcefully rejected by Beerbohm Tree in an address to the Oxford Union in 1900, arguing that Shakespeare would have used elaborate scenery had the techniques for its manufacture been available—a suggestion that the carpenters and shipbuilders of Shakespeare's day would surely have found deeply insulting. Yet the new approach also drew strong support. Shaw, hearing Shakespeare's word music at last being given full attention, was generous in his praise: 'the effect was magnificent, unforgettable'. Edmund Gosse, seeing the 1903 revival of *Twelfth Night*, called it 'one of the most inspiring and most poetical at which I have ever been present'. In 1899, Poel produced *Richard II* with the title role played by Harley Granville Barker; later, Barker continued Poel's work in returning to something approaching Shakespearian performance conditions. While, in Barker's work, authenticity of staging was modified in its minimalism by modernist drops and costumes, the emphasis on verse speaking remained, to become one of the dominant features of English Shakespeare production for at least the next half century.

Taken together, these strands of Shakespeare activity from the final years of the Victorian period suggest, as much through controversy as consistency, that criticism of the texts and performance of the plays were both entering a vigorous new phase. It would not be quite true to say that performance rested on the discoveries and revisions made by two generations of editors and scholars: then as now, the stage had its own priorities when forming a text. But at least the editorial work had been done, and was there for those who, like Poel, chose to make use of it. The Cambridge edition, and the single-play volumes of Pitt Press, Clarendon, and Warwick Shakespeares, along with the newly launched Arden, gave scope and fuel to academic study at all levels; and the lectures of Bradley and the writings of other critics offered directions in which this study might proceed. It was a lively, dynamic ending to the period, its controversies powerful and continuing, giving to the new generation of performers, critics, scholars, and readers a forceful range of Shakespeares with which they could disagree and debate according to their own tastes and directions.

Queen Victoria died on 22 January 1901: opinions differ as to when the Victorian age ended. In December 1914, as the first year of war neared its close, *The Sphere*, a journal launched in the last year of the century to rival the *Illustrated London News*, devoted a full page to a picture of the cliffs at Dover with, facing it, an extended quotation of John of Gaunt's speech from Act 2 of *Richard II*—'This royal throne of kings,/This earth of majesty, this seat of Mars'. It did not, though, include the culmination of the speech—'Is now leased out, I die pronouncing it,/Like to a tenement or pelting farm'. If, as some would have it, the Victorian age ended only at the moment war came, its confident appropriation of Shakespeare to reflect its own self image did not falter. Every age reconfigures the poet and his works for its own ideologies, and in this brief, fragile statement of certainty the Victorian construction of Shakespeare seems, in its brittle earnestness, as clear as ever.

1837 Charles Heath: *The Shakespeare Gallery*
C. R. Leslie: *Florizel and Perdita*
Charles Dickens: *Posthumous Papers of the Pickwick Club*
1837–9 William Charles Macready manager at Covent Garden
1838 William Mulready: *Seven Ages of Man*
Dickens: *Oliver Twist*
Charles Darwin: *The Voyage of the Beagle*
Charles Lyell: *Elements of Geology*
Regular transatlantic steamship service begun
Macready restores Fool to *King Lear*
1838–43 Charles Knight's *Pictorial Shakspere* and *The Works of Shakspere*, edited by
  Barry Cornwall and illustrated by Kenny Meadows, issued in serial parts
1839 Henry Rowley Bishop: incidental music to *Love's Labour's Lost*
Henry Fox Talbot invents photographic prints on treated paper
Dickens: *Nicholas Nickleby*
1839–41 Madame Vestris manager at Covent Garden
1840 Shakespeare Society founded
Thomas Carlyle: 'The Poet as Hero' lecture
Anna Brownell Jameson: *Shakespeare's Heroines* (earlier published as *Charac-
  teristics of Women, Moral, Poetical and Historical*)
Daniel Maclise: *Letter Scene in Twelfth Night*
Queen Victoria marries Prince Albert of Saxe-Coburg Gotha
Penny post established
1841 first Bradshaw's railway guide
Thomas Carlyle: *On Heroes and Hero-worship*
James Orchard Halliwell: *Shakespeareana*
John Keble: *Tracts for the Times*
John Henry Newman: *Remarks on Certain Passages in the Thirty-Nine Articles*
Punch founded
1841–3 Macready manager of Drury Lane
1841–51 Barry Sullivan tours England, Scotland, New York, and Australia
1842 John Payne Collier: *Reasons for a New Edition of Shakespeare's Works*
Daniel Maclise: *Play Scene in Hamlet*
Alfred, Lord Tennyson: 'Ulysses' published (written 1830)

Copyright Act—works in copyright for 42 years after publication or seven after author's death

Mudie's Circulating Library founded

Illustrated London News founded

1842–4 John Payne Collier: *Works of Shakespeare*

1843 Theatre Regulation Act abolishes patent theatres' exclusive rights

F. W. Fairholt: *Home of Shakespeare Illustrated*

Thomas Babington Macaulay: *Critical and Historical Essays*

A. W. N. Pugin: *Apology for the Revival of Christian Architecture*

John Ruskin: *Modern Painters*, i

1844 Ben Webster and James Robinson Planché produce *Taming of the Shrew* in Elizabethan manner.

Musical Times founded

Sir Thomas More, edited by Alexander Dyce

1844–5 Charles Calvert manager at Surrey Theatre

1844–62 Samuel Phelps manager at Sadler's Wells.

1845 Mary Cowden Clarke: *Complete Concordance to Shakespeare*

Disraeli: *Sybil, or The Two Nations*

1846 *The Two Noble Kinsmen* edited by Alexander Dyce

1847 Shakespeare's Birthplace purchased

Shakespeare Birthplace Trust founded

Currer Bell (Charlotte Brontë): *Jane Eyre: An Autobiography*

Ellis Bell (Emily Brontë): *Wuthering Heights*

Acton Bell (Anne Brontë): *Agnes Grey*

1847–8 Fanny Kemble's final stage appearances

1847–55 Madame Vestris manager at Drury Lane

1848 Pamphlet *A Home for Shakespeare* begins campaign for a national theatre

J. O. Halliwell: *A Life of William Shakespeare*

Royal Command performances begun

Charles and Ellen Kean perform in New York

Brunel commissions paintings for 'Shakespeare Room'

Marx and Engels: *Communist Manifesto*

John Stuart Mill: *Political Economy*

Pre-Raphaelite Brotherhood founded

1849 N. J. Halpin: *The Dramatic Unities of Shakespeare*

John Everett Millais exhibits *Ferdinand Lured by Ariel*

Charlotte Brontë: *Shirley*

Notes & Queries founded

Macaulay: *History of England*, i and ii (iii and iv, 1855)

1849–50 Dickens: *David Copperfield*

1850 Elizabeth Barrett Browning: *Sonnets from the Portuguese*

Tennyson: *In Memoriam A. H. H.*

Wordsworth: *The Prelude* (rev. 1851)

Household Words founded

1850–59 Charles Kean manager at Princess's Theatre

1850–1 'Tallis Shakespeare', edited by Halliwell, with engravings copied from daguerreotype photographs.

1851 Mary Cowden Clarke: *Girlhood of Shakespeare's Heroines*

Holman Hunt: *Valentine Rescuing Sylvia from Proteus* and Collins: *Convent Thoughts*

Millais: *Mariana*

Henry Mayhew: *London Labour and the London Poor*

Ruskin: *Pre-Raphaelitism*

Great Exhibition

1852 Mendelssohn's *Midsummer Night's Dream* music played at Norwich festival

Millais exhibits *Ophelia*, and Holman Hunt *The Hireling Shepherd*

Collier claims to find 'Perkins Folio', with his own forged notes

Matthew Arnold: *Empedocles on Etna, and other poems*

1852–3 Dickens: *Bleak House*

1853 William Holman Hunt: *Claudio and Isabella.*

Arnold: *Poems* (first collected edition)

1853–9 John Hatton musical director and composer for Kean at the Princess's Theatre

1853–65 *Works of Shakespeare* edited by Halliwell

1854 *Works of Shakespeare* edited by Nikolaus Delius

W. S. Walker: *Shakespeare's Versification*

August Manns founds Crystal Palace Orchestra

Crimean War begins (ending 1856)

Dickens: *Hard Times*

Coventry Patmore: *The Betrothal* (*The Angel in the House*, i) ii, 1856

1854–6 'Stratford Edition' of works, edited by Charles Knight

1855 Sidney Dobell and Alexander Smith: *Sonnets on the War*

Elizabeth Gaskell: *North and South*

Fall of Sebastopol

1855–9 William Chappell: *Popular Music of the Olden Time*

1856 Ruskin: *Modern Painters*, iii and iv

Elizabeth Barrett Browning: *Aurora Leigh*

National Portrait Gallery founded (opened 1896), with Chandos portrait of Shakespeare its first item.

Delia Bacon: *Philosophy of the Plays of Shakespeare*

1856–60: *The Plays of Shakespeare*, edited by Howard Staunton, illustrated by John Gilbert, issued in serial parts

1857 *Works of Shakespeare* edited by Dyce

Charles Bathurst: *Difference in Shakespeare's Versification*

Dickens: *Little Dorrit*

Opening of railway to Stratford-upon-Avon

1857–61 Henry Buckle: *History of Civilization in England*

1858 Mendelssohn's wedding march from *Midsummer Night's Dream* played at marriage of Princess Royal

East India Company gives powers to crown

Hallé orchestra founded (Manchester)

Sinn Fein founded

William Morris: *Defence of Guinevere and Other Poems*

Herbert Spencer: *Essays: Scientific, Political and Speculative*

1858–9 facsimiles of *Hamlet* Q1 and Q2

1859 Parallel text of *Romeo and Juliet* Q1 and Q2, edited by Tycho Mommsen

George Eliot: *Adam Bede*

Tennyson: *Idylls of the King*

Darwin: *On the Origin of Species by Natural Selection*

Samuel Smiles: *Self-Help*

1859–60 *Works of Shakespeare* edited by Mary Cowden Clarke

1859–75 Charles Calvert manager at Theatre Royal, Manchester

1860 John Bucknill: *Medical Knowledge of Shakespeare*

Augustus Morgan: *The Mind of Shakespeare*

George Eliot: *Mill on the Floss*

1861 Charles Fechter performs Hamlet

Shakespeare Fund established

Palgrave's Golden Treasury

American Civil War begins

1861–71 E. W. Ashbee and J. O. Halliwell: Quarto facsimiles, 48 vols.

1862 George Meredith: *Modern Love*

Mary Elizabeth Braddon: *Lady Audley's Secret*

Christina Rossetti: *Goblin Market*

John Stuart Mill: *Utilitarianism*

1862–4 Lionel Booth: Typographic facsimile of First Folio

1863 Georg Gottfried Gervinus: *Shakespeare Commentaries*

John Connolly: *Study of Hamlet*

Metropolitan Railway opened—first underground railway in London

1863–6 *Works* (Cambridge Shakespeare), edited by W. G. Clark, J. Glover, and W. Aldis Wright published in nine volumes by Macmillan

1863–88 Edward Saker at Alexandra Theatre, Liverpool

1864 Tercentenary celebrations in London and Stratford-upon-Avon

Works (Globe edition), using the Cambridge text

Early English Text Society founded

The Complete Works of Shakspere, edited by John Dicks

Halliwell: *Historical Account of New Place*

John Ruskin: 'Of Queens' Gardens'

Arthur Sullivan: incidental music to *The Tempest*

Robert Browning: 'Caliban upon Setebos'

J. Hain Friswell: *Life Portraits of William Shakespeare*

1864–5 Dickens: *Our Mutual Friend*

1864–6 Howard Staunton: photolithographic facsimile of First Folio

1864–9 Charles and Mary Cowden Clarke: *Plays* (*Cassell's Illustrated Shakespeare*)

1865 Charles Knight: *Life of Shakespeare*, expanded edition

Shakespeare's Songs and Sonnets edited by Palgrave

Arnold: *Essays in Criticism*

1867 Matthew Arnold: 'Dover Beach' published (written c.1851)

Second Reform Bill

1868 Shakespeare Museum opened next to New Place, Stratford

William Barnes: *Poems of Rural Life in Common English*

Wilkie Collins: *The Moonstone*

1868–97 Clarendon Shakespeare, 17 vols, each with separate editor, for school use

1869 Arnold: *Culture and Anarchy*

F. D. Maurice: *Social Morality*

E. A. Abbott: *A Shakespearean Grammar*

1870 E. Cobham Brewer: *Dictionary of Phrase and Fable*

Forster's Education Act makes possible education from ages 5–12

Franco-Prussian war (–1871)

1870–72 Eliot: *Middlemarch*

1870–81 Dante Gabriel Rossetti: *The House of Life*

1870–1911 Editions of separate plays by William J. Rolfe for use in American schools

1871 German empire founded

Hardy: *Desperate Remedies*

Samuel Smiles: *Character*

Variorum Shakespeare edited by Horace H. Furness and Horace H. Furness Jr begun in USA (completed 1928)

Thomas Hardy: *Under the Greenwood Tree*

1873 Frederick Gard Fleay and Frederick James Furnivall found New Shakspere Society (–1894)

Louisa Starr: *Imogen inside the Cave of Belisarius*

Millais: *Bare ruined choirs*

Leichner introduces grease paint

Walter Pater: *The Renaissance*, revised 1877

John Henry Newman: *The Idea of a University*

1873–5 *The Library Shakspere*

1873–6 *The Works of Shakespeare* (Charles Knight's '*Imperial Shakespeare*')

1873–9 *Collins' School and College Classics* in separate volumes

1874 Halliwell-Phillips: *Illustrations of the Life of Shakespeare*

E. W. Godwin begins articles on 'Architecture and Costumes of Shakespeare's Plays'

Hardy: *Far from the Madding Crowd*

Fleay's *Metrical Tables* published by New Shakespeare Society

1874–75 Alexander Schmidt: *Shakespeare-Lexicon*

1875 Edward Dowden: *Shakspere: A Critical Study of His Mind and Art*

W. W. Skeat, (ed.): *Shakespeare's Plutarch*, translation by North

Tennyson: *Queen Mary*

Gilbert and Sullivan: *Trial by Jury* (first comic operetta)

1875–8 Collier's 4th edition of Shakespeare's *Works*, including *Edward III*

1876 Halliwell-Phillipps reduced photolithographic facsimile of First Folio

Mrs G. Linnaeus Banks: *Manchester Man*

1877 *Leopold Shakespeare*, including *Two Noble Kinsmen*, introduction by Furnivall

Edward German: Symphonic poem *Hamlet*

Dowden: *Shakspere*

The Nineteenth Century founded

1878 Henry Irving and Ellen Terry as Hamlet and Ophelia

James Hamilton Clarke musical director for Irving, with first permanent theatre orchestra

Hardy: *The Return of the Native*

1878–92 Irving manager at Lyceum

1879 Shakespeare Memorial Theatre, Stratford-upon-Avon, opens, with Barry Sullivan as manager (–1886)

William Poel founds The Elizabethans

Walter Bagehot: *Literary Studies*

1880 Saxe-Meiningen Company performs *Julius Caesar* in London

Algernon Charles Swinburne: *Study of Shakespeare*

David Main (ed.): *Treasury of English Sonnets*

The Stage founded

Education Act makes schooling compulsory to age 10

1880–82 Helena Modjeska performs in London

1880–91 Quarto facsimiles edited by Furnivall and others

1881 William Poel produces *Hamlet* First Quarto

Elizabethan Stage Society founded

Halliwell-Phillipps: *Outlines for the Life of Shakespeare*

T. H. Huxley: *Science and Culture*

1882 'Standards' introduced in schools, including reading passages from Shakespeare

1884 Tommaso Salvini as Hamlet

First part of the *Oxford English Dictionary* published

Third Reform Bill

1885 Richard Moulton: *Shakespeare as a Dramatic Artist*

Helen Faucit: *On Some of Shakespeare's Female Characters*

Dictionary of National Biography begun

1886 Frank Benson directs Shakespeare Theatre Festival at Stratford-upon-Avon (–1919)

Ben Greet establishes his own company, for open-air productions and performances at Stratford

English Historical Review founded

1887 Hardy: *The Woodlanders*

1887–97 Beerbohm Tree manager at Haymarket.

1888 Sarah Bernhardt as Lady Macbeth in Edinburgh and London

Arthur Sullivan: Music for Irving's *Macbeth*

Frederick Corder: *Prospero* overture

W. E. Henley: *Graphic Gallery of Shakespeare's Heroines*

Conan Doyle: *A Study in Scarlet*

1888–90 'The Henry Irving Shakespeare'

1889 Walter Pater: *Appreciations*, including 'Shakespeare's English Kings'

Oscar Wilde: 'The Portrait of Mr. W. H.'

W. B. Yeats: *The Wanderings of Oisin*

1890 Ward & Lock's *Sixpenny Shakespeare*

Henry James: *The Tragic Muse*

1890–1936 Pitt Press Shakespeare, Cambridge University Press

1891 Edward German: Music for Irving's *Henry VIII*, later an orchestral suite

Birthplace Trust takes over management of New Place

Hardy: *Tess of the d'Urbervilles* (rev. 1892)

George Bernard Shaw: *The Quintessence of Ibsenism*

Wilde: *The Picture of Dorian Gray*

1892 Millais: *Blow, blow thou winter wind*

Birthplace Trust purchases Anne Hathaway's Cottage

Gustav Mahler conducts Wagner's *Ring* in London

1893 Augustin Daly opens Daly's Theatre in London, with Ada Rehan as leading woman actor

1893–1938 *Warwick Shakespeare*, general editor C. H. Herford H. Herford

1894–6 *Temple Shakespeare* (40 vols.) edited by Israel Gollancz

1895 Poel produces *Comedy of Errors*

Henry Irving knighted

John Bartlett: *Shakespeare Concordance*

Hardy: *Jude the Obscure*

Henry Wood Promenade Concerts begun

H. G. Wells: *The Time Machine*

1895–8 George Bernard Shaw theatre critic of *Saturday Review*

1896 Thomas Donovan, editor of *English History Plays* adds plays by Shakespeare's contemporaries to complete the historical canon

George Saintsbury: *A History of Nineteenth-century Literature*

1897 Poel produces *Twelfth Night* in Middle Temple Hall

Her Majesty's Theatre opened by Henry Beerbohm Tree

1898 *Shakespeare's Poems*, edited by George Wyndham

Sidney Lee: *A Life of William Shakespeare*

Elizabeth Forbes: *Imogen Lying among the Flowers*

Hardy: *Wessex Poems*

1899 Sarah Bernhardt as Hamlet

Poel produces *Richard II* with Harley Granville Barker as the King

Tree acts death of King John as first Shakespeare film

First Arden Shakespeare edition, *Hamlet*, edited by Dowden

Shakespeare's Sonnets, edited by Samuel Butler

1900 Labour party founded

Tree's *A Midsummer Night's Dream* at Her Majesty's Theatre

1901 Arthur Quiller-Couch: *The Oxford Book of English Verse 1250–1900*

George Bernard Shaw: *Three Plays for Puritans*

Death of Queen Victoria, 22 January

1904 A. C. Bradley *Shakespearean Tragedy*

Further Reading

There are several general works on Shakespeare in the Victorian period. A fine introductory study is *Shakespeare and the Victorians*, by Adrian Poole (London: Arden Critical Companions, 2004). Two volumes of essays, exploring a range of topics treated here, are collected in *Victorian Shakespeare*, edited by Adrian Poole and Gail Marshall (2 vols, London: Palgrave Macmillan, 2003). Covering a slightly longer period is another collection, *Shakespeare in the Nineteenth Century*, edited by Gail Marshall (Cambridge: Cambridge University Press, 2012); it has important lists of productions in London theatres and tables of productions of each play by year, although strangely these stop at 1899, not 1900. Wider perspectives are taken by Gary Taylor in the relevant parts of *Reinventing Shakespeare: A Cultural History, from the Restoration to the Present* (London and New York: Weidenfeld and Nicholson, 1989). The annual publication *Shakespeare Survey* (Cambridge: Cambridge University Press) is especially valuable for articles on individual performers, directors, editors, and critics. Many Victorian editions of Shakespeare, including that of the Bowdlers and the 'Henry Irving Shakespeare', and other works of relevance, have been reissued in the Cambridge Library Series of reprints using texts from Cambridge University Library by Cambridge University Press; others are available through Project Gutenberg or other free download services.

CHAPTER I: SHAKESPEARE THE VICTORIAN

The best account of the tercentenary celebrations is given in *The Shakespeare Tercentenary of 1864* by Richard Foukes (London: Society for Theatre Research, 1964). The wider frames of Shakespearian activity are covered by Andrew Murphy in *Shakespeare for the People* (Cambridge: Cambridge University Press, 2010) and Nicholas Rose, *The Intellectual Life of the British Working Classes* (New Haven and London: Yale University Press, 2002). A more specific approach is taken by Gail Marshall in *Shakespeare and Victorian Women* (Cambridge: Cambridge University Press, 2009), and an overview of reading practices is offered by Richard Altick's *The English Common Reader: a Social History of the Mass Reading Public, 1800–1900* (Chicago: University of Chicago Press, 1957), still invaluable in many areas, including sales figures. Alan R. Young's *Punch and Shakespeare in the*

Victorian Era (Bern and New York: Peter Lang, 2007) is a fascinating, copiously illustrated study. Commercial activity is explored by various essays in *The Cambridge Companion to Shakespeare and Popular Culture*, edited by Robert Shaughnessy (Cambridge: Cambridge University Press, 2007). Works discussing areas covered in greater detail elsewhere will be given in the relevant later chapters.

CHAPTER 2: SCHOLARSHIP, EDITING, AND CRITICISM

The indispensable guide to the history of editing is Andrew Murphy's *Shakespeare in Print* (Cambridge: Cambridge University Press, 2003). As to the editions themselves, many are easily found with second-hand and antiquarian booksellers, either online or in the flesh. Single volumes of the larger editions are often much cheaper; collectors often prefer complete sets with luxurious bindings, so odd copies can provide a very good way of gaining the Victorian reading experience at first hand. Charles Knight's *Passages of a Working Life* (2 vols, London: Bradbury and Evans, 1864) is intriguing, although one suspects that in places it is more than a little economical with the truth. An important editorial issue is discussed by Stanley Wells and Gary Taylor in *Modernizing Shakespeare's Spelling* (Oxford: Oxford University Press, 1979). The history of illustrated editions is covered in *The Illustrated Shakespeare, 1709–1875* by Stuart Sillars (Cambridge: Cambridge University Press, 2008); Jonathan Bate's 'Pictorial Shakespeare: Text, Stage, Illustration' in *Book Illustrated: Text, Image, and Culture, 1730–1930*, edited by Catherine J. Golden (New Castle, DE: Oak Knoll Press, 2000, 31–59); and 'Performing Shakespeare in Print: Narratives in Nineteenth-Century Illustrated Shakespeares' by Peter Holland in Marshall and Poole (2. 47–72). More specialized is Alan R. Young's *Hamlet and the Visual Arts 1709–1900* (Newark, NJ: University of Delaware Press and London: Associated University Presses, 2002). The history of criticism is not an area that has attracted a great deal of scholarship, but Aron Y. Stavisky in *Shakespeare and the Victorians: Roots of Modern Criticism* (Norman, OK: University of Oklahoma Press, 1967) is important. General histories of criticism, such as Arthur M. Eastman's *A Short History of Shakespeare Criticism* (New York: Random House, 1969) and Augustus Ralli's *A History of Shakespeare Criticism* (2 vols, Oxford: Oxford University Press, 1932) are also helpful. More specialized are William Benzie, *Dr. F. J. Furnivall: Victorian Scholar Adventurer* (Norman, OK: Pilgrim, 1984) and Clyde K. Hyder, *Swinburne as Critic* (London: Routledge and Kegan Paul, 1972). On the broader changes in scholarly activity, see T. W. Heyck, *The Transformation of Intellectual Life in Victorian England* (Chicago, IL: Lyceum, 1982) and *Learning in a Liberal Education: the Study of Modern*

History in the Universities of Oxford, Cambridge and Manchester 1800–1914 (Manchester: Manchester University Press, 1986).

CHAPTER 3: PERFORMANCE

Here the position is quite otherwise, with a large and growing number of books covering all aspects of theatre history, the work of individual performers and the history of individual plays in performance. All of the major editions of the plays today have introductory material that covers their stage histories, and general works on theatre history or Shakespeare studies all have sections on changing patterns and techniques of performance. Some general accounts are Michael R. Booth's *Theatre in the Victorian Age* (Cambridge: Cambridge University Press, 1991); *Performing Shakespeare in the Age of Empire* by Richard Foulkes (Cambridge: Cambridge University Press, 2002); *Victorian Spectacular Theatre* by Michael R. Booth (London: Routledge and Kegan Paul, 1969); and the collection of essays *Shakespeare and the Victorian Stage*, edited by Richard Foulkes (Cambridge: Cambridge University Press, 1986). Alicia Finkel's *Romantic Stages: Set and Costume Design in Victorian England* (Jefferson, NC and London: McFarland, 1996) gives valuable coverage to these aspects of performance. Victor Glasstone's *Victorian and Edwardian Theatres* (London: Thames and Hudson, 1975) is a fine pictorial survey, with images of many theatres now long gone, while Michael Dobson's *Shakespeare and Amateur Performance* (Cambridge: Cambridge University Press, 2011) explores a much-overlooked tradition.

In addition to these present-day surveys are a number of important works from the period itself, or shortly after it. Russell Jackson's *Victorian Theatre: The Theatre in Its Time* (London: A & C Black, 1989) collects important articles on all aspects of theatre from original Victorian sources. Also important is the three-volume *Shakespeare on the Stage* by William Winter. First published in 1911, these were reissued in 1969 (New York and London: Benjamin Blom) and give play-by-play histories of performance practice, the Victorian passages written from personal experience.

The work of individual performers is also well covered, not least by their own writings. *The Journal of William Charles Macready*, edited by J. C. Trewin, is an invaluable source for the earlier period; *The Life and Theatrical Times of Charles Kean F.S.A.* by William Cole (2 vols, London: Richard Bentley, 1859) is a highly detailed account of the years at the Princess's Theatre, with some valuable discussions of Kean's approach to historical staging. Charles Kean's editions of many of the plays have been reissued commercially as both online and print-on-demand productions; *Emigrant in Motley*, edited by J. M. D. Hardwick, presents the letters of both Keans during their visits to America and Australia.

W. May Phelps and John Forbes-Robertson offer valuable insights in *The Life and Work of Samuel Phelps* (London: Sampson Low, 1886). *Mr and Mrs Bancroft on and off the Stage, written by themselves* (London: Richard Bentley, 1889) is a joint autobiography that is revealing about the practical side of theatre management. Beerbohm Tree's *Thoughts and After Thoughts* (London and New York: Cassell, 1915) is also helpful. Two books by Hesketh Pearson discuss the figures from personal knowledge: *Beerbohm Tree* (London: Methuen, 1956) and—especially useful on Forbes-Robertson, Benson, and Waller—*The Last Actor-Managers* (London: Methuen, 1950). The Continuum *Great Shakespeareans* series contains valuable material, by both contemporary writers and later scholars, particularly on women performers.

There are many more recent accounts. Shirley S. Allen gives a full discussion of *Samuel Phelps and Sadler's Wells Theatre* (Middletown, CT: Wesleyan University Press, 1971). In *Shakespeare's Victorian Stage* Richard W. Schoch explores the staging practices of Charles Kean; *Henry Irving, Shakespearean* by Alan Hughes (Cambridge: Cambridge University Press, 1978) gives detailed descriptions of each of the main productions. Jeffery Richards' *Henry Irving: A Victorian Actor and his World* (London and New York: Hambledon and London, 2005) is valuable on both Irving and Ellen Terry as regards their public and private performances. The Saxe-Meiningen company is covered in detail by Ann Marie Koller in *The Theatre Duke* (Stanford, CA: Stanford University Press, 1984). Also important is *Actresses on the Victorian Stage* by Gail Marshall (Cambridge: Cambridge University Press, 1998).

First hand accounts from the auditorium are available in *Shakespeare in the London Theatre 1855–58* by Theodor Fontane, translated and edited by Russell Jackson (London: Society for Theatre Research, 1999); *Shaw on Shakespeare*, edited by Edwin Wilson (London: Cassell, 1961); *Henry James: the Scenic Art*, edited by Allan Wade (New York: Hill and Wang, 1957) and *Queen Victoria Goes to the Theatre*, by George Rowell (London: Elek, 1978). A more general collection is offered in *Victorian Dramatic Criticism* (London: Methuen, 1971) edited by George Rowell. The quotations from reviews cited in the text are taken from the journals named. Other valuable contemporary sources are *Dramatic Notes* and *The Dramatic List*, published annually in the later Victorian period, and still available from specialist bookshops as well as academic and many public libraries. Arthur Colby Sprague's *Shakespeare and the Actors: The Stage Business in his Plays (1660–1905)* (Cambridge MA: Harvard University Press, 1944) is also a fine resource.

CHAPTER 4: MUSIC AND VISUAL ART

There is no single full-length study of Shakespeare in Victorian music, a highly regrettable omission, so those wishing to explore further should look in general histories of English music in the period. Entries on some individual composers may be found in *The New Grove Dictionary of Music and Musicians*, edited by Stanley Sadie (London and Washington, DC: Macmillan, 1980) and *The New Grove Dictionary of Opera*, edited by Stanley Sadie (London: Oxford University Press, 1997). Even here, however, many Victorian composers remain unmentioned. Two works provide general listings of compositions: *A Shakespeare Music Catalogue* edited by Bryan N. S. Gooch and others (5 vols, Oxford: Clarendon, 1990–1991), of which the final volume is a bibliography, is the more comprehensive; *Shakespeare in Music*, edited by Phyllis Hartnoll (London: Macmillan, 1964), has a series of essays by various hands as well as a catalogue of musical works. *My Life in Music* by the conductor and founder of the Promenade Concerts, Henry Wood (London: Gollancz, 1938) is a fine account of the working life of a Victorian musician. A short general essay, 'Music for the Theatre: Style and Function in Incidental Music' by Michael Pisani appears in *The Cambridge Companion to Victorian and Edwardian Theatre*, edited by Kerry Powell (Cambridge: Cambridge University Press, 2004, 70–92). A few recordings are available, generally from second-hand or specialist suppliers.

Visual art is better covered. Martin Meisel's *Realizations: Narrative, Pictorial, and Theatrical Arts in Nineteenth-Century England* (Princeton, NJ: Princeton University Press, 1983) is as all-embracing as its title suggests. For paintings of the plays, the standard work remains *Shakespeare and the Artist* by W. Moelwyn Merchant (London: Oxford University Press, 1958), supplemented by *Shakespeare, Time and the Victorians: A Pictorial Exploration* by Stuart Sillars (Cambridge: Cambridge University Press, 2011), which also discusses the visual identities of stage design and photography. Richard Altick's *Paintings from Books: Art and Literature in Britain, 1760–1860* (Columbus, OH: Ohio State University Press, 1980) is good in placing the works within larger settings; *Shakespeare in Pictorial Art: The Studio* Special Number (London: The Studio, 1916) is important in giving an earlier view; *Shakespeare in Art*, edited by Jane Martineau, (London and New York: Merrell, 2003) is a finely illustrated exhibition catalogue that includes comments on many of the images mentioned here. A major resource are the web pages of the relevant galleries as given in the chapter, as well as the galleries themselves; of course there is no substitute for seeing the paintings in the pigment. Little has been written on the photograph, but three articles are important: Richard Foulkes, 'The Laroche Photographs of Charles Kean's Theatre Revivals', *Theatrephile* 2 (8): 29–32; David Mayer's 'Quote the Words to Prompt the Attitudes: The Victorian Performer, the Photographer and the Photograph', *Theatre Survey* 43 (2) (November 2002): 223–51; and the same author's 'The Actress as Photographic Icon: From Early Photography to Early Film', *The Cambridge Companion to the Actress*, edited by Maggie B. Gale and John Stokes (Cambridge: Cambridge University Press, 2007, 74–94). Margaret F. Harker's *Henry Peach Robinson: Master of Photographic Art 1830–1901* (Oxford: Basil Blackwell, 1988) contains brief but useful references to the Shakespearian images. As yet there is no critical study of the Shakespeare photographs of Julia Margaret Cameron, but Victoria Olsen's *From Life: Julia Margaret Cameron and Victorian Photography* (London: Aurum, 2003) provides a biographical approach.

CHAPTER 5: SHAKESPEARE, THE NOVEL, AND POETRY

Here the invaluable resource is the works themselves, all of which are available in modern editions, which come with introductions and suggested critical reading. In his *Shakespeare and the Victorians*, Adrian Poole has important things to say about the novels. Valerie Gager's *Shakespeare and Dickens: The Dynamics of Influence* (Cambridge: Cambridge University Press, 1996) is a comprehensive survey and list of quotations and allusions. *Engaging with Shakespeare: Responses of George Eliot and Other Women Novelists* by Marianne Novy (Iowa City: University of Iowa Press, 1998) and the collection edited by the same scholar, *Women's Re-visions of Shakespeare: On the Responses of Dickinson, Woolf, Rick, H.D., George Eliot, and Others* (Urbana: University of Illinois Press, 1990) address the influence of Shakespeare within a larger view of women novelists. Robert Sawyer's *Victorian Appropriations of Shakespeare: George Eliot, A. C. Swinburne, Robert Browning, and Charles Dickens* (Madison, NJ: Fairleigh Dickinson University Press and London: Associated University Presses, 2003) discusses both poetry and the novel. Three essays in the *Victorian Shakespeare* collection edited by Poole and Marshall are more specific in aim: 'Implicit and Explicit Reason: George Eliot and Shakespeare' (pp. 84–99) by Philip Davis; 'Shakespeare's Weeds: Tennyson, Elegy and Allusion' by Robert Douglas-Fairhurst (pp. 114–30) and 'Shakespeare and the Death of Tennyson' by Christopher Decker (pp. 131–49). The major authors are all freely available, and many of the less well known can be found in print-on-demand editions or online in sites such as Project Gutenberg.

CHAPTER 6: SEARCHING FOR SHAKESPEARE, POEMS, LIVES, AND PORTRAITS

The essential, if a little dated, account of all writings on Shakespeare's biography is Samuel Schoenbaum's *Shakespeare's Lives* (Oxford: Clarendon, 1971). This gives acute, extensive and often very witty readings of the major biographies, as well as exploring and criticizing their various readings of the sonnets. Marvin Spevack's *James Orchard Halliwell-Phillipps* (New Castle, DE: Oak Knoll and London: Shepheard Walwyn, 2001) covers the life and work of the scholar in full. *Shakespeare's Sonnets* by Paul Edmondson and Stanley Wells (Oxford: Oxford University Press, 2004) includes a discussion of Victorian interpretations; Joel Fineman's *Shakespeare's Perjured Eye: The Invention of Poetic Subjectivity in the Sonnets* (Berkeley and Los Angeles, CA: University of California Press, 1986) gives a broader view of the idea of autobiographical poetry. The Stratford pilgrimage cult is covered extensively by Julia Thomas in *Shakespeare's Shrine: The Bard's Birthplace and the Invention of Stratford-upon-Avon* (Philadelphia: University of Pennsylvania Press, 2012) and more selectively in her essay for the 2010 Marshall collection. *Stratford-on-Avon from the Earliest Times to the Death of Shakespeare* by Sidney Lee and Edward Hull (1885) is now available in the Cambridge Library Series (Cambridge: Cambridge University Press, 2012). F. E. Halliday's *The Cult of Shakespeare* (London: Duckworth, 1957) takes the approach further afield; Judith Flanders' *Consuming Passions: Leisure and Pleasure in Victorian Britain* (London: Harper, 2006) places the visit to Stratford in a much wider frame. Discussions of the portraits are largely concerned with advancing the claims of one or other images. The catalogue to the 2006 National Portrait Gallery exhibition *Searching for Shakespeare*, edited by Tarnya Cooper (London: National Portrait Gallery, 2006) is, however, measured and reliable, and also contains a great deal of other valuable information and fine illustrations. David Piper's *The Image of the Poet* (Oxford: Clarendon, 1982) places portraits of Shakespeare within a longer perspective. The authorship controversy is forcefully terminated by Paul Edmondson and Stanley Wells in *Shakespeare Beyond Doubt* (Cambridge: Cambridge University Press, 2013), while more specialist interests are catered for in *The Shakespeare Ciphers Examined* by William S. and Elizabeth S. Friedman ([1957]: Cambridge: Cambridge University Press, 2011).

CHAPTER 7: SHAKESPEARE BEYOND SHAKESPEARE

Writings on Carlyle are in general little concerned with his discussion of Shakespeare. The most recent edition of *On Heroes, Hero-Worship and the Heroic in History* (usually referred to as '*On Heroes and Hero-worship*') is that edited by Michael K. Goldberg (Berkeley and Los Angeles, CA: University of California Press, 1993); Philip Rosenberg's 'A Whole World of Heroes' appears in the *Modern Critical Views* volume on Carlyle, edited by Harold Bloom (New York: Chelsea House, 1986). Ruskin has fared better, with *John Ruskin and the Victorian Theatre* by Katherine Newey and

Jeffrey Richards (Basingstoke: Palgrave Macmillan, 2010); Richard Foulkes' essay '"A Truer Peep at Old Venice": *The Merchant of Venice* on the Victorian Stage' in *Ruskin, The Theatre and Victorian Visual Culture*, edited by Anselm Heinrich, Katherine Newey, and Jeffrey Richards (Basingstoke: Palgrave Macmillan, 2009, 169–86); and Francis O'Gorman's '"The Clue of Shakespearean Power over Me": Ruskin, Shakespeare, and Influence' in the Marshall and Poole collection (2.203–18). Especially valuable is David-Everett Blythe's 'A Stone of Ruskin's Venice' in *New Approaches to Ruskin* edited by Robert Hewison (London: Routledge, 1981, 157–73). The edition of *Sesame and Lilies* by Deborah Epstein Nord (New Haven and London: Yale University Press, 2002) contains a valuable introduction, as well as an essay by Seth Koven on the range of Victorian responses to the work. Bagehot's Shakespearean writing is discussed briefly in Schoenbaum's *Shakespeare's Lives* (pp. 342–3).

Cowden Clarke's Shakespeare adaptations are discussed by several scholars in the larger context of writing for children. Significant among them are Carol Rutter, in *Shakespeare and Child's Play* (Oxford and New York: Routledge, 2007); Erika Hately in *Shakespeare in Children's Literature: Gender and Cultural Capital* (Oxford and New York: Routledge, 2010), and the essays in *Reimagining Shakespeare for Children and Young Adults*, edited by Naomi J. Miller (London and New York: Routledge, 2003). A broader view is taken by George C. Gross in *Mary Cowden Clarke, The Girlhood of Shakespeare's Heroines, and the Sex Education of Victorian Women* (Bloomington: Indiana University Press, 1972). Volume 7 of the *Great Shakespeareans* series (London and New York: Continuum, 2011) includes an essay on Mary Cowden Clarke by Gail Marshall and Ann Thompson, and one on Jameson by Cheri Larsen Hoeckley. The fullest discussion of Jameson, however, is Judith Johnston's *Anna Jameson: Victorian, Feminist, Woman of Letters* (Aldershot: Scolar, 1997). Biographical studies dominate the approach to Helen Faucit, the most extensive being *Helen Faucit: Fire and Ice on the Victorian Stage* by Carol Jones Carlisle (London: Society for Theatre Research, 2000), with more specific focus provided by the same author's 'Helen Faucit's Lady Macbeth', *Shakespeare Studies* 16 (1983): 205–33 and Julie Hankey's 'Helen Faucit and Shakespeare: Womanly Theatre' in *Cross-Cultural Performances: Differences in Women's Re-visions of Shakespeare*, edited by Marianne Novy (Urbana and Chicago, IL: University of Chicago Press, 1993, 50–63).

CHAPTER 8: LAST YEARS

The work and influence of Bradley is covered in different ways in *A. C. Bradley and Shakespeare's Tragedies: A Concise Edition and a Reassessment* by John

Russell Brown (London: Palgrave Macmillan, 2007) and Katharine Cooke in *A. C. Bradley and his Influence in Twentieth-Century Shakespeare Criticism* (Oxford: Clarendon, 1972). There is no shortage of biographies of Oscar Wilde; the most valuable is Richard Ellmann's *Oscar Wilde* (London: Hamish Hamilton, 1987). The final, extended text of *The Portrait of Mr W. H.* is available in the standard edition of the *Collected Works*, edited by Vyvyan Holland (London: Methuen, 1958); other relevant material may be found in *The Artist as Critic: Critical Writings of Oscar Wilde*, edited by Richard Ellmann (New York: Random House, c.1969). For discussions of the theatre of the last decades, see the works on Irving and Tree already listed, as well as Terry's *The Story of My Life* (London: Pearson, 1907). Michael Holroyd's *A Strange Eventful History: The Dramatic Lives of Henry Irving, Ellen Terry and their Remarkable Families* (London: Chatto and Windus, 2008) links them to a later generation of performers. A collection of essays edited by Richard Foulkes, *British Theatre in the 1890s* (Cambridge: Cambridge University Press, 1992), offers a range of views; James Woodfield looks further forward to discuss changes in production styles in *English Theatre in Transition 1881–1914* (London: Croom Helm, 1984). The standard work on Poel is Robert Speaight's *William Poel and the Elizabethan Revival* (London: Heinemann, 1954); his work is compared with others by Jean Chothia in 'Varying Authenticities. Poel, Tree and Late-Victorian Shakespeare' (Marshall and Poole, 2. 161–78).

Index